MANHUNT!

James Morton is the best-selling co-author of the *Mad Frank Fraser* books, as well as many other crime titles including the *Gangland* series published by Little Brown. He worked as a solicitor for over twenty-five years, and was previously the editor of *New Law Journal* and *The Criminal Lawyer*. He is now a full-time writer.

MANHUNT!

The Definitive History
of Criminal Detection

JAMES MORTON

EBURY PRESS
LONDON

This edition first published in the UK in 2002

First published in the UK in 2001 as Catching the Killers

Text © James Morton 2001

1 3 5 7 9 10 8 6 4 2

James Morton has asserted his right to be identified as author of this
work under the Copyright, Designs and Patents Act 1988

Ebury Press
Random House, 20 Vauxhall Bridge Road, London SW1V 2SA

Random House Australia Pty Limited
20 Alfred Street, Milsons Point, Sydney, New South Wales 2061,
Australia

Random House New Zealand Limited
18 Poland Road, Glenfield, Auckland 10, New Zealand

Random House (Pty) Limited
Endulini, 5A Jubilee Road, Parktown 2193, South Africa

The Random House Group Limited Reg. No. 954009

A CIP catalogue record for this book is available from the British
Library

ISBN 0 09 188475 6

Jacket design by the Senate
Typeset by Lovelock & Co.

Printed and bound in Great Britain by Bookmarque Ltd, Croydon,
Surrey

Papers used by Ebury Press are natural, recyclable products made from
wood grown in sustainable forests.

Contents

Whenever the human element enters
into an interpretation of anything,
there is always a possibility of error.

J.Edgar Hoover

CHAPTER 1

Fingerprints

I

On 23 December 1983 an horrific murder took place in the Finger Lakes region of Upper State New York. An intruder interrupted the Christmas preparations of the Harris family. Before he left, setting the house on fire, the man had sexually assaulted Shelby Harris and killed her along with Do and Tony who had been shot twice with a .22 calibre rifle modified as a pistol. Mark Harris had been shot three times as had Shelby. All had been hog-tied, wired and had pillow cases over their heads.

The bullets matched a gun from the prime suspect, 31-year-old Michael Kinge, who was later killed in a shoot-out with the police. On a petrol can at the scene was a fingerprint of his mother, Shirley, which Officer David Harding said he found in the living room. She was arrested and charged with complicity in the murder of the Harris family.

The road which led to the arrest of Mrs Kinge and the seemingly incontrovertible evidence of her fingerprint had been a long and hard one for the various men from France, India, the Argentine, Scotland and Japan who, almost simultaneously, proposed their own versions of ensuring identification. Like an American presidential candidate in the face of a recount, they often jealously and gracelessly clung to a position when it was demonstrable that another's method was superior.

Two early observations on fingerprints had come to nothing. The first was in 1686 when Marcello Malpighi, Professor of Anatomy at the University of Bologna, put down his thoughts which were promptly ignored, as were those of Johann Purkinje at the University of Breslau who did the same in 1823.

So it is the Frenchman, Alphonse Bertillon, who has the unquestioned title of being the first to establish a modern means of identification. He started with the undeniable asset that he was grandson of Achille Guillard, a noted naturalist and mathematician and the son of Louis Adolphe Bertillon, a distinguished physician, statistician and, even better from his son's point of view, the Vice President of the Anthropological Society of Paris. Both had keenly studied and measured the skulls of men, trying to establish a relationship between the shape of the head and intellectual development. They were not alone. The Belgian scientist and statistician Adolphe Quetelet had, for some years, been trying to demonstrate an even distribution of human nature – there were as many dwarfs as giants but the majority of men fell within a certain physical range.[1] Quetelet's theory had already attracted some attention and in the 1850s the director of the Louvain prison had suggested that rudimentary measurements be taken of the head, length of ears, feet, height and the circumference of the chest of adult prisoners – the system would not, of course, work with juveniles. He argued that this would defeat disguises, false names and mutilations. His suggestion was largely ignored.

Had Bertillon not come from such a respected family he might well have been regarded as totally unemployable because he had been expelled from a number of schools for poor conduct and had been sacked by the bank to which he had been apprenticed. He suffered from violent headaches and a poor digestive system, which may have explained his totally unsociable nature and bad temper. He had a tendency to pedantry and was regarded as lacking any cultural qualities at all. He was so unmusical that during his short career in the Army, to help him distinguish the bugle calls for reveille and roll call he had to count the actual notes. Sent to England as a tutor he had made such a poor job he was swiftly shipped back across the Channel. More or less in despair his father obtained a position for him as a clerk at the police headquarters at the Sûreté in Paris.

Nor, initially, was he any great success in this position. Ignored by his colleagues he was set to work compiling cards in a corner, which was boiling hot in the summer and so cold in the winter that he was forced to wear gloves. His job was transferring arrest data to these cards. Each card had general remarks on the physical features of the prisoners such as 'tall', 'small', 'average'. Additionally, there was a photograph, often badly taken, of the man to whom the card referred.

By this time in its career the archive section of the Sûreté had effectively outgrown itself. Criminals were categorised in sections of burglars, pickpockets, forgers and so on, with no thought that a robber might also be a coiner and so might fall into two or more categories. Then there was the problem of the collection of 80,000 photographs. Even if the photographs were a likeness – and the arrested man had usually grimaced at the camera in an effort to make himself unrecognisable – it was physically impossible to compare the library with newly arrested criminals.

To the amusement of his fellow clerks, Bertillon began comparing the photographs, studying the ears and noses side by side. He applied for permission to measure suspects brought into the building and, possibly because of the status of his father, permission was eventually granted. From these studies he decided that, while people might have similar measurements of their ears or noses, they never had four or five characteristics the same. By August 1879 he was convinced that he had devised a system for the easy and correct identification of criminals and accordingly he wrote a report to Louis Andrieux who, since the previous March, had been the Prefect of Police in Paris. It was ignored. Undaunted, Bertillon went on amassing data and obtained permission to take measurements at La Santé prison before he commenced work in the mornings.

On 1 October 1879 he was promoted from assistant clerk to clerk when he sent a second and much more detailed report. Now he could say that the chance of two people being exactly the same height was 4 to 1. If a second measurement was added then the chance of the two being the same decreased to 16 to 1. If eleven measurements were taken then the mathematical probability of finding another criminal with exactly the same measurements was 4,191,304 to 1. He had also developed a system of arranging the cards on which the measurements were recorded so that there would be only 23 in each sub-section of a file.

Unfortunately Bertillon had a double misfortune, only the first part of which was of his own making. His basic lack of syntax made his report repetitive, complicated, obscure and basically incomprehensible to the ordinary person. Andrieux made no sense of it and passed it to Gustave Mace, the head of the Sûreté.[2] This was Bertillon's second misfortune. Mace had no time for theories and theorists. He believed in the detective's 'nose' and practical experience. He reported back to Andrieux that the police should not be troubled with theorists' experiments. There was far more important work to be done. Andrieux called in Bertillon who made a blundering and incoherent attempt to explain his system. He was told that as a clerk of only eight months he was getting ideas above his station and that if he continued to trouble senior management he would be looking for another job.

Sometimes that vastly misunderstood breed of people, parents, are useful. Bertillon's father, told by Andrieux to keep his son's nose out of matters that did not concern him and horrified by the prospect of another filial failure, called for the report. This time he was not, however, disappointed. On reading his son's work he began to champion his cause. In turn he also ran into the stumbling block of Andrieux. Despite Bertillon *père's* influence and that of his friends the prefect could not be shifted. His son would have to wait for a change of prefect.

He had to wait seven years for the change and then one of his father's friends, the lawyer Edgar Demange, persuaded the new incumbent, Camecasse, to give Bertillon the opportunity to prove his system. He was given the assistance of two clerks and three months for his system to root out one recidivist criminal. It was an incredibly short time for a man to be charged, sentenced, released and re-arrested but it was all that was available for Bertillon. Once again his assistants, currying favour with Macé, mocked Bertillon. He took his data to a young Austrian woman, Amélie Notar – whom he had met crossing the street and who, possibly because of her short-sightedness, was almost as anti-social as himself – for her to complete the registration cards. Halfway through February 1883, with only two weeks of his trial period remaining, his index had grown to 1,800 cards. Then his luck changed. While he was taking the measurements of a man who gave his name as Dupont, a regular alias among the criminal classes of the time, he correctly challenged the man, who had been arrested on 15 December for stealing bottles, as being called Martin. The newspapers reported the case and the politically astute Camecasse extended the trial indefinitely. Bertillon was given more assistants and an office of his own. In March he made another identification and by the end of the year he had identified 49 recidivists.

From then on his system and his own doggedness gained grudging acceptance. Detectives, questioning whether he could identify a dead person by his methods, took him to mortuaries and watched him fight back nausea as he took his measurements. And identify bodies he did. But detectives wanted more. How could they be expected to stop criminals and measure them in the street to see if they were wanted men? So Bertillon began a rudimentary identikit, taking photographs of, say, noses and cutting and pasting dozens side by side, eventually deciding that a photograph of the face in profile was the most satisfactory.

In 1884 he identified another three hundred criminals and the previously unwanted Bertillon and his methods became fashionable. The Home Office sent Edmund Spearman to talk with him and Camecasse paraded him before politicians as well as Hébert, Director of the French Prison Administration, who announced to the press that he was going to introduce Bertillon's system, which he now called anthropometry, into French prisons. From then on the ugly duckling indeed became a swan with newspaper headlines championing him. 'Young French Scientist Revolutionises the Identification of Criminals'. On 1 November 1888 Bertillon moved into a set of, admittedly run-down, offices of his own. Now he was called Director of the Police Identification Service. Journalists coined the word *bertillonage*.

> Thanks to a French genius, errors of
> identification will soon cease to exist not only
> in France, but also in the entire world. Hence
> judicial errors based upon false identification
> will likewise disappear. Long live *bertillonage!*
> Long live Alphonse Bertillon![3]

Next came improvements to the photographing of criminals with Bertillon devising a chair in which the suspect was sat and which ensured regularity in the composition of the portraits. And after that came his pride and joy, the *portrait parlé*. He devised a series of words and phrases to describe visible characteristics; each was given a letter and so a group of the letters explained and identified the man's features.

His major triumph was to come in 1892 after a violent explosion blew up the house of Judge Benoit who the previous year had presided over the trial of a group of anarchists. Although the solution of the case was Bertillon's, the initial breakthrough came when one of the Sûreté's informers known as X2SI reported in. X2SI was female and had learned from the wife of Professor Chaumartin of the Technical School at Saint-Denis that her husband, a known sympathiser, had planned the outrage. The motive was, as surmised, revenge for the previous year's conviction. Chaumartin was arrested and implicated Légér, whom he knew under a number of aliases including Ravachol, as the man who had planted the bomb.

Ravachol's abandoned room on the Quai de la Marne was searched and bomb-making equipment was found. He was already wanted by the police for the theft of dynamite from a quarry in Soiry-sous-Etoiles. Chaumartin described him as being 5ft 4in in height with a sallow complexion and a dark beard.

The 43-year-old Ravachol, a known smuggler and burglar with a reputation for violence, had been arrested under the name of Koenigstein in 1889 and released through lack of evidence. His measurements and characteristics had, however, been taken and they included a scar on his left hand near the thumb. From then on he had indulged himself in a one-man crime-wave across France. On 15 May 1891 he had broken into the funeral vault of the Baroness de Rocher-Taillier in St-Étienne and stolen a cross and medallion from the coffin. Just over a month later he had strangled a recluse, who lived in the Forez mountains, and had stolen 35,000 francs. He had been arrested but had escaped. Then six weeks later, on 27 July, he killed two women who ran a hardware store in St-Étienne. This time his take had been a mere 48 francs.

On 27 March 1892 another bomb exploded in Paris, this time at 39 rue de Clichy, seriously injuring five people. On 30 March the owner of the Restaurant Very on Boulevard Magenta sent a message to the police to the effect that a man with a scar on his left hand was breakfasting. He had been there before and, rather carelessly, had been spouting anarchism to the waiter. The man was arrested after a violent struggle during which he was said to have called out 'Long live anarchy! Long live dynamite!' The day after his arrest he posed willingly for Bertillon and the measurements proved him to be Claudius Francois Koenigstein. In time he would admit that his anarchism was merely a cover for his professional activities and that he had robbed the grave in St-Étienne and killed the recluse. Ravachol sang on the way to the guillotine, 'If you want to be happy, hang your masters and cut the priests to pieces.' His last words were recorded as 'You pigs, long live the Revolution!'

This was a coup of the highest order for *bertillonage*. Now its deviser could hope it would become standard police practice worldwide. It was not such a coup for the proprietor of the Restaurant Very. On 25 April, two days before Ravachol was due to stand trial in Paris, a bomb exploded on the premises killing him and a customer.

One of the great problems of the Bertillon system, and it was one recognised by Mace from the start, was that it required some skill and commitment to record the measurements accurately. Since much of the measuring in prisons was left to marginally supervised prisoners who had no possible incentive in assisting the authorities it is hardly surprising that there were considerable variations. For example the celebrated American confidence trickster and jewel thief Annie Gleason had her measurements given variously as 5ft ½in, 5ft 2in and 5ft 3in on arrest records in the Pinkerton files.[4]

II

Almost from the time of his arrival in India in the late 1850s as a junior secretary assigned to the highland district of Hooghly, William Herschel began taking fingerprints. In a country where agreements and timescales were at best overlooked and more often forgotten, initially he had done so as a *proces d'impressement,* reasoning that this might instil some sense of commitment. It was nothing new. Chinese orphanages took the fingerprints of abandoned babies and a handprint was usual on a Chinese divorce contract.

As early as 1858 Herschel had made a supplier of road building materials, Rajadar Konai, seal a contract with a palm print. At first Herschel had only been interested in the contractual side of things but, as the years passed, he became fascinated by the differences in the prints themselves and began to accumulate a collection of impressions of the first two fingers of the right hand. He found it no more difficult than making a fair stamp of an office seal and by the middle of the 1860s he was using his system to ensure that pensioned

Indian soldiers did not make multiple applications for money. Over the years he had taken thousands of impressions. No one had refused to give an impression and he noted that not only was everyone's impression different but that, while the face, hair, stature might change over the years, fingerprints did not. He had made each prisoner place a fingerprint after his name in the register and almost instantly he had eliminated a wide variety of practices such as having a substitute serve one's sentence.

On 15 August 1877 he wrote to the Inspector General of the prison in Bengal saying that by using his method he was able to identify every person in what he called his sign-manual.

The English legal system had just undergone one of its more tortuous cases, that of the Tichborne claimant. In 1854 Roger Charles, the eldest son of Lord James Tichborne, had apparently been drowned near Brazil. In 1866 he seemingly reappeared in Wagga-Wagga writing to his mother for money. The lost son migrated to Europe where his mother saw him in a hotel room in Paris. In his missing decade the once thin young man had ballooned to a massive 26 stones but his mother was able to recognise him. He was allowed £1,000 a year by her until he could legally inherit and his case became a *cause célèbre* as he fought those more sceptical than his mother to establish himself. He elicited vast sums of money for a fighting fund on the basis that, once he won, substantial dividends would be paid to his supporters, something which sounded suspiciously like the illegal practice of champerty. But supporters he did have and the noted Sergeant Ballantine took his case.[5]

The case ran over a year and cost in the region of £200,000. A commission of inquiry visited Australia and found that the new baronet was in reality a butcher, Arthur Orton. One of the clinching pieces of evidence was a pocket book in which, he admitted, he had written:

> Some men has plenty money and no brains,
> and some men has plenty brains and no
> money. Surely men with plenty money and no
> brains were made for men with plenty brains
> and no money.

The jury quickly ruled against him and Orton was tried for perjury, receiving a sentence of 14 years of which he served ten. Now Herschel wrote in India:

> As an instance of the value of the thing, I
> might suggest that if Roger Tichborne had
> given his 'sign-manual' on entering the Army
> on any register, the whole case would have
> been knocked on the head in ten minutes.

But just as Bertillon had fought against unbelievers to establish his measurement system so Herschel went unrewarded. The letter in reply led him to think the Inspector General knew he was an ill man and believed his suggestions were simply delirious ramblings. Two years later he sailed for England and home.

Meanwhile in Tokyo, a Scottish doctor, Henry Faulds, who seems to have shared some of Bertillon's less admirable qualities, noticed fingermarks in some 'pre-historic' Japanese pottery and remarked on 'skin-furrows'. In 1880 he wrote to the English publication *Nature* pointing out his discovery.[6] In fact, what is so curious is that no one had 'discovered' it before. Just as the Chinese had used fingerprints as a form of signature so had the Japanese. Mail would be acknowledged in country inns by a thumbprint. Initially Faulds seems to have been interested in prints from an ethnological point of view but his interest became a practical one when the police arrested a thief who had, they said, left a clear sooty impression on a wall. Faulds was called for and was able to show not only that the prints were not of the detained man but a few days later that they were those of a second man who had been arrested.

He continued with his amateur detection when he was able to find prints on a mug. This time he discovered that it was not necessary for the print to be sooty or inky, a print could be left by the oily secretion of the sweat glands. He also wrote of the Tichborne case saying there might be a recognisable Orton type or a recognisable Tichborne type. He also pointed out the potential value of prints in identifying the former ownership of a severed hand where there were no other parts of the body.

It is curious that Herschel, convalescing in Littlemore from the amoebic dysentery which had ruined his heath, read the issue of *Nature* which printed Faulds' letter. He wrote to the editor saying that he had studied the subject for the last twenty years and only the recalcitrance of his superiors and his illness had prevented him from making his findings public. Faulds took up what he saw as a challenge to his discovery with enthusiasm. Off went letters to the Home Secretary, Charles Darwin, the Police Commissioner in

London and to Andrieux, the Prefect of Paris Police, defending his claim of discovery. His contract ended in Japan and he too set sail for England.

There was, however, a third player on the English scene and it was he who undoubtedly would make the greatest contribution of the three. Sir Francis Galton, born in 1822 the son of a wealthy Birmingham manufacturer, dabbled in science throughout his life. At the age of 20 he had been to Giessen to see the German chemist Justus Liebig and had then gone on to Budapest, Belgrade and Constantinople before turning for home and visiting Athens, Venice, Milan and Geneva on the way. Throughout his life he had an interest in anthropometry and for the London International Exhibition in 1884 he had devised a highly popular show which for the admission price of 3d gave the visitor the chance to have his physical and mental characteristics measured.[7]

In the spring of 1888 it was learned that Bertillon had been appointed head of the police identification bureau in Paris and Galton was invited to present a paper on the great man and his system on 25 May 1888 at one of the Royal Institution's Friday meetings. Accordingly he set forth to meet the Frenchman. He was fortunate that Bertillon was in one of his more receptive moods because he was shown the system in operation and noted the dexterity with which assistants, under Bertillon's supervision, took and recorded the measurements. Nevertheless he had doubts. He had not had 'the means of testing its efficiency with closeness'. He also thought the system was flawed in that different measurements of the same person were treated as independent variables. For example he found it unsurprising that a tall man should have a bigger foot or finger than a smaller one.

He also recalled the correspondence in *Nature* and wrote asking the editor for Faulds' and Herschel's addresses. Faulds was now a police surgeon in England. He had tried without any success to interest Scotland Yard and the Home Secretary in fingerprinting and, totally embittered, he had continued his studies privately. As indeed had the self-effacing Herschel. Unfortunately for Faulds, the editor sent Galton only Herschel's address.

Once Galton had seen Herschel's papers he at once recognised the deficiencies in *bertillonage* which he had been prepared to adopt wholeheartedly. At his lecture to the Royal Institution he gave an early indication that fingerprinting was a superior method of identification. Immediately after the lecture he began work and within three years he had a greater print collection than Herschel. He also devised a system of classification based on four definitive types of print:

1 Prints containing only arches
2 Prints with a triangle on the right hand side
3 Prints with a triangle on the left hand side
4 Prints with triangles on both sides

In 1891 he too wrote an article for *Nature* acknowledging his debt to Herschel. It elicited no great interest except for an angry response from Faulds. Galton was undeterred. In 1892 he published his book *Fingerprints*. This time it did create attention.

There was still, however, one remaining major participant in the development of fingerprinting in

Europe and he too came from India: Edward Henry, son of a London doctor. In 1873 he entered the Indian Civil Service and from 1891 he held the position of Inspector General of Police for Nepal.

The story goes that having no paper with him he set down a comprehensive system for classifying fingerprints on his starched cuffs on a train journey to Calcutta in 1896. What he had already done was to establish *bertillonage* in the police force. This had proved a substantial success with 23 former convicts picked out in 1893, a figure which had risen to 207 in 1895. But the process was laborious. Measurements had to be checked and re-checked with two millimetres accepted as a margin of error. It took an hour to complete a card and another to locate one.

In 1894 the Troup Committee reported to the Home Office. It had been established to report on the merits of adopting either fingerprinting or *bertillonage* and the members, Charles Edward Troup, a Home Office official, Major Arthur Griffith, Inspector of Prisons, and Melville Macnaghten, then Assistant Chief Constable of Scotland Yard, went to see Galton's laboratory at the South Kensington Museum where he was still trying to work out an improved system of sub-classifications. He felt he was getting there but, when pressed, he admitted it would probably be another two or three years before he had the problem solved.

Here was the nub of the problem. The committee admired Galton's system but classification was a serious problem. Should they therefore go for *bertillonage*, only to find that in a relatively short period the more accurate system had overtaken it?

The Committee had travelled to Paris to see the great man as well as Louis Lépine, the Prefect of Paris, who later in his career would break the Bonnot gang which had originated the use of the motor car in bank robberies,[8] and Goron, the head of the Sûreté. Goron had his own version of the Third Degree with deprivation of food and light followed by meals and prostitutes in return for confessions. He also used his men as infiltrators, posing as prisoners, questioning their cell mates and then, when they had the information, moving them to other prisons where they died and were reborn to start the process all over again.

Bertillon did what he could to convert them, allowing them to take measurements to show how easily it could be done. He also demonstrated some of his new devices which included a camera on a high stand equipped with a metric grid overlay which could be used to photograph a crime scene. They were impressed but not completely converted.

The Committee delivered its report on 19 February 1894. It was part Bertillon and part Galton. Anthropometry should be introduced but with only five instead of Bertillon's eleven measurements and the cumbersome *portrait parlé* was out. Instead all ten fingerprints of convicts should be preserved on cards and for the present classification would be à la Bertillon. The acceptance by the Home Secretary of the Troup Committee did not meet with favour among the officers at Scotland Yard. In particular a doubter was Detective Inspector Stedman who had travelled to Paris to find Bertillon in a major sulk over the refusal by the English to adopt his system wholeheartedly, but also overjoyed to find police forces from Russia, Belgium and Berlin queuing to sign up allegiance.[9] *Bertillonage* also became the classification of choice in Portugal, Holland and Denmark as well as Austria. Britain was becoming isolated.

Henry had met Galton at his home in Rutland Gate and had been given a free run of his laboratory and files. Now on the train he devised a system which needed nothing more complicated than a magnifying glass and a needle for counting ridges. It was the beginning of the system we know today of plain and tented arches, radial and ulnar loops and whorls. There was also a division into the sub-patterns based on Galton's work.

The following year, 1896, Henry ordered his officers to take not only Bertillon measuring cards but also all ten fingerprints of convicts, and a year later he suggested to the Governor General of India that an independent commission be appointed to consider the merits of the respective systems. On 12 July 1897 the Governor General ordered the abandonment of anthropometry in favour of fingerprinting. What India did today Britain did three years later. In November 1900 a committee under Lord Belper recommended that *bertillonage* be dropped. In March 1901 Henry was appointed Acting Police Commissioner of London and it was through his personal efforts that he converted doubting officers to the cause. In the first year over 1,700 convicts were identified.

One case in which fingerprinting would have solved the problems in five minutes flat and went some way to turn opinion against *bertillonage* was that of Adolph Beck.

In 1877 a John Smith was convicted at the Old Bailey of frauds on demi-mondaine women whom he deprived of their money and jewellery. The *modus operandi* was to pose as a member of the aristocracy, Lord Willoughby, with a home in St John's Wood and then offer the woman a position as his mistress. She would be purchased a new outfit on a forged cheque and he would decamp with her jewels and whatever money he could borrow from her. He was sentenced to five years' penal servitude and remained in prison until 1881.

In 1894 the swindles began again, carried out by a Lord Wilton or Lord Winton de Willoughby still living in St John's Wood. Unfortunately for Adolf Beck, a Norwegian seaman, quite by chance he met an Ottilie Meissonier on 16 December 1895 in Victoria Street and she identified him as Lord Wilton. She called a policeman; he denied his guilt but was arrested and charged. A rudimentary identification parade was held and several other women identified Beck. After the committal proceedings a man, not a policeman, communicated with Scotland Yard to say that Beck was the swindler John Smith. He was then identified by PC Spurrell and another officer who had arrested Smith 15 years previously. Handwriting evidence was given by the expert Guerin who said the handwriting and exhibits 'must have been written by the same person'. Beck's solicitor made two applications to the Commissioner of the Police to inspect John Smith's record. Both applications were turned down and Beck, prosecuted by Horace Avory, went on trial at the Old Bailey.

Charles Gill, defending Beck, asked for leave to cross-examine Guerin to the effect that the 1877 exhibits had been written by Beck. If Guerin confirmed this there was an immediate defence available. There was clear evidence in 1877 that Beck had been in South America. Avory objected on the grounds that this was a collateral issue and should not be enquired into until the jury had reached its verdict. His objection was upheld and Beck received a sentence of seven years' penal servitude.

In prison he was treated as the ex-convict Smith. Dutton, his solicitor, appealed to the Home Office to show that Beck had been in Peru when Smith was convicted. His appeals were turned down and Beck had been in prison for two years before it was discovered that he could not be Smith. Smith was a Jew and circumcised. Beck, a gentile, was not. The prison governor consulted the trial judge, the Common Sergeant, Forrest Fulton, but it was decided that while Beck, since he could not be Smith, should now be treated as a first offender, nothing had happened which invalidated his conviction. His further petitions were turned down and he was released on licence in 1901.

During his time in prison the swindles ceased, only to begin again in 1903. The next year Beck was once more arrested, committed for trial and convicted. Again the swindles stopped but while Beck was in custody a William Thomas was arrested trying to pawn the rings of two actress sisters, Violet and Beulah Turner, who had been swindled. Mr Justice Grantham postponed sentence on Beck for a period for further enquiries to be made. Thomas was found to be Smith, alias Lord Wilton; Guerin withdrew his evidence and Beck was released to general acclaim on 19 July 1904.

Public opinion now ran high in favour of the unfortunate Norwegian and the £2,000 offered to Beck as an Act of Grace was roundly condemned. An internal Home Office inquiry was pooh-poohed in the *Daily Mail* by Sir George Lewis, the eminent solicitor now acting for Beck. There must be an inquiry held by a judge. And indeed there was. The Home Secretary appointed the Master of the Rolls to head it. Curiously the Tribunal did not recommend a Court of Appeal. The fault in the present case was that of the judge. In future the right to compel the court to state a case would be sufficient.

Another case, while not so damaging as that of Beck but in which fingerprinting would have cleared things up in a matter of hours, was recalled by Tighe Hopkins:

> A certain J— C— was convicted at the Clerkenwell Sessions of larceny from the person. A warder from a London prison swore of his having been convicted ten years previously under the name of Hart. The prisoner denied this in court and though the jury, after seeing Hart's photograph, gave a verdict in accordance with the warder's evidence, sentence was postponed and further inquiry made. It was then found that the distinctive marks ascribed to Hart did not tally with those of J— C—, who had been, he alleged, serving a short sentence at Lewes at the time when Hart was in penal servitude. Here was a clear case of mistaken identification.[10]

III

It was also a hard road for Ramon Velasquez in Necochea, on the Atlantic coast of Argentina. It was there on 29 June 1892 that a double murder took place in a slum area of the small town. The victims were the two illegitimate children of a part-time worker, a young woman Francisca Rojas. The principal suspect was Velasquez, said to be trying to persuade Rojas to marry him. Rojas had run to the hut of a neighbour about 50 yards from her own screaming. When she had been calmed down she said 'My children ... he killed my children ... Velasquez.' It would be the first murder case worldwide to be solved by the use of fingerprints.

Just as Bertillon was enjoying one of his greatest triumphs, in the Argentine a young immigrant, Juan Vucetich, born in Dalmatia, was making gigantic forensic strides of his own. He had arrived in South America in 1884 with a gift for mathematics and boundless enthusiasm for his new home. Within a year he had joined the police force and after five years had become the head of the Statistical Bureau of Police in La Plata. Now on 18 July 1891 he was ordered by his chief, Guillermo Nuñez, to set up an office for anthropometry. He was handed a number of articles on *bertillonage* and also a copy of *Revue Scientifique* of 2 May which contained an article by Francis Galton on identification through fingerprints.

Within a week Vucetich had a small office at work measuring prisoners but, dazzled by Galton's article, he was not content with the Bertillon measuring system. Leaving his assistants to take the Bertillon measurements he became obsessed with fingerprinting, visiting morgues and testing the mummies in the La Plata museum. Papillary lines held firm over centuries. By 1 September he had identified the four basic types of print which Sir Francis Galton had formulated in England:

1 Prints containing only arches
2 Prints with a triangle on the right-hand side
3 Prints with a triangle on the left-hand side
4 Prints with triangles on both sides

and he worked out a practical system for classifying fingerprints. As Galton had done he initially encountered problems, and so he had counted the papillary lines which provided enough sub-classifications to make distinctions between sets of prints. From his own pocket he paid for filing cabinets and cards to hold and record his system. He no longer had any enthusiasm for establishing Bertillon bureaux in other provincial cities but, as with many other pioneers, his early efforts were regarded with suspicion by his superiors. Then came the savage murder in Necochea of the two young children of Francisca Rojas who had blamed her former friend Velasquez.

Rojas, when questioned, told the police that Velasquez had been madly in love with her but that she was in love with another man. He had pestered and pestered her until on the day of the killing she had told him she would never marry him. He had flown into a rage and threatened to kill those whom she most loved. When she returned home from work she had found the door to her hut open and the children dead in the bedroom.

Velasquez was arrested and questioned. He accepted that he loved Rojas and had wanted to marry her but had been rejected. He also accepted he had made threats but, he said, he had no intention of carrying them out. The police then, using the standard investigative techniques of the time and place, and many others, gave him a sound beating. When this did not produce a confession he was bound and laid beside the corpses of the two children overnight. This also was a practice which had been used by New York police for the past two decades.

Velasquez must have been made of stern stuff because he still did not confess, nor did he after a further week of beatings. Instead it was the police who began to weaken and to make more general enquiries. They learned that Rojas had, indeed, had another admirer who, according to general gossip, had said he would not marry her while the two 'brats' were in the way.

The police inspector now turned his attentions to Rojas but she also was not easily frightened. So when he knocked on her windows at night, calling out that he was an avenging spirit come to punish her for killing her children, this had no effect whatsoever and she continued to blame Velasquez. The inspector now sent for help to La Plata. Nuñez sent Inspector Alvarez, one of the few policemen who understood and accepted the fingerprint classification. He soon found that Velasquez had an unshakeable alibi which, through his limited intelligence, he had omitted to mention.

Alvarez examined the bedroom and found a greyish-brown spot on the wooden door, something he recognised as a fingerprint dried in blood. He had the section cut from the door and, obtaining a stamp pad and paper from the local police chief, took Rojas' prints. He showed her the result through a magnifying glass and she confessed. She had killed the children with a knife which she had thrown in a well. She had washed her hands carefully but had forgotten she had touched the door. There is no existing record of her trial and punishment nor whether Velasquez received compensation for his beatings but it is a fairly safe assumption that he did not.

It was however the first murder case solved by finding a fingerprint at the scene of the crime. The story created a sensation in the police department and in the newspapers.

> I hardly dare to believe it but my theory has
> proved its worth. No doubt my opponents will
> call it fortuitous. But I hold one trump card
> now, and I hope I shall soon have more.[11]

And soon he did. Within a matter of weeks he was able to identify a suicide as a former convict, and after that the fingerprints of Audifrasio Gonzales on a counter convicted him of the murder of the shopkeeper.

His was not, however, an unmitigated triumph. His superiors were still in favour of *bertillonage* and, despite a pamphlet published at his own expense in which he pointed out that he had identified over twenty criminals in a single day in June 1893, he was ordered to abandon his fingerprinting scheme. He was obliged to sell his personal library to pay for the printing of his second book *Sistema de Filacon* but, for the time being, he was at his lowest ebb. Within the year and with the arrival of a new chief of police, Narcisco Lozano, he and fingerprinting were back in favour. The same year he was awarded 5,000 gold pesos to compensate him for the money he had personally spent. In fact the Senate voted against the payment and he never received it. Within a further two years, however, the provincial police abolished anthropometry and Argentina became the first country to have a system of identification based only on fingerprinting.

IV

One of the great days of the English social sporting and criminal calendars was the Derby meeting run at Epsom, a mecca for thieves from around the country. It was usual for temporary magistrates' courts, with the power to impose six months' imprisonment, to be set up behind the stands to deal with the stream of pickpockets. It was here that the usefulness of the fingerprinting system proved itself. In 1901 54 men were arrested on Derby Day and fingerprint officers found that 29 of them had previous convictions. In his autobiography, Melville Macnaghten recalled:

> The first prisoner on this occasion gave his
> name as Green of Gloucester and assured the
> interrogating magistrate that he had never
> been in trouble before, and that a racecourse
> was, up to this time, an unknown world to
> him. But up jumped the Chief Inspector in
> answer to a questions as to whether 'anything
> was known' and begged their worships to look

at the papers and photograph which proved the innocent to be Benjamin Brown of Birmingham with some ten convictions to his discredit. 'Bless the fingerprints,' said Benjamin with an oath, 'I knew they'd do me in!'[12]

It was, however, one thing to convince tame magistrates that a prisoner's record was correct but a completely different matter convincing a jury that fingerprints correctly identified a defendant.

The opportunity occurred when, in the summer of 1902, a burglary took place in Dulwich, south-east London, where Stedman the Scotland Yard detective, once a committed opponent of fingerprinting, found a print on a newly painted board. It was identified as that of a Henry Jackson who had previously served a sentence for burglary. He was arrested and taken to Brixton prison where he was once again fingerprinted. It was essential that fingerprinting could be explained in simple terms to a jury and the barrister chosen to do so was Richard Muir.[13]

Muir was known as an extremely hard worker and one of the rising men who prosecuted. He was said to allow himself no more than five hours sleep a night and he would appear in court with a number of cards with notes in different colours to assist his cross-examination. He distrusted eyewitness evidence. To Edward Henry he seemed ideal. Contrary to the usual practice of the Bar of the day, when barristers never left their chambers except for court or to go on circuit, Muir spent four days at Scotland Yard being briefed by Collins on how the system worked. His preparation paid off. Jackson appeared at the Old Bailey in front of the Common Sergeant. The odds were stacked against him because he was unrepresented. *The Times* reported that Muir told the court that fingerprint evidence was commonly used to identify criminals in India and Sergeant Collins' demonstration, with the use of photographs, of how fingerprints were identified had been received 'with much interest by the jury'. Jackson was convicted in short order and received seven years penal servitude.[14]

It was a dramatic step in the acceptance of fingerprinting but it would be a quantum leap to convince a jury that they should convict a man of murder, and so sentence him to death, on fingerprint evidence.

The opportunity came three years later when at 7.15 a.m. on 27 March 1905 a milkman saw two young men rush from a small paint shop at 34 High Street, Deptford, a depressing south-east London suburb. A quarter of an hour later an apprentice arrived for work and found the door locked and there was no answer to the bell. He climbed over a fence, looked in a window and ran calling for help to a nearby shop.

The body of the 70-year-old owner, Farrow, was on the floor of a room behind the shop which served as an office. He had been badly beaten. Upstairs his wife lay dying from her injuries. She survived four days in a local hospital but, during that time, was unable to speak. The local Detective Inspector Fox found two masks made from women's black stockings and also a cashbox under Mrs Farrow's bed from which something in the region of £9 had been taken. Melville Macnaghten arrived and examined the box for fingerprints and there was indeed a smudge on the varnished inner tray. A young sergeant admitted he had pushed the box under the bed so that the stretcher-bearers would not trip over it when they were taking Mrs Farrow to hospital. He was sent with the box for fingerprinting, along with the apprentice, and, for the first time in London, fingerprints were taken from a corpse.

The next morning the reports came through. The fingerprint did not belong to the victims, the apprentice or the police officer. That was the good news. The bad news was that it did not correspond with any of the 80,000 prints currently on record. It was, however, a good print which, when it had been enlarged, was particularly clear.

The investigation proceeded on the usual lines with enquiries being made in the neighbourhood and in a public house one evening a detective overheard a conversation to the effect that the Stratton brothers were 'capable of it'. The police found Alfred Stratton's mistress, Helen Cromarty, living in squalor in Brookmill Road. She had been given a recent beating by him and was now prepared to say that he had wanted her to give him an alibi for the night of the murder. He had also dyed his brown shoes black and she had not seen him since wearing the overcoat he had when he left her.

The brothers, Alfred and Albert, had no previous convictions but locally they were regarded as small time ponces with no regular work. From the prosecution's point of view it was a good murder in which to try to introduce fingerprint evidence. Defendants such as the brothers, alleged to have battered two old people to death for a few pounds, were not likely to garner much public sympathy.

There was little evidence against them – a revengeful girlfriend and a woman, Ethel Stanton, who had seen two men running up the high street. The first problem, therefore, was persuading the magistrate to remand the pair in custody and allow the police to take their fingerprints. Eventually the magistrate agreed and, when it came to it, the brothers were rather amused. The process tickled, they said.

They would not have been tickled to know that the mark on the cashbox tray was that of Alfred Stratton. The milkman, however, failed to recognise them but a woman identified them. The magistrate committed the brothers for trial at the Old Bailey and now Muir, who once again had been briefed for the Crown, was faced with the very serious problem of getting a jury to understand fingerprinting in a capital case. Meanwhile the Strattons' lawyer indicated he would be calling two experts to challenge the prints.

One of the experts turned out to be a Dr J.G.Garson who had so long argued in favour of *bertillonage* and had then developed his own, inadequate, system of fingerprinting. The other was the unfortunate Dr Henry Faulds who was still smarting because Herschel rather than he had been given the credit for the discovery of fingerprinting.

The way in which prosecuting counsel opens a case to the jury can, very often, have a significant effect on the outcome and Muir made the most of his opportunity in having the first word.

In the hundreds of murder cases in which he prosecuted for the crown, Muir never revealed such animosity towards prisoners in the dock as he did towards the two Strattons. He looked upon it as the most brutal crime he had ever come across, saying the manner in which the faces of the poor old couple had been battered about made it quite impossible to extend the slightest human consideration towards the murderers. He spoke perhaps even more slowly and deliberately than usual, but with a deadly effect which made the men in the dock look at him as though he, and not the judge, might at any moment order their execution.[15]

As for the fingerprint evidence, after further lessons from Collins he had arranged for a large blackboard so that Collins could clarify his evidence with examples. He displayed a substantially enlarged photograph of the thumbprint on the cashbox tray, displayed it side by side with the one of Alfred Stratton and pointed out no less than eleven similarities.

Unfortunately for the Strattons, neither Curtis Bennett nor Harold Morris who appeared for them had any great understanding of dactyloscopy and had to rely heavily on their experts. Nor did they know much, if anything, of the in-fighting which had gone on in the scientific journals to establish supremacy. Faulds had, for some years, kept up a running fight to show that it was he who was the progenitor of on-the-scene fingerprinting, as he undoubtedly was. Unfortunately he was also claiming the discovery of fingerprinting for himself. Now Faulds argued that Collins's photographs showed discrepancies which were clear to anyone examining the prints carefully — another example of careless behaviour at the Yard.

Muir and Collins, now an Inspector, met this challenge by having the latter fingerprint every member of the jury several times. They were then given their prints to examine so they could see for themselves that the discrepancies were simply the result of different pressure being applied to the fingers during the printing process and nothing at all to do with the basic characteristic patterns. Faulds lapsed into silence. At least he maintained his integrity.

The defence, after some lengthy deliberation, decided to call Dr Garson. He did not last long under cross-examination. Had he written to the Director of Public Prosecutions offering himself as a witness for the prosecution? How could he explain this behaviour? 'I am an independent witness,' he told the court and Mr Justice Channell added as he ordered him to leave the witness box, 'I would say a completely untrustworthy witness...'. The judge regarded the mark made through perspiration as less satisfactory than if the murderer had made a definite impression in ink but he instructed the jury that fingerprint evidence could, to an extent, be regarded as corroborative evidence. The jurors retired for two hours before returning the verdict of guilty.[16]

Even before that trial the star of Alphonse Bertillon had begun to fade. In 1902 Hungary began fingerprinting, as did Austria, along with Denmark and Spain, followed by Switzerland. In the next year Saxony introduced fingerprinting followed by Hamburg and Berlin. A Belgian anarchist was traced by his fingerprints on anonymous letters. A man broke into a morgue where his wife's body lay. Through fingerprinting he was identified as her murderer. That convinced the Belgian authorities. Italy followed suit and Russia adopted fingerprinting in all major prisons in 1906. Six years later a Russian jury convicted a man of murder on fingerprint evidence. It was only a matter of time before *bertillonage* was completely outmoded. Really only Rumania, Luxembourg and Monaco were left among European adherents.

Part of the trouble was that Bertillon was unwilling to shift his stance. His colleagues Dr Lacassagne and Dr Locard in Lyons had been urging him to do so but he would not listen. Locard had, for example, been burning his own fingers with oil and hot irons to prove that fingerprints never changed.

In a more practical demonstration of the immutability of fingerprints in the early 1900s, an old lag who had not been recognised in court, but who had been remanded in custody for a week, 'excoriated (with a pluck and perseverance worthy of a better cause) the papillary ridges of his thumbs and fingers by means of a metal tag attached to his bootlace'. On his arrival at Brixton prison his hands were in such a state that it was feared that if the ink for fingerprinting were applied it might result in blood poisoning. As a result he was remanded from week to week until his fingertips had healed and the impressions revealed his identity.[17]

Perhaps Bertillon's downfall came with the theft on 22 August 1911 of Leonardo da Vinci's *Mona Lisa* from the Salon Carré in the Louvre. The theft caused an international political scandal with suggestions that the painting had been stolen on the orders of Kaiser Wilhelm II. In fact the answer was much more mundane. It had been taken by an Italian house painter, Vicenzo Perrugia, who simply removed it from the wall, hid it under his painter's smock and walked out with it. The painting remained under his bed in a room on the rue de l'Hôpital Saint-Louis for over two years until he offered it to a Florentine art dealer, Alfredo Geri. The suggestion was that he wanted to return the painting to Italy because it had been stolen by Napoleon. In fact it hadn't.

The difficulty for Bertillon was that Perrugia's fingerprints were on the files. His prints had been taken in 1909 when he had tried to steal a prostitute's purse but unfortunately the files had become far too cumbersome to search. The matter was hushed up by the resourceful Lepine who did not want to cause damage to a national treasure such as Bertillon even if he had, by now, become a liability. The good news for Lepine was that Bertillon was dying of pernicious anaemia and progress could soon be made.

In the autumn of 1913 Vucetich, whose star was definitely in the ascendancy at the time and who was on a triumphant world tour, tried to pay a call on the now desperately ill Bertillon in Paris. After being kept waiting, Bertillon said 'Sir, you have tried to do me great harm' and shut the door on him. Bertillon, now blind, died on 13 February 1914.[18]

In the spring of that year an International Police Conference was held in Monaco, one of the last strongholds of *bertillonage*. There his successor David proposed that the standard method of identification be fingerprinting.

V

Meanwhile for the past 30 years the police forces in the United States had been experimenting with *bertillonage* and fingerprinting. As far back as 1882 Gilbert Thompson, a railroad engineer, had been taking a thumbprint from each of the workers on wage slips to safeguard himself against forgeries. In 1885 it had been suggested that thumbprints were stamped on railroad tickets and the same year there was another suggestion, this time that the ever-increasing number of Chinese immigrants be registered by their thumbprints.

It was not, however, until 1903 that the great value of fingerprinting over *bertillonage* was recognised. Quite by chance McCloughty, the Warden of Fort Leavenworth, had been sent a copy of the Henry book on fingerprints together with a rudimentary test kit. Apparently the warden had experimented and had not been impressed. Then some months later a black prisoner, Will West, was being measured and photographed under Card No. 3246 when one of the guards discovered his exact measurements (within the tolerated discrepancies) on Card No. 2626. West protested that he was not the same man, who was found, in fact, to be in one of the workshops. The discovery spelled the slow death of *bertillonage* in the States.

Fingerprinting came to New York through Police Commissioner William McAdoo who heard of the identification of West. Fingerprinting had been a great attraction at the Louisiana Purchase Exposition in St Louis and he sent a Detective Sergeant Joseph A. Faurot to London to learn the techniques. However, by the time he returned, full of enthusiasm, McAdoo had been replaced and Faurot was told to forget the system. Like so many other pioneers he continued with his own experiments and with assembling a private collection of fingerprints.

On 16 April 1906 Faurot, on patrol for hotel creepers, saw a shoeless man, otherwise in full evening dress, leaving a suite in the Waldorf-Astoria. The man explained that he was British, that his name was James Jones and that he had just been leaving following an assignation. He demanded to see the British Consul. He nearly bluffed his way out of the situation but Faurot insisted on having the man give his fingerprints which he wired to Scotland Yard. Back came the reply that he was in fact Daniel Nolan, otherwise known as Henry Johnson who had twelve previous convictions for burglary.

The first American murder case officially solved with the use of fingerprinting was the strangling of a nurse, Nellie Quinn, in 1908. As in the Stratton case, the crime scene had become contaminated with beat policemen and others on the premises who had touched a number of objects in the room. They had not, however, touched a whisky bottle on the table. Faurot was able to obtain prints, some of which were the nurse's and some of a neighbour. Faurot was able to establish that the girl had only purchased the bottle earlier in the evening and the man confessed.[19]

Another early American case in which fingerprinting was used to convict and hang a suspect was that of Thomas Jennings in Chicago. On 19 September 1910 Clarence Hiller awoke at his home on W 104th Street and, going out on to the landing, found a burglar. The men fought and Hiller was shot dead. The evidence was strong. Jennings was arrested within a mile of the shooting and he was carrying a loaded revolver. Three bullets were found by Hiller's body. Jennings was wearing bloodstained clothing caused, he said, when he fell from a street car.

More important, however, were the fingerprints found in paint in the kitchen. With echoes of the early discovery by Herschel, Hiller had been painting the kitchen railings and the paint was still wet. Four perfect prints had been left by Jennings.

So far these had been cases where there was either a confession or a good deal of corroborative evidence. It was a wholly different thing to persuade a jury to accept fingerprint evidence on its own, particularly when ranged against a defence which called five alibi witnesses. In May 1911 Caesar Cella, a well-known New York burglar, raised $3,000 for his defence to a charge that he had broken into a millinery shop. His alibi was that on the night of the burglary he had been to the Hippodrome and then home with his wife.

Faurot had found and photographed the prints of several dirty fingers on the shop window and identified them as those of Cella. Just as Collins had done in the Stratton case 15 years earlier, Faurot enlarged the prints so the jury could see the points of identification more clearly. During Faurot's evidence the judge stopped the case, ordering him from the room and again, as in the Stratton case, an experiment began. In Faurot's absence various lawyers and court personnel pressed their fingers on panes of glass in the windows of the court, noting carefully whose print was where. Additionally one man placed his fingerprint on a glass desktop. When Faurot returned and, after examining the prints, made the correct identification, Cella changed his plea to one of guilty.

Before he was sentenced Judge Rosalsky promised there would be no indictments against his alibi witnesses if Cella told the court he had really committed the crime and how:

> It is most important in the cause of justice and science that you tell the whole truth. It is invaluable to us to know whether the expert testimony given during this trial was correct.

Cella said that his alibi had in part been correct. He had been at the theatre and had returned home with his wife. While she was asleep he had gone out and committed the burglary. He received six months' imprisonment.

It was reported that before the plea of guilty the jury was split seven for a conviction, because of Cella's previous record, while five, in view of the strong alibi, would not have convicted on fingerprints alone. 'That is beautifully characteristic of the jurybox – conservatism', commented the editorial.[20]

VI

Now it fell to criminals, sometimes with the help of their lawyers or doctors, to devise ways of getting round fingerprinting. Gloves were an obvious answer but, even at the end of the twentieth century, despite countless crime shows first on radio and then on television, and newspaper reports, it was apparent that some participants were not taking even this rudimentary precaution. Enough criminals, however, did take to wearing gloves for gloves to be included in the list of equipment which could be said to be housebreaking implements. Even that was not sufficient and one enterprising detective extracted fingerprints from the inside of gloves.[21]

More painful and no more successful was the removal or changing of fingerprints. A crucial day occurred on 6 January 1935 when FBI agents and a Sergeant Healey from the Chicago police trapped Jack Klutas at a bungalow in the Bellwood suburb of the city. In the exchange of fire Klutas was killed. It had become routine for police to take the fingerprints of dead criminals so they could be crossed off the wanted list but when an attempt was made to take those of Klutas he was found to have none.

There must have been panic among the FBI hierarchy, and the head of the bureau, J.Edgar Hoover, called for skin specialists from Chicago's Northwestern University to make a careful examination of Klutas's hands. The result was predictable. They found that he had had the skin of his fingertips removed. Two days later order was restored. Just as the early European experiments had shown thirty years earlier, the new skin growing over the wounds showed the old papillary lines.[22]

The news did not, however, filter through to other criminals of the era and doctors, very often struck-off abortionists, had their own 'secret' formulas which were sold as doing the trick. Both John Dillinger and Horace Van Meter went through the agonising process of undergoing treatment by Dr William Loeser's 'secret' formula of two parts of hydrochloric acid and one of nitro-hydrochloric acid to be used with an alkaloid, usually of caustic soda. And in May 1934 Alvin Karpis and Freddy Barker of the Barker-Karpis gang put themselves in the shaky hands of the alcoholic Dr Joseph Moran.

Moran was drunk and he botched all his work, leaving the men in extreme pain for weeks. When the bandages came off Karpis was even uglier than before and Moran had merely burned away the top skin on the men's fingers. He was taken by Barker and Karpis to Toledo where he was shot and dumped in a lake. Fred Barker is said to have remarked, 'Doc will do no more operating, the fishes probably have eat him up by now.'[23]

At least Loeser survived to be returned to prison when, after the shooting of Dillinger outside the Biograph Cinema in Chicago on 22 July 1934, the rest of the gang was rounded up and prosecuted.[23]

There were two more challenges for fingerprint experts in America in the 1930s. The first came when the bullet-ridden body of Gus Winkler was found in a Chicago suburb. He was well-known and wanted for murder and robbery. When his fingerprints were taken as a routine measure there was some consternation. They should have matched up with his card but they did not do so. What had happened was that the unknown doctor who had treated him had been more successful than either Loeser or Moran. He had only treated one detail of the pattern but, in so doing, had left an identifying scar. It was decided that there was only one way of altering fingerprints permanently and that was by grafting skin from the palms. However, this did not present any great problem since the grafts always left scars at the edges of the fingers. Provided care was taken in the fingerprinting itself this, coupled with any scars on the body which indicated a transplant, would always show up.

The second test came on 31 October 1941 when Robert Pitts was arrested for not carrying a draft card. He was fingerprinted and, to considerable embarrassment, was found not to have any fingerprints at all. What he did have, however, were sets of five scars on either side of his chest from where grafts had been taken. Pitts declined to answer questions. His photograph, age and general description fitted Robert J.'Roscoe' Phillips who had been in Alcatraz and who had last been arrested on 28 March 1941. His operation must therefore have taken place during the previous six months. Enquiries of previous cell inmates led to a Dr Leopold Brandenburg who had himself been arrested for abortion and a mail fraud. He was interviewed and confessed that he had done the transplants in the May. Pitts had been obliged to hold his fingers against the transplantation sites on the chest until skin had grown. It was then peeled away and the fingerprints 'modelled'.[25]

VII

The general public has often shown a healthy dislike of compulsory fingerprinting. When an 'enquiring reporter' carried out an admittedly tiny straw poll, only one in three said they would have no objections to being fingerprinted. One replied, 'Who knows, I might yet become another Dillinger ... I wouldn't want my prints on file.'[26] Indeed it was the reason that Vucetich fell out of favour. In 1916 he had proposed that all of Buenos Aires be fingerprinted and for a time it appeared that his suggestion might be followed. Both houses of the provincial parliament had accepted the suggestion but in May 1917 the federal government cancelled the law. Vucetich was forbidden to carry on his work, ordered to hand over his files and was banished to the country with a nominal pension.[27]

It was therefore surprising when in 1948 the male population of Blackburn, Lancashire, agreed *en masse* to be fingerprinted following the abduction of a three-year-old girl from her hospital bed in the children's ward at Queens Park Hospital. The reason may well have been the revulsion caused by the horrific death of the child who had been due to be released the next day after she had recovered from a slight case of pneumonia.

A nurse had checked the ward at 11 p.m., seeing to a child in the next bed to the victim's. At 11.30 she had been working in the kitchen when she thought she heard a child's voice in the corridor. She went outside and saw a door to the garden open. It had been a windy night and, not unnaturally, she thought it had blown open. She shut it and went back to work until, a quarter of an hour later, she made another tour of Ward CH III. This time she noticed what appeared to be adult footprints, either barefoot or with thin socks, on the polished floor. In that era it was something no matron would have tolerated for two seconds and so the nurse knew they had to be fresh. They led from a bay window to the girl's bed which was empty and under which was a bottle of distilled drinking water. After checking the lavatory, the nurse raised the alarm. Two hours later, after a search of the grounds and buildings found no trace of the child, the police were informed. Her body was discovered about 3 a.m. in long grass near a wall.

She had been raped and the killer had then smashed her head into the wall.

There had been a number of child killings in the area, and Scotland Yard, in the form of Chief Inspector John Capstick who liked to be known as Artful Johnny, was called in. He arranged for the area to be fingerprinted and photographed. Elimination prints were taken from doctors, staff and visitors and when it came to it the only print which could not be matched was the one on the bottle of water.

The print was sent to Scotland Yard, which at the time had a collection of some million and a quarter prints, but there was no match. Photographs were sent to all identification bureaux outside Great Britain in the hope that the killer had been a sailor or foreigner whose prints might be on record abroad. Again there was no positive response.[28]

A week after the murder on 20 May Chief Inspector Campbell, head of the fingerprint bureau of Lancashire County police, proposed that the fingerprints of all males in Blackburn and all those who commuted to Blackburn to work be taken. Given that the town then had a population of around 110,000 it was estimated that some 50,000 prints would need to be taken.

It was decided that to encourage co-operation the appeal would be made, not by the police, but by the Mayor of Blackburn. He announced that all prints would be compared with the print on the bottle and then destroyed. They would not be checked against a list of wanted men nor would they be used to solve any other crime. The work would be done on a house-to-house basis. There would be no need for anyone to attend a police station.

By August, 45,000 had been collected and sent to the North Western Forensic Science Laboratory at Preston with no result and it was feared that the person was indeed a stranger. Then, when a check was made on those to whom ration cards had still been sent, it was discovered that a further 800 males had been overlooked.

On 11 August PC Calvert called at 31 Birley Street occupied by a Mrs Griffiths and her 19-year-old son Peter. He was one who had been overlooked and willingly gave his prints. At 3 p.m. the next day a match was made. The print of his left thumb and index finger tallied with the prints on the distilled water bottle. When questioned he confessed. He had spent long periods as a child in Queens Park Hospital and knew the layout well. Fibres from a suit he had pawned matched those found on the child and bloodstains on it were of the same group as that of the victim. The defence argued that he killed the child while suffering from schizophrenia – his father had been in a mental hospital – but the jury rejected this in 23 minutes.

Two weeks before Griffiths was hanged on 19 November 1948 at Walton Prison all the fingerprints were publicly pulped at a local paper mill. Many regard the death of June Devaney as a good argument for general registration of fingerprints.

More claims for nationwide fingerprinting came when 'Aunt Polly' Mary Ornesher and her sister Margaret were battered to death in Ormskirk, Lancashire in May 1956. Fifteen thousand fingerprints were taken over a period of six months of every male over 16 years of age but none matched with the prints left behind. Three years later Paul Bennett, VC, the magistrate at Marlborough Street Magistrates' Court, suggested that 'If everybody's prints were taken from the Prime Minister downwards it would save the police tens of thousands of pounds.' But when 73-year-old Florence Gooding was found battered to death in Oxted, *Daily Herald* reporters found rather less than universal agreement that fingerprints should be taken. Curiously, they found that resistance was as high among older people as among younger ones.[29]

A proposal was examined by the Home Office in 1966 for compulsory fingerprinting. It came after the mass fingerprinting in Reading following the murder of 71-year-old 'Auntie Bea' Annie Cox who was suffocated at her home on 31 March. A disused dance-hall was turned into the murder headquarters. Ten thousand sets of prints were taken when, apparently without dissent, all males over 14 in the town were fingerprinted. A man was convicted in July 1966 and sentenced to life imprisonment.

The suggestion of compulsory fingerprinting produced considerable debate and *Punch* ran a series of mock letters for and against the scheme. They included one from a lady whose husband's penchant was for disregarding *Do Not Touch* notices in stately homes and instead 'leaving a loving finger' on Sèvres teapots 'but mostly I am sorry to say, on statues of nymphs and such. If any of these articles he has touched should be stolen and afterward recovered, my husband's fingerprints may well be found on them. We cannot sleep at nights for worrying.'[30]

On the other hand C.H. Rolph, a writer and former policeman very much in favour of compulsory printing, said that from his own straw poll he believed most would accept it.[31]

Nothing came of the suggestion but it was renewed from time to time. In April 1973 former Deputy Assistant Commissioner of Scotland Yard John Du Rose was one who maintained that 'thousands of unsolved crimes in Britain including murders, muggings, armed hold-ups and thefts could be cleared up tomorrow – if everyone was compulsorily fingerprinted'. He argued that no person had ever been convicted in Britain on fingerprint evidence alone and suggested that there were only two kinds of people who opposed compulsory fingerprinting:

Do gooders – anxious to protect crooks – and the public have suffered enough violence because of the kid-glove treatment of thugs, and those who are scared of fingerprints because they do not understand what part they play in prosecution.[32]

A third category could well be criminals who have never been arrested.

His was a call renewed in January 1979 and this time Tony Smythe, general secretary of the National Council for Civil Liberties, commented:

It would be a large stride towards a police State, which we would deplore. In some ways I can see the point of view of the police. They have more than two million unidentified prints on their files. But we like to think of ourselves as a law-abiding State, where things are not just geared to catching the criminal. Despite the block of the social advantages put forward,

people want to remain as individuals rather
than numbers. I would deplore any return to
the days of the identity card.[33]

In America from 1941 to 1958 all foreign visitors had to
leave their fingerprints recorded as a condition of entry.
The last all-out attack on fingerprinting came in 1938
when the American Civil Liberties' Union denounced
the FBI's voluntary programme as 'an early – and
effective – move in the direction of the regimentation
of the people'. The year that fingerprinting for visitors
was abolished it was calculated that only one in five
sets of prints on FBI files belonged to criminals. The FBI
had exchange facilities with 76 foreign countries and
six US territories or possessions with over 19,000 prints
being received a year including contributions from
Ghana and Iceland.[34]

VIII

Mistakes can always be made. There has been a
tendency to believe in the infallibility of the expert
witness but, in recent years in Britain, a number of
cases have caused hands to be thrown up in horror.
Unfortunately those who believe that the reading of
fingerprints is an infallible science received a setback
in their devotion when, in April 1997, it was
disclosed that an error had been made in a
comparison test between fingerprints found at the
scene and those of the suspect. Even more
unfortunately, the disclosure came during a relatively
high-profile case.

In March 1995 a burglary had taken place at the Mayfair, London home of Dr Miriam Stoppard, the estranged wife of the playwright Tom Stoppard, during which £30,000 of property had been taken. The fingerprints, which had been, it was said, triple-checked, showed that a 20-year-old man had been involved and he was duly charged. Unfortunately for the prosecution it was accepted after an examination by an independent expert that the match was wrong.

Adrian Clarke, of solicitors Bindman & Partners, commented that:

> Fingerprint comparison is all quite Neanderthal and an innately subjective process. I would imagine it is susceptible to error, particularly if you are doing it for considerable periods of time.

Anne Rafferty, QC, then chairman of the Criminal Bar Association, later to become a High Court judge, voiced the general feeling of practitioners:

> If fingerprint evidence emerges when you are defending a client, then you tend to put your head in your hands. There is not really a question mark over it.[35]

An even more serious example had occurred in 1991 in Nottinghamshire when a 39-year-old man was arrested for the rape of an 11-year-old girl because of matching fingerprints. He was only released when someone in prison confessed. By that time he had suffered the usual assaults in jail doled out to child sex offenders and his home had been wrecked by vigilantes.

In recent years two more cases have shaken the absolute faith in Britain as to the accuracy of fingerprint identification. They have come at a time when there has been a move by the Association of Chief Police Officers (ACPO) to abandon the tried and tested 16-point formula in favour of a non-numerical system backed by 'standardised and accredited quality procedures', whatever that may mean.

For years, faced with witnesses from the Metropolitan Police and other laboratories, each of whom had many years' experience in comparing prints, defendants and their lawyers have tended to cave in when the expert said he had found 16 standard points of comparison. In 1999 the barrister Michael Mansfield commented:

> We were constantly being told that to question
> fingerprints was like questioning two and two
> and so we didn't. They thought that it was a
> science. We now discover it is no more
> exacting than comparing two shades of blue.[36]

Mansfield had said in the earlier case involving the burglary of Dr Stoppard's home:

> I think, however, that we tend to be too
> blinded by science. It is time that fingerprint
> techniques were subjected to the same rigour of
> questioning as DNA comparisons.

This time his comments followed the case of Danny McNamee, convicted in 1987 of the 1982 Hyde Park bombing in which four troopers from the Household

Cavalry and seven horses were killed. The explosion had been triggered by a remote-controlled device near Kensington Barracks. In 1986 he was arrested near Crossmaglen, Co Armagh and brought to stand trial at the Old Bailey. McNamee's fingerprints had allegedly been found on a Duracell battery and circuit boards for the Hyde Park bomb which, said the prosecution, linked him to two IRA arms dumps and a defused bomb in Kensington.

During his appeal 14 fingerprint officers from different forces gave evidence regarding the thumbprint on a bomb defused in Kensington. They were divided on whether it could be linked to Mr McNamee which, said Lord Justice Swinton Thomas in the Court of Appeal in December 1998, was enough to render unsafe the conviction on the Kensington bomb. As to the Hyde Park bomb it had become clear that there had been significant non-disclosure to the defence at the time of the trial. Scotland Yard reports showed another man was more likely to have been responsible than Mr McNamee for making the Hyde Park bomb. The court accepted there had been a material irregularity and the conviction would be quashed.

The court went on to say that this did not automatically mean he was innocent, something Mr McNamee, unsurprisingly, resented. 'It was a grudging judgement', he told reporters.[37]

The second case revolved around whether Detective Constable Shirley McKie had been present or not at a murder scene. On 6 January 1997 Marion Ross was found stabbed through the eye and throat with a pair of scissors at her home. The prosecution alleged that

David Asbury, who had been working at Miss Ross's semi-detached bungalow, had returned there to steal money. Pretending to wish to use the telephone he had conned his way into the house and stabbed her with a pair of scissors. Much of the evidence against him concerned a Marks & Spencer biscuit tin said to belong to Miss Ross, found at his home and on which was her fingerprint. He claimed the police had taken the tin to the morgue and put the dead woman's print on it.

The case was clouded by the finding of a fingerprint on the bathroom doorpost near where the body of Miss Ross was found. In the prosecution of the Detective Constable for perjury, the Crown claimed that it was her print. She had been excluded from the crime scene but it was alleged she had gone back 'for a peep' and so had contaminated the scene. Four fingerprint experts from the Scottish Criminal Records Office identified the print as hers while two experts from America, including David Grieve who trains police fingerprint experts in Illinois and is the editor of *The Journal of Forensic Identification*, told the court the print was not Ms McKie's.

Finally she was acquitted and Donald Findlay QC, who appeared for Ms McKie, commented:

This is not the death knell of fingerprinting. That would be a ridiculous point of view. What it means is that lawyers should do their job properly in the questioning of all evidence against an accused.

It is the lawyers' duty to check everything to an enormous degree and maybe to an extent we have accepted fingerprint evidence at face value. Fingerprinting is always going to be crucial evidence and more often than not will be the compelling evidence.[38]

In August 2000 David Asbury was freed on bail pending an appeal. An American expert used by the FBI, Pat Wertheim, said, 'A first-day student could have dismissed any link to the murder victim within two minutes. It is not her print.'

IX

Even more worrying is the police officer or, occasionally, the criminal who sets out to obtain a conviction by faking prints.

One criminal obtained the copy of the right index finger of a fellow criminal. It was actually taken from a book called Fingerprints of My Friends which the owner of the fingerprint had forgotten was in existence, containing the right index finger impressed in Indian ink.

The print was made into a rubber stamp with a fine, very good quality rubber. The stamp was carefully cleaned after it was made and the criminal who owned it took it with him when he broke into an office, where he made a good haul of petty cash.

He held the rubber stamp in his own cupped palm for some minutes until he was sure the fingerprint was damped with body sweat, and lightly impressed the print on a corner of a polished desk, departing with the knowledge that he had laid a false trail.

By chance he was caught leaving the premises.[39]

On one occasion an accused brought his own fingerprint kit to court to demonstrate how tampering could take place. In January 1938 David Pearce, alleged to have broken into a club pavilion in Surrey, demonstrated how a fingerprint could be taken and planted. He produced a small mirror and a pad of plastic substance in which he pressed the finger of a warder. He then pressed the substance on the mirror, producing a perfect print. He was acquitted despite the evidence of his co-accused who maintained he had been on the raid with him.[40]

Four years later the murder of Sir Harry Oakes still ranks as one of the great unsolved crimes of the twentieth century. It involved the alleged planting of a print which was the main plank of the prosecution.[41] The 69-year-old self-made, socially inept, millionaire who had made his fortune in gold mining was found dead on 3 July 1943 in his bed at his ocean front home at Westbourne in Nassau in the Bahamas. His head had been repeatedly battered and an attempt had been made to set him on fire. The only other person in the house at the time was his great friend and real estate dealer, Harold Christie. It was he who discovered the body.

Nassau, during the war, was full of interesting people. The Governor General was the former Edward VIII, who was now the Duke of Windsor, exiled as an embarrassment to the British Government. As well as senior Mafia figures and at least one suspected Nazi spy, there was also Oakes's son-in-law, the 34-year-old Count Marie Alfred Fouquereaux de Marigny who had married the 18-year-old Nancy in a secret wedding ceremony in America the previous year. It was he who was selected by the authorities as the most likely murderer. It was known that Oakes had not favoured the twice divorced, womanising, socially adroit, failed chicken farmer, playboy.

The evidence against him came down to singed hairs on his beard, arms and hands said to have happened when he tried to set fire to Sir Harry's body. More damning was a fingerprint, said to have been found on a Chinese screen by Sir Harry's bed.

The investigation, in the hands of the Duke of Windsor, was handled with less than skill and was marked by a series of blunders. Inexplicably he decided to call in two officers from the Miami Police Department instead of using the local police or, what would have been perfectly usual in a Crown Colony, sending for Scotland Yard officers. The reason given was that Captain Edward Melchen had been the bodyguard for the Duke when he had visited Miami and had impressed him with his efficiency.

When arrested, de Marigny asked for his lawyer, Sir Alfred Adderley. He never arrived and said he had never been told of the request. Instead Sir Alfred appeared as a special prosecutor. When the Commissioner of Police, Lieutenant Colonel R.A. Erskine-Lindop, at first declined to charge de Marigny he was transferred to Trinidad. He maintained that another suspect had broken down during cross-examination. It was learned that on the night of the murder a watchman at Lyford Cay had seen a powerful boat pull in and drop off two strangers. The men had later returned to the boat which had left. The lawyers for de Marigny were never able to trace the watchman who was said to have drowned.

It was the fingerprint which caused the trouble. The second Miami policeman, Captain James Barker, said to be a fingerprint expert, alleged he had lifted the print from the screen. He certainly lied about the time of the first interview with de Marigny who otherwise could have touched the screen during his interview.

De Marigny owed his life to the efforts of his young wife who travelled to New York to hire Raymond Schindler, possibly the most famous private detective of his day. In turn he contacted Professor Leonard Keeler, who developed the lie-detector in its present form.

The defence lawyers were able to show that Barker had, deliberately or ignorantly, destroyed much of the fingerprint evidence in the case, including a bloody handprint on the wall. Photographs of the handprint were exposed to the light before they were developed and there was no second opportunity because the Bahamian police were told to wash off the handprint because it did not match that of the accused. Godfrey Higgs, de Marigny's barrister, had also been to New York to study fingerprinting and he forced Barker into admitting that he had informed no one, not even Melchen, of the existence of the fingerprint for a week. Nor could he say exactly from where he had 'lifted' the print.[42] He maintained he had lifted scores of prints without first photographing them but could not recall a specific instance. Nor had he remembered to bring a fingerprint camera and he had not bothered to borrow one from the local Royal Air Force station. Barker was in the witness box for three days contradicting himself time after time and becoming increasing disturbed. He also admitted he had failed to take samples from de Marigny of the allegedly singed hair.

De Marigny was found not guilty by a 9–3 vote and the next day Schindler wired his client to a lie detector, a test he passed. Thereafter, despite offers of assistance from President Truman and Schindler himself, no great effort was made to pursue the case. Suggestions for the death of Oakes have been numerous. De Marigny was meant to have killed him because they were on bad terms but, it seems, Oakes had recently given him £5,000 to start a new business. It has also been suggested that the Duke of Windsor 'wanted' de Marigny whom he disliked intensely. A more likely explanation is that Harold Christie killed Oakes because of his refusal to see that legalised gambling – to be run, in fact, by the Mafia although this was not made clear – would do much for the Bahamian economy. It is also said that Oakes was about to call in loans he had made to Christie, which would ruin him. Another suggestion is that Sir Harry was planning to move his funds off the island to Mexico, an act which would cause economic damage. Another, relatively fanciful but not wholly dismissible, is that Oakes knew of a plot involving a Swedish industrialist Axel Wenner-Gren, a good friend of Goering, Mussolini and the Duke, to move funds, frozen by the allied government, to Mexico where he owned a bank. Such a move would have considerably assisted the Axis powers who needed finance for petroleum and arms. A final suggestion is that Oakes was killed by racists who disapproved of his efforts to assist the black indigent community.[43]

De Marigny and his wife were exiled from the Bahamas and, none too welcome in Cuban society, were entertained there by Ernest Hemingway. They soon split up and he went to Canada where he joined the Canadian Army. Afterwards he worked in a shoe shop and was for a time reduced to selling his blood to hospitals. He returned to the United States where he lived in obscurity until, in June 1990, he published *A Conspiracy of Crowns* in which he alleged that it was Christie who had Oakes killed and that the Duke of Windsor was behind the attempt to frame him.

Nancy de Marigny fell in love with a Dutch airman who was killed. Later she married a titled German and when this marriage failed married a third time. Christie was knighted in 1964 and died in Germany nine years later. In 1952 Captain James Barker was shot by his son in Miami. It was revealed that, as with many police officers of the time, he had been on the payroll of the Mafia for a number of years.

X

On 30 August 1988 a man walked to the door of 81-year-old Joe Meeker in Enfield, New York and asked for a glass of water. The old man was then savagely beaten. New York State Trooper David Harding went to investigate and a local man, Mark Prentice, was arrested after being named by two other suspects. Prentice strongly denied that he had ever been at Meeker's home but Harding said he had found matching fingerprints in two places: on Meeker's sink and in a shed adjacent to Meeker's house, on some old Budweiser bottles. It was Harding's crucial evidence which brought Prentice a sentence of 7–15 years in prison and which Prentice recalls most vividly:

> He had to go through the points system of the fingerprints, so many identifiable points on the card, and – when it got to the point where he said, yes, these are 12 comparison points on this fingerprint and he said, yes, there are the defendant's and, yes, I did lift these off the kitchen sink in the victim's house – and you can see the jurors looking at me like you're worthless, you know. And it was hard, it was hard to deal with. I kept asking the judge if I can sit in the other room, because I couldn't – I couldn't tolerate the lies, I couldn't stand it. I couldn't deal with it.

The following year Harding went to upstate New York to deal with the Harris murder. There he organised an undercover operation and police identified Michael Kinge and his mother Shirley as being involved. Their house was raided and Michael Kinge was killed trying to escape. Shirley Kinge was arrested and was found to have credit cards belonging to the Harris family in her possession. As to the murders and arson, all the evidence against her consisted of a print on a gas canister Harding had found in the living room. She received a sentence of 20 years' imprisonment. As she was led away she was asked if she had anything to say and replied 'Yeah, but it's not printable. It's called truth and it's called justice and it's called the American way.'

Now Harding was a police hero with a seemingly limitless career horizon. In fact his downfall came in a curious way. He applied for a job with the CIA and was routinely asked to take the lie-detector or polygraph test. While he was speaking about covert operations he was asked if he had committed any crimes and the detector registered he was lying when he said he had not. Eventually the tape was played to special prosecutor Nelson Roth. The lies were about the prints supposedly found in Meeker's home. In fact, a Labatt's beer bottle had been taken by Harding from Prentice's home and he had lifted the prints, saying they came from the scene. Prentice was released after five and a half years and Harding served four, the minimum which could be imposed under his plea bargain. He was still able to justify his conduct:

In forensic investigation, fingerprint evidence is some of the best evidence you can have as far as convicting someone. It doesn't take a lot of information to arrest someone, it takes a lot to convict. And that's what we want to do, to take the violent people off the street, we have to convict them. Fingerprint evidence is some of the best evidence we had to do that. But we don't – we don't steal, don't profit from this. We're doing what we thought was right, what needed to be done to protect the public.

Harding was found responsible for four fingerprint fabrications and the 'we' to whom he was referring, his unit, was responsible for a further thirty. Theirs may have been the most celebrated instance of faking fingerprints in recent times but it has not been the only one. The problem is greatest in small jurisdictions. It is a difficult type of case to prosecute and the perpetrator is often fired or allowed to resign. He then goes to another jurisdiction where he begins again or leaves behind others who are already doing it.

Shirley Kinge's 20 year sentence was overturned. She had served two years in prison and in November 1992 was allowed to plead to a single count of using a stolen credit card belonging to a member of the family. She received a one-year conditional discharge and agreed to pay $600 restitution.[44]

As Special Prosecutor Nelson Roth says:

Anybody who thinks that fingerprint evidence tampering is a thing of the past now is a fool. You simply cannot assume that any scientific evidence is above reproach. Anything that has human involvement has to be questioned like any other evidence in a criminal case. Nothing is foolproof.

CHAPTER 2

Ballistics

I

Almost everyone concerned with the early days of fingerprints had some scientific background and was acting, if sometimes mistakenly, in good faith. The same could not be said for the early gun experts. For a good twenty years charlatans moved through rudimentary police laboratories and the courts selling their 'expert' evidence to whichever side paid the better. And, of course, they produced some terrible and tragic results.

In fact the early solving of crime by the use of firearms evidence can be dated back to Henry Goddard, one of the Bow Street Runners who pre-dated the Metropolitan Police. In 1835 he removed a bullet which had a curious ridge from the body of a householder. In those days bullets were often home-made and at the home of a suspect he found a bullet mould with a slight gouge and the ridge on the bullet corresponded to the gouge in the mould. The suspect confessed.

On 9 December 1860 a labourer Thomas Richardson stood trial at Lincoln charged with the murder of Constable Alexander McBrian on 25 October that year. At about 4 a.m. McBrian had been on duty patrolling near the churchyard at Wyberton when he saw Richardson wearing a billycock hat pulled over his eyes and with something in his pocket. When McBrian went to question him, Richardson shot the officer and fled. Badly wounded McBrian managed to rouse the vicar but he died later that morning after giving a description of his attacker.

This time the murder was solved not by matching the bullet but with the paper plugs used to stuff powder and bullets into the barrels of muzzle-loaders. Superintendent Manton found the singed remains of a tampion made from a page of *The Times*. The home of Richardson was searched and he was found to have a double-barrelled pistol, one barrel of which had been fired and the second contained a matching piece of *The Times* from 27 March 1854. At his trial the jury was invited to return accident, manslaughter or wilful murder with the judge seeming to favour a manslaughter verdict. They returned a verdict of wilful murder and Richardson was sentenced to death. The sentence was respited on 20 December.[1]

One of the first cases in America in which ballistics played a part took place in Oregon in 1852 when the sheriff was asked to examine a hole in a victim's shirt and give an opinion whether it had been caused by a bullet hole or a tear. Using the firearm which might have been used, the sheriff fired the gun into the shirt and produced a similar hole.

The American Civil War produced two cases of rudimentary ballistic examination, the first in 1863 when Confederate General Stonewall Jackson was fatally wounded. When the bullet was removed, tests measuring both the calibre and bullet shape showed that he had been shot by his own troops. They used a 67 calibre ball projectile while the Union forces used a

58 calibre minie ball. The second came when a year later Union General John Sedgwick was killed by a Confederate sniper at a distance of 800 yards. Tests carried out on the calibre and the bullet's hexagonal shape showed that it had come from a Whitworth rifle imported from England for use by the Confederates.

Another landmark case was in 1879 when a man, Moughon, charged in Georgia with murder, maintained that he had not used his gun for a year before the prosecution claimed he had fired the two fatal shots. The trial judge sent for a gunsmith who examined the weapon, found the barrels mildewed and was prepared to say that it had not been fired for 18 months. Three years later another gunsmith in Minnesota gave evidence about rifling marks which tended to show one rather than another gun had been used.

An early use of ballistics in England traced the 1882 killer of PC George Coles who was shot while trying to arrest a young man he had seen acting suspiciously outside the Baptist chapel opposite the Reeves paint factory in the Dalston Road, London. The man drew a pistol and fired two shots, one of which killed the policeman. A set of housebreaking tools was found behind a low wall of the chapel but for nearly two years there was no sign of the officer's killer.

The bag of tools did provide one clue. A chisel had the letters 'ROCK' marked crudely on the handle and it was believed that a tool repairer had scratched Orrock into the wood when the owner had left the tool for sharpening.

Enquiries led the police to believe that a young man Thomas Henry Orrock had acquired a pistol from

Exchange & Mart. Initially he was placed on an identification parade but was not picked out and was released. Later Sergeant Cobb was told that Orrock had used a tree on Tottenham Marshes for firing practice and the detective went there, found the tree, took out the bullets and matched them with the one which had killed Coles.

The police were also able to find youths who had been drinking with Orrock on the night of the murder and they confirmed that they had all planned to burgle the church undercover of the prevailing fog.

Orrock was traced to the jail at Coldbath Fields where he was serving a short sentence. He was convicted at the Old Bailey and hanged by James Berry on 6 October 1884 at Newgate Prison.[2]

Throughout the century manufacturers developed the design of guns in an effort to improve both range and accuracy. Once the breech-loader and cartridge were developed then rifling became possible. This technique, spiralling grooves cut into the inner surface, gave the bullet a rotational movement rather than tumbling end over end during flight. Now, with some manufacturers making barrels with five and others with six or more grooves, identification became easier, and in France Professor Lacassagne became the first to make a comprehensive study.[3] Shortly after, an article by Dr Albert Llewellyn Hall dealt with a variety of issues including how measurement of groove markings are made on bullets. He also discussed the deposits of gunpowder residue.[4]

An early German case cited by magistrate Hans Gross in his book of 1894, is of A.M., a grain merchant found dead one morning on a bridge with a single gunshot wound behind the ear. There was no gun by the body. He had been seen in the company of an 'unknown wretched-looking man' and A.M. had been noticed taking out his pocket book which seemed to have been well-filled. When the body was found his watch-chain and ring as well as the pocketbook were missing. The man's alibi was that he had spent the night in a barn which he could not point out to the police. He was naturally arrested.

The police investigator seems to have been unusually observant because he noticed a fresh mark on the structure of the bridge and he believed that something had been thrown over, struck the wood and damaged it. The bed of the stream was dragged and a cord attaching a large stone at one end and a revolver at the other was found. Experiments showed that A.M. had hung the stone over the parapet and as he fired the pistol he let it go. The stone then dragged the gun over the bridge damaging it in the process. It was a case of suicide. The gun belonged to A.M. who had been hopelessly in debt. He had taken out a large insurance policy for his wife and family but, since the company did not pay out on suicide, had faked his own murder.[5]

Two years later a Massachusetts court permitted the introduction of expert testimony on the effects of rifling on bullets. The following year came a major development in English cases. Camille Holland, a wealthy late-middle-aged spinster, had disappeared in 1899. She had been living at Moat House Farm, Audley End in Essex with Samuel Herbert Dougal, who had been married twice and both of whose wives had died from oyster poisoning. After Dougal had been found in the room of a frightened servant girl and had tried to excuse himself by saying he had only wanted to wind up the clock in her room, Miss Holland decided to leave him. He shot her and buried her body in a filled-in moat trench. Enquirers were told 'Mrs Dougal' was away on a yachting trip. In 1903, after police had seen him trying to teach a naked girl to ride a bicycle and one of Miss Holland's cheques was found to be forged, a full-scale investigation began and her body was found. Dougal claimed the shooting had been accidental. E.J. Churchill, uncle of the celebrated firearms examiner Robert Churchill, after carrying out a series of tests using a .32 revolver and a number of sheep skulls, gave evidence that the shots had been fired from a distance of between 6 inches and a foot.

On 13 August 1907 came the so-called Brownsville (Texas) Affray when it was claimed that a number of soldiers from an infantry regiment rioted in the small town. It was alleged that in a ten minute period no less than 150 shots and probably substantially more were fired. Afterwards some 39 fired .30 calibre cartridge cases and some spent bullets were found in a back alley. These and rifles from the infantry company were sent to Frankfort Arsenal for examination. Thirty-three of the fired cases were said to have come from four of the rifles. There was, however, no evidence linking a specific gun to a particular soldier and on 4 October President Theodore Roosevelt warned that if the troops would not give up the culprits then all would be discharged 'without honour'. They remained silent and 167 were discharged. Fourteen were later allowed to re-enlist and the decision was finally quashed on 22 September 1972 when the discharge was changed to 'with honour'. It was the first time that a serious study had been undertaken to attempt to identify and link fired cartridge cases to specific rifles.[6]

II

So far all relatively seemed well and the science of ballistics was developing nicely. Then came two cases which set things back on their heels. Both involved the participation of one of the great forensic quacks of the time as a prosecution witness, the *soi-disant* self-proclaimed expert, 'Dr' Albert Hamilton. As was the case with a number of charlatans of the time, 'Dr' was a self-bestowed title. Hamilton had begun his professional career as a patent medicine salesman. He called himself a Micro-Chemical Investigator and published a pamphlet, *That Man from Auburn*, in which he praised himself as an expert in chemistry, microscopy, handwriting analysis, toxicology, identification of bloodstains, causes of death, embalming and anatomy, as well as being well-versed in gunshot wounds, guns, identification of bullets, gunpowder and high explosives. Like all good conmen he was certainly something of a psychologist. He knew that enlarged photographs appealed to juries and, with his very basic knowledge of the literature, camera and microscope, at a fee of $50 a day plus expenses, he provided them.

The first of the two cases concerned an illiterate tenant farmhand, Charles Stielow. On the morning of 22 March 1915 at West Shelby, New York the bodies of farmer Charles Phelps and his housekeeper, Margaret Wolcott, were discovered at around 6 o'clock by the immigrant Stielow. They had been shot to death. Stielow walked through the snow to the cottage of his brother-in-law, Nelson Green, described as being, if anything, even more backward than Stielow, who then went to inform the sheriff, Chester Bartlett. When a doctor arrived he removed three .22 bullets from the body of Phelps. Both Stielow and Green denied they owned any firearms at all but, after lengthy questioning, Green broke down and confessed that Stielow had once owned a revolver, a rifle and a shotgun. All were .22 calibre weapons. After more questioning he confessed that both he and Stielow had killed Phelps.

In turn Stielow was again questioned and was offered the opportunity of seeing his wife and going home if he confessed. Nevertheless it took two days before he finally admitted to the murder. Robbery was the motive and he said they had been interrupted by Phelps and then the housekeeper whom they shot and left dying in the snow. Stielow refused to sign the confession and retracted it in court.

Stielow was seriously unfortunate that Hamilton had arrived and had examined the man's revolver. Hamilton claimed that Stielow's weapon had in the muzzle an abnormal scratch which showed up on the bullets found in Phelps' body. Stielow was doubly unfortunate. His case was the first murder trial handled by his lawyer, David A. White, whose inexperience was compounded by the fact that there was no money to obtain an expert to contradict Hamilton. White did what he could and pointed out that Hamilton's photographs showed no traces of scratches. Hamilton also explained away the suggestion that flaws at the muzzle of a weapon rarely left marks on the bullets. In this case, he said, the barrel fitted the cartridge so tightly that no explosive gasses escaped to the rear. This meant that the lead had expanded close to the muzzle and filled in the scratch at the end of the barrel. And the jury accepted it. On 23 July 1915 Stielow was convicted and sentenced to electrocution in Sing Sing.

Now his fortunes took a turn for the better. He impressed Spencer Miller, one of the crusading warders of the period, who referred his case to three women, one of whom was a lawyer, from the Humanitarian Cult of New York. They discovered that two tramps, King and O'Connell, had been in West Shelby on the night of the murder and had been heard discussing it before the facts were made public.

King made a voluntary confession to the trial judge but later retracted it and it was not until 1917 that an independent commission was appointed to examine the case. Headed by a Syracuse lawyer, George H. Bond, it included an employee in the office of the New York State Prosecutor Charles E. Waite, who called on Captain Jones of the New York City police force along with Inspector Joseph Faurot for assistance. When Stielow's guns were fired the bullets were covered in dirt and they immediately disproved Hamilton's flash theory when, on firing the gun, a dart of flame leaped back and set alight the piece of paper placed over the revolver. So far as the scratches were concerned they used Max Posner, a specialist in applied optics and microscopy, who could not find any allegedly seen by Hamilton.

Stielow, who had once actually been strapped in the electric chair before a stay of execution came through, was pardoned and once more King confessed. He was fortunate. The Grand Jury of Orleans County, not keen to waste any more money on abortive trials, refused to indict him. Waite went on to interest himself in the science of ballistics, becoming one of America's founding fathers in the subject. By 1922 he had accumulated data on all types of guns manufactured in the United States since the middle of the nineteenth century and had discovered that no type of gun was identical to any other in detail.

The second case in which Hamilton disgraced himself was in one of the great trials in American criminal and social history. It followed the killing on 15 April 1920 of Frederick Parmenter, the paymaster of a shoe factory in South Braintree, Massachusetts, and Alessandro Berardelli, his guard, when the payroll of $15,776 was stolen. There had been a similar attack in nearby Bridgewater on the White Shoe factory on the morning of 24 December 1919.

At about 3.05 p.m. Parmenter and Berardelli were shot as they carried the money in two metal boxes across the street. Two strangers snatched the money and jumped into a car in which three others were waiting. Berardelli died on the street. Parmenter survived for some 14 hours. One bullet had penetrated his ventral cave, the largest vein in the body. When it was extracted it was marked with a white cross. A bullet from the lung of Berardelli which had slightly flattened as it hit the hip-bone was marked with III in Roman numerals. All the cartridges found were manufactured by either Peters, Remington or Winchester.

It was a time of great social unrest. The Wobblies, the Industrial Workers of the World, were at their height, struggling for proper pay and working conditions. It was also a period of anarchy, the central tenet of which was that social justice could only be achieved by the violent overthrow of government. Bombs had been sent to senators and millionaires such as John D. Rockefeller. On 7 November 1919 a bomb had exploded in front of the Washington home of the Attorney-General, A. Mitchell Palmer. The Government struck back; arrests and deportations were plentiful.

Two days after the robbery, on 17 April, an abandoned Buick was found in a wooded area of Massachusetts. It fitted the description of the car used in the hold-up. The police learned that an Italian named Boda had been seen in the Buick. Watch was maintained on a garage where he kept another car. When the police swooped, Boda and a companion escaped on a motorcycle. Boda would eventually reach the safety of Italy. The two who were caught were Nicola Sacco and Bartolomeo Vanzetti.

Unfortunately for them they denied they knew Boda. Sacco was carrying a loaded .32 Colt automatic and in his pockets were 23 .32 cartridges manufactured by the firms of Peters, Remington and Winchester. Vanzetti had a .38 Harrington & Richardson revolver with five cartridges and four shotgun cases. Both lied consistently throughout their first interviews.

At the time of his arrest Sacco, who had been born in southern Italy on 22 April 1892 and had come to the United States in 1908, was working in a shoe factory. Vanzetti, born on 11 June 1888 near Turin, had been a pastry-cook before coming to America after his mother died, also in 1908. He had a cart from which he sold fish. There is no doubt that both were active in anarchist circles but Sacco had a cast-iron alibi for the Bridgewater robbery. Vanzetti was picked out and charged. They were both charged with robbery and murder following the South Braintree pay snatch. The trial of Vanzetti began in June 1920 and of the pair for murder in May 1921. As is often the case, the trial was muddied by politics. They might have done better to have simply run their defence on the basis of mistaken identity. Instead the anarchists supporting them saw the trial as an opportunity to 'unmask the criminal nature of the American government'. A radical lawyer from California, Fred H. Moore, was brought in for the defence.

It is now accepted that, whether Sacco and Vanzetti were actually guilty, the prosecution evidence was flawed and fabricated and at best the trial judge Webster Thayer may not have been wholly impartial. He was later admonished for making rash public – at his golf club – comments after the trial. The first prosecution ballistics expert, Captain William Proctor, claimed that the bullet marked III had been fired by Sacco's Colt. He had previously tried to push a bullet through the pistol and, when he had, failed, said it was not necessary. A second expert, Charles Van Amburgh, said that he was inclined to believe that the bullet marked III had come from the Colt. Neither of the prosecution experts could distinguish between types of weapons and Proctor had no experience with even the simplest kind of microscope work.

Two witnesses called for the defence said that III could never have been fired by the Colt. Both the defence experts, James Burns who had worked as a technician for the US Cartridge Company for 30 years and J. Henry Fitzgerald who had been in the arms business for nearly as long, had serious credentials. Burns was adamant. Asked if bullet III had been fired from Sacco's pistol he answered, 'In my opinion, no. It doesn't compare at all.'

On 14 July 1921 the jury retired and after five hours convicted both men, Vanzetti as an accessory which in law made him equally guilty.

Moore continued to challenge the convictions and by 1932 he had lost two motions for a retrial. Unfortunately he then latched on to Dr Albert Hamilton. The man's business had flourished and on a train to Boston he fell into conversation with a reporter from the Boston *Globe* and boasted that had he been giving evidence at the trial the result would have been different. The reporter told Moore who wrote asking what Hamilton's fees would be. Within a matter of days Hamilton arrived uninvited in Moore's office.

Then came a significant piece of evidence. Proctor decided that he was not convinced the bullet had come from Sacco's gun and although he died soon afterwards he left an affidavit to the effect that no one had asked him the question point blank because they knew what the answer would have been.

Armed with this Moore presented a fifth supplementary motion for a retrial but when, at the end of October 1923, Judge Thayer reconsidered the evidence of Van Amburgh for the prosecution, Dr Hamilton tried to switch the exhibit with a gun he had brought into court. He was seen by the judge who instituted an inquiry. Hamilton, brazen to the end, suggested the switch must have been made by a member of the prosecutor's staff. Unsurprisingly the motion for a new trial was rejected.

Nor did Van Amburgh always cover himself with glory. In the 1924 case of Father Hubert Dahme, who was shot in Main Street, Bridgeport, Connecticut, he produced photographs which showed the bullet had come from the gun of suspect John Reynolds. He was contradicted by five experts and when the prosecutor examined the photographs it was clear that there was not the remotest possibility that this was so.

Sacco and Vanzetti died in the electric chair on 23 August 1927. Sacco cried, 'Long live anarchy!' Vanzetti said, 'I am an innocent man.' The executions were marked by worldwide demonstrations. Socialist and Communist newspapers appeared with black borders. Millions paraded through city streets. Meanwhile Judge Webster Thayer's home had been fire-bombed and his wife and maid injured.

In 1961 two experts, Frank Jury, a former Lieutenant Colonel in the New Jersey State Police Laboratory, and Jac Weller, who had revised Major Julian S. Hatcher's 1935 forensic bible *Textbook of Firearms Investigation, Identification and Evidence,* re-examined Sacco's gun and were convinced that bullet III had indeed come from it.

The best view of the case, and that of Carlo Tresca, the campaigning and politically committed journalist who did so much to help the defence of his fellow anarchists, was that Sacco was guilty and Vanzetti was not. One thing is certain and it is that at the time of their arrest these men of peace, as they portrayed themselves, were armed to the teeth, something they were never ever able to explain satisfactorily. Of course that does not mean they were guilty of the robberies and murders. In any event they were both pardoned in 1977 by Governor Dukakis five years before another panel of experts, assembled to consider the evidence in the case, confirmed the Jury-Weller report.[7]

III

In 1917 Dr Sydney Smith, from Edinburgh University, accepted the post of Principal Medico-Legal Expert in Cairo, Egypt. There he arranged that he should have a series of laboratories for his own use and he began to collect information regarding the examination of firearms. He constructed his own comparison microscope which allowed examiners to look simultaneously at two different bullets, one on the left lens and one on the right, something which, of course, made comparison more simple but more reliable. It was he who in 1925 gave evidence in the murder of Sir Lee Stack Pasha, the Sirdar of the Egyptian Army. Smith demonstrated in court how easy it was to turn an ordinary bullet into a dum-dum and his unchallenged evidence led to the conviction of the assassins. In January 1926 he contributed a paper on the case to the *British Medical Journal* and, perhaps immodestly, wrote:

> It brought me a whole host of inquiries from police authorities throughout the world. I hope I may be pardoned for claiming that the scientific examination of firearms and projectiles in Great Britain had its beginning as a result of the publication of my report in this case.[8]

It certainly attracted the attention of Robert Churchill, the London gunsmith who had been giving evidence on a slightly more hit than miss basis for the previous 15 years. Immediately he obtained a comparison microscope for himself and sailed to speak with the American expert Calvin Goddard in New York. The next year he was involved in one of the most sensational murders of the time and one which could not have been solved without the use of the comparison microscope. It was the shooting of PC George Gutteridge at Stapleford Abbots, again in Essex.

On 27 September 1927 PC Gutteridge was found shot dead on the road between Romford and Ongar. A particular feature of the case was that he had been shot through both eyes, the belief in some circles being that the pupils reflect the last thing a dying person sees and the imprint would have been that of his murderer. Shortly afterwards a Dr Powell reported that his car, in which he had left his medical bag, had been stolen in nearby Billericay. The car was later found abandoned and in it was an empty cartridge.

The bullets which had shot out Gutteridge's eyes were examined and found to be obsolete types which had not been used for several decades but the shots to his head had come from more modern cartridges. The shells came from a .455 Colt, Webley or Smith & Wesson. That was all experts at the Royal Arsenal could say. Churchill, with the aid of his comparison microscope was in no doubt that they had come from a Webley.

Four months later a Frederick Guy Browne was arrested at a garage in South London after he had sold a stolen car. In another car at the garage was Dr Powell's bag, along with a Webley revolver and ammunition of the type which had killed the officer. William Kennedy, Browne's employee, was arrested in Liverpool and blamed his employer.

Churchill compared the Webley and the case found in Dr Powell's car and found that the patterns on the breechblock of the Webley and the base of the case matched, marking for marking. William Fox, an arms inspector from Enfield Lock, examined 1,374 small arms which were at the Royal Arsenal for repairs and it was not until he had failed to find a single breechblock whose markings corresponded to those on the case that he agreed with Churchill. It was the first time in the twentieth century in a British court that modern forensic ballistics had played a part. Kennedy confessed and both were hanged at Wandsworth on 31 May 1928, Browne to the end maintaining his innocence.[9]

IV

It was always known that Al Capone was behind the St Valentine's Day Massacre of 1929 when seven men from Bugs Moran's gang, which had been causing Capone trouble in Chicago, were slaughtered. The problems were identifying the actual shooters and proving it.

Although, as Prohibition ran towards its tenth year, there were many factions in Chicago who formed and re-formed alliances, the main opposition to Capone was Bugs Moran. After the death of Drucci, the last surviving leader of the O'Bannion gang, Moran had formed an alliance with Joey Aiello and was now harrying Capone's lorries. On 1 July 1928 Frankie Yale, Capone's mentor in New York, was shot dead in that city as he tried out his new automobile; the first man there to die from machine gun wounds.

On 7 September, Moran and Aiello shot Tony Lombardo, the president of the Unione Siciliano in Chicago and a Capone supporter, as he walked with his bodyguards along Dearborn and Madison. On 2 January Aiello killed another Capone supporter, Pasquale Lolordo, who had taken over the lethal position of president of the Unione.

It was this killing, for which no one was ever charged, which prompted perhaps the most famous murders in gangland Chicago – the St Valentine's Day Massacre. It was planned by Capone who called on the services of 'Machine Gun' Jack McGurn and Frank Nitti while he was well away from the scene in Florida. In turn they hired members of Detroit's notorious Purple Gang, Fred 'Killer' Burke and Fred Goetz. The gunmen were, in all probability, McGurn, Burke, Goetz and Capone's ubiquitous henchmen, John Scalise and Albert Anselmi. The aim was to trap Moran and the remaining members of his entourage.

At about 10.30 a.m. on 14 February 1929 a fake Chicago Police Department car drew up outside Moran's headquarters at the SMC Cartage Company, 2122 North Clark Street. Burke and Goetz, dressed as police officers, walked inside and lined the Gusenberg brothers, John Snyder, James Clark, John May, Albert Weinshank and Dr Rheinhardt H. Schwimmer, who was not a member of the ensemble but who had dropped by for a game of cards, against a wall. The gunmen opened fire, killing all but Frank Gusenberg instantly. Moran survived because he had been late arriving at the office that day. He had seen the police car and had stopped off at a cafe until it was over. The look-outs, mistaking Weinshank for Moran, had signalled that he was inside the building. Moran then had himself driven to the haven of a hospital where he remained under guard, blaming Capone for the outrage.[10]

There were no less than 70 sub-machine gun cartridges on the floor of the garage. Although Burke, Goetz and McGurn had been seen in the area, there was no other evidence against them nor could any help be expected from the Chicago police who, because of the uniforms, were themselves under suspicion over the murder. The coroner, Dr Herman Bundesen, called a Grand Jury and those citizens decided they needed the help of Calvin Goddard, the new star of American forensic science.

From this would come his dream, the establishment of a national laboratory for scientific criminology. Goddard was given the shells and bullets and he gave his opinion that the killings had been done with two .45 calibre Thompson sub-machine guns. One of them had a magazine which held 20 bullets per loading and the other had a much greater capacity of 50 bullets. He examined all the Tommy guns from the Chicago Police Department. He then fired the guns into a waste bin filled with cotton wadding and, with the help of the comparison microscope, was able to determine that the firearms marks on the bullets did not match those left at the scene of the massacre.

In fact, as is often the case, luck played a considerable part in the case. Today any criminal who is less than a 32nd cousin to a fool will dispose of weapons used in case they are found and so can be matched. In 1929 there was no need at all for criminals to think, if think they could or did, that ballistics was a sufficiently exact science to link bullets with guns. Indeed all the previous evidence was that it was not. There was therefore no reason not to use and reuse a perfectly good machine gun until it fell apart in your hands. After all they were moderately expensive to acquire.

On 15 December 1929 a patrolman, Charles Skelly, in the small town of St Joseph, Michigan was called to an altercation following a minor traffic accident. Fred Burke was refusing to give a farmer $5 for damage he had caused to a bumper. When the officer asked his name Burke shot him and fled the scene. On 26 May 1930 he was arrested at his father-in-law's farm in Milan, Missouri, where an arsenal of weapons, including two Thompson guns, was found. At first he gave a false name and it is interesting that the *New York Times* reported, long after the system had been discredited and fingerprinting was the norm, 'After Bertillon experts had confronted him with records he admitted his name.'[11]

These guns were now sent to Goddard who again fired test bullets into containers of cotton. He was sure that the guns were those used in the St Valentine's Day Massacre and that one of them had been used in the New York killing of Frankie Yale. The gun was also matched to the killing of Frank Marlow in Queen's Borough, New York, in the summer of 1929.

Burke escaped the electric chair. He was wanted in both Illinois and Michigan and was sent to the latter where Circuit Judge Charles E.White held that he had been intoxicated at the time he shot Skelly and therefore had not been able to premeditate the act which would have turned it into a capital offence. He was sentenced to life imprisonment with hard labour on 27 April 1931 and survived a little under a decade, dying of a heart attack in the State prison in Marquette on 10 July 1940.[12]

V

George Bernard Shaw had not been happy with the Gutteridge case, writing an open letter in which he protested, 'Anyone with access to a discharged cartridge case and to a revolver can tamper with the revolver.' Jurgen Thorwald in his *The Marks of Cain* is dismissive of the querulous Irish dramatist.

But such cavilling sounded very thin, when set against the massive evidence of scientific ballistics, for Churchill had exorcised the element of error from forensic ballistics.[13]

Thorwald was writing in 1965. Just as doubts crept into the accuracy of fingerprint evidence, once thought to be beyond reproach, so they did into ballistic evidence. Ironically it was again in Chicago where the damaging incident occurred. It involved the then leader of the Black Panthers in Illinois, the charismatic Fred Hampton.

The late 1960s was again a time of considerable social unrest and a number of organisations such as the Weathermen and the Black Panthers were targeted as subversive groups.[14]

At 4.45 a.m. on 4 December 1969 the police raided the Panthers' headquarters on Monroe Street claiming they were after an arms cache. A violent shootout was reported and Hampton was killed. He had, said the police, been given the opportunity of surrendering several times before he was shot. The police claimed that the Panthers had fired at least 15 shots at them and this was backed by a police forensic expert, John Sadunas.

Hampton's girlfriend Akua, who was with him at the time, told a different story:

> The next thing I remember was someone
> coming into the rear bedroom, shaking Fred
> and saying 'Chairman, chairman, wake up,
> wake up, the pigs are vamping'. And I can see
> plaster flying off the wall and smell the cordite,
> gunfire.

She escaped from the bedroom and then heard a police officer's voice say he was barely alive or he would barely make it. And then the shooting started again.

After the apartment had been forensically examined, the police did not seal the crime scene and left it unguarded. It was a move that the Panthers saw as their opportunity to give their own interpretation of events and they told visitors that here was the bedroom where the Deputy Chairman Fred Hampton had his brains blown out as he lay asleep at 4.30 in the morning.

Other black organisations such as the organisation for a better Austin and the Organisation for Southwest County voiced their fears and asked that a probe be conducted by Mayor Daley. Charles Wise, President of the Organisation for Southwest County, told the *Chicago Tribune* that the black community would no longer tolerate this kind of police oppression, brutality, harassment and killing of black youths.

General public concern led to the summoning of a Federal Grand Jury into whether the civil rights of the Panthers had been violated. In turn the Panthers organised their own ballistics expert. Initially Herbert MacDonell was sceptical:

> I just had the feeling this was another black militant group that had a shootout with the police and with very little question the police were in the right and, in this case, the Black Panthers were in the wrong. That was my first reaction based upon similar experience in the past.

MacDonell was refused access to the police firearms and so in an effort to work out who had fired the shots he used the science of trajectory to trace the paths of the bullets:

> Trajectory can be determined very easily if the projectile goes through more than one surface. For example if we have a wall here and a bullet goes through it, we can simply take two points and depending on where they are, we can determine the angle very easily. Then once you have the two holes lined up you have the trajectory. I determined there were a minimum of 99 shots fired into the apartment and one out of it.

MacDonell determined that:

> The head wounds that Fred Hampton received
> were from two different shots and he was
> completely immobilised and incapacitated with
> either of those two shots, didn't matter which
> one. So he never moved after the first shot and
> if he was shot again there seems to be no
> reason for it, unless they simply wanted to
> make sure Fred Hampton was dead.

Some of the charges against the surviving Panthers
were dropped at the trial in April 1977 and by
December all had been acquitted. In 1983 $1.8 million
was paid in an agreed settlement by the city of
Chicago to them and the families of those killed in
the raid.[15]

CHAPTER 3

Offender Profiling

In the autumn of 1974 a group of grouse hunters in the American North West made a gruesome discovery. In the hills, east of Seattle, they stumbled across some human remains. After that discovery the police mounted a search of the hillside for other bones and the officer in the case, Robert D. Keppel, recalls:

> *...before we were finished we had found literally hundreds of bones, about all the remains of at least three people, quite possibly four. We had no information about how they had died. Only the fact that there were just bones spread out over the hillside.*[1]

So began the hunt for one of America's most notorious serial killers in a case which did much to popularise the investigative approach known as criminal or offender profiling.

I

In fact criminal profiling, which uses the analysis of crime scenes and a vast amount of crime data to try and predict as accurately as possible what kind of person may be the criminal, is nothing new. It is the application which has produced a troubled history, particularly in recent years.

The traditional approach to detective work has been that the only clues of value were fingerprints, discarded equipment, blood stains and the like, whereas profiling relates to the 'invisible' clues which help to define the perpetrator. These will include the location and choice of victim, whether the victim is allowed to live and the type of assault. These factors are applied to create a profile and also to eliminate suspects. Many might say that this is only good police work based on experience. A burglar will usually operate within a limited range of his own home; unless the killer is a transient he is also likely to operate in a known area in which he feels comfortable. Even if he is a transient he is still likely to operate in an area which is 'safe' to him – a railway or bus station, a fast food complex and so on.

Offender profiling is the art – profilers will say science – of making correct deductions based on both physical and psychological clues such as the background of a likely offender. It is also a combination of appraisal and statistics. Another factor will be the type of similar offences committed by similar offenders. So if, for example, rapists statistically are shown to have previous convictions for indecent exposure, a profile of a rapist is likely to include a man who has at least one previous conviction for that offence.

The father of the criminal profile, as indeed of criminology itself, was undoubtedly Caesare Lombroso, an Italian army doctor. In the 1860s he began seeking the answer to whether criminals were physically different from ordinary people, and to this end he conducted studies of criminals imprisoned in Turin and Pavaia.

In 1871 he made what he considered to be a breakthrough when he studied the skull of an Italian thief, Vilela:

> I found in the occipital part, exactly on the post where the spine is found in a normal skull, a distinct depression as in inferior animals, in particular rodents. I suddenly saw, lit up as a vast plane under the flaming sky, the nature of the criminal. An atavistic being who reproduced the ferocious instincts of primitive humanity and of the inferior animal.

Lombroso believed he had found evidence that a criminal's brain was different from that of a non-criminal and he claimed that this was clearly displayed in the shape of the criminal's face:

> A criminal's ears are often of a large size. The nose is frequently upturned or of a flattened character in thieves. In murderers on the contrary, it is often aquiline like the beak of a bird of prey.

As for the rapist:

> The lips of violators of women are fleshly, swollen and protruding. Swindlers have thin and straight lips.

He also deduced that women with excessive pubic hair were more likely to become prostitutes and thieves than their more lightly endowed sisters.

Lombroso's controversial criminal typology does not stand up to modern scientific scrutiny. Indeed it was substantially discredited in the early part of the twentieth century when experiments showed that criminals and public schoolboys had similar skull measurements, but at the time when it was fashionable it was hugely influential. Now the studies he conducted can be ridiculed in their simplicity, but it was a beginning. He laid the foundations on which later generations would build houses.

In 1929 a series of horrific murders took place in and around Düsseldorf. It was one of the first times that a rudimentary form of offender profiling was tried in an attempt to track down a killer – Peter Kürten, a man who came to be known as the Vampire of Düsseldorf.

An annual carnival or *kirmes* was held in Flehe, a semi-rural district on the outskirts of the city, and it was from there on 24 August that two girls were seen leaving with a fairly nondescript man. The next morning in a nearby field the bodies of five-year-old Gertrude Hamacher and her 14-year-old friend Luise Lenzen were found with their throats cut.[2]

However much horror they caused, the murders of the two girls were only part of a series of indiscriminate killings in the Düsseldorf region. All the victims had been stabbed, often in the genitalia, and most were women and children. The most experienced police officer in Prussia, Ernst Gennert, was drafted from Berlin to assist with the manhunt.

Some three weeks earlier Maria Hahn had failed to return from an afternoon's walk. Then in the November the police received a letter, 'Murder. The body can be found at the marked location on this map.' In a field on the outskirts of Düsseldorf the police found Maria Hahn's body.

By this time, throughout 1929 there had been at least 19 attacks on women and children and Gennert, using all the available information from the crime scenes, tried to deduce what kind of person could commit such crimes:

> From the killer's description of the crime scene
> I deduce that he is familiar with Düsseldorf.
> The killer seems to have been in close contact
> with his victims prior to the attack. This means
> that he is perceived as friendly and good-
> natured by the people who are in contact with
> him. They'd never suspect he was a killer.

This was certainly correct in a number of the cases. Kürten had met Maria Hahn in early August and they has arranged to meet the following Sunday. They had spent the afternoon together and had gone for a walk by the river. They had sex and then went into a meadow at which time Kürten decided to kill her.

In the case of the two young girls, Hamacher and Lenzen, he had persuaded the older girl to go and get him some cigarettes whilst he killed her adopted sister. In that of Maria Maas, whom he tried to kill on 21 July 1929, he met her and asked her to go to the Heerdter Festival with him. They had been together for some hours before he decided to strangle her. Fortunately she escaped. This was the pattern of much of his behaviour. He picked up young women and after behaving normally with them, often having intercourse with their consent, he then stabbed or strangled them.

Gennert continued his deduction:

The killer has shown exceptional cruelty in his
attacks. He is sexually abnormal and has a
history of mental illness. He must be mad.

In principle it is difficult to disagree with Gennert. His
logic, given the horror of his crimes, that the killer was
mad was simply common sense. But his deduction then
took a wrong direction. He presumed that the man
must have a recorded history of mental illness and the
police were now set to trawl the records of psychiatric
institutions. Nothing turned up.

In fact, as is often the case, Kürten was caught
almost by accident. On 14 May 1930 he had seen a man
accost a young girl, Maria Butlies, near the Düsseldorf
railway station and had followed them. The man had
tried to persuade the girl to go to a park but she had
refused and Kürten then intervened, offering to take
her to a room he kept at Mettmannerstrasse 71. There
she said she did not want intercourse and wanted to be
taken to a hostel. He took her on a tram and down a
dark street near the Grafenberger Wald where he more
or less forced her into having sexual intercourse while
standing. He then took her towards the tram but when
he saw a police officer he feared she might complain
she had been raped and made off, convinced she would
never find his room again.

In fact Maria Butlies took the tram back and went to
the *Gertrudishaus* run by nuns. Three days later she
wrote to a friend telling her she thought she had fallen
into – and out of – the hands of a murderer. By chance
it was delivered to the wrong person, a Frau Brugmann

instead of Frau Bruckner, and this woman started making enquiries of her own volition as well as taking the letter to the police.

Kürten was extremely surprised when on 21 May he looked over the banisters and saw Maria Butlies and even more surprised when she was back at lunchtime with a police officer. According to the version of events he gave to Professor Karl Berg, Kürten seems then to have behaved with admirable calmness. Two days later he persuaded his wife that she should give him up in the anticipation that she would receive some substantial reward money.

In any event he was arrested near Rochus Church during the afternoon of 24 May. Frau Kürten had told the police she was to meet him there and the square was surrounded.

Much of Kürten's story told to Berg in the 12 months from June 1930 could never be checked but he told the examining magistrate that his father was a drunkard who in 1897 had been imprisoned for incest with his eldest daughter. Now Kürten maintained that his early crimes had been of necessity. He had stolen to eat. In 1909 he received a week in prison, the following year a series of short sentences and later longer terms as he became an arsonist. His wife had shot the man who jilted her in 1911 and for this she had received a sentence of five years. After that she met Kürten's sister and then him.

As to his career as a sadist and murderer, he said he had tried to have intercourse with one of his sisters and at the age of nine had pushed two young boys off a raft so that they drowned. He had started having sex with animals and his first orgasm had come at the age of 13 when he had stabbed a sheep and at that moment ejaculated. This pattern continued for two or three years before he graduated to women.

Probably his first killing, in 1913, was of a 10-year-old girl, Christine Klein, who was found dead in her bed in a tavern kept by her father, Peter. Suspicion fell on the girl's uncle Otto who had quarrelled with and threatened her father, Peter, the night before that he would do something his brother 'would remember all his life'. A handkerchief with the initials P.K. was found by the bed and it was assumed that Otto had taken it from his brother to implicate him. Otto Klein was arrested but acquitted.

Despite his catalogue of mutilation and bizarre sexual conduct, the court doctors decided that Kürten was definitely not mad. He was sentenced to death and now expressed remorse saying that he was a changed man. During one of his last conversations with the doctors he wanted to know whether his severed head would still be able to hear the blood rushing from his torso. This, he explained, would give him his ultimate pleasure.

It might not have been but, always a man with a healthy appetite, he had *Wiener Schnitzel* and potatoes together with a bottle of wine for his last meal. He enjoyed it so much he asked for it to be repeated. He was guillotined on 2 July 1931.

II

Nine years after the execution of Kürten, on 16 November 1940, a man began his career, albeit in a small way, in New York. On this occasion he placed a very carefully made small pipe bomb on the windowsill at the Con Edison building at 170 W 64th, Manhattan. It failed to explode not by any basic defect in design but because of faulty assembly. A second was placed also in Manhattan in September the next year. Over the next decade and a half he would come to be known as the Mad Bomber. His career was interrupted by a patriotic break during the Second World War when he sent a note signed 'F.P.' saying that the bombing would stop during the duration but 'I will bring Con Edison to justice – they will pay for their dastardly deeds'. His career continued until the late 1950s, by which time what was perhaps the first successful criminal profile had been drawn.

In fact he did not resume his career until 29 March 1951 when a bomb was found on the lower level of Grand Central Station. It was better made than the two previous ones but it also failed to explode. For the first year after resumption the bombs, which as the years passed became bigger and more dangerous, did not cause serious damage. They had been placed in telephone boxes and public lavatories at places such as the New York Public Library. Then in 1953 the bomber moved up a notch. He began to place the devices in theatres and cinemas including Radio City Music Hall and, when he placed a bomb there on 28 November 1954, four people were injured.

In 1955 there were five separate bomb attacks and the following year six including, on 2 December 1956, one at the Paramount Theatre in Brooklyn where seats were slashed to conceal the bombs. This time six people were injured.

Each bombing was followed by a letter to a newspaper, signed F.P., which suggested an unspecified grievance against Con Edison, New York's main power supply company. One read:

> The bombings will continue until Con Edison
> is brought to justice. My life is dedicated to this
> task. It must anger the New York authorities
> that an individual can be just as mean, dirty
> and rotten as they are.

Now the letters became more hysterical, suggesting that his life was limited.[3] Desperate measures required desperate remedies and one detective in the case, Al Gleason, was sent to see a psychic.

III

Although in the early 1990s the American police acknowledged they had spent some $13 million on psychics in the fight against terrorism, police forces worldwide have generally had a love–hate, often unacknowledged, relationship with them. There is little doubt that on occasions they have proved extremely useful in finding missing people or bodies. For example Dutch psychic, Gerald Croiset, enjoyed a long and, in his case, public relationship with the police, particularly in America.

In England one of the first times a psychic had helped the police had been in the winter of 1936 when the medium Estelle Roberts in the south of England said that Mona Tinsley had appeared to her and explained how she had been abducted, strangled and then dumped in the River Idle by Fredrick Nodder. She identified the place where the body would be found but a search revealed nothing. Later there was a drought in the area and Mona's body was found wedged in a drain below the water level but in the place identified by the medium.[4]

Again in England, in June 1993, a dinner in honour of Nella Jones was given by the Metropolitan Police honouring her 20-year career of assisting officers. She had first been involved following the 1974 theft of Johannes Vermeer's *The Guitar Player* from Kenwood House in Hampstead, London. She telephoned Scotland Yard to tell them where they would find the frame of the picture and she then began to receive visions or 'psychic' clues telling her the painting would be found in a cemetery in east London. It was found undamaged in St Bartholomew's churchyard in the City. After that there was a steady if irregular series of knocks on her door by baffled policemen. She was able to tell the police that the first name of the Yorkshire Ripper was Peter and that the initials of his last victim would be J.H. She identified the day as either the 17th or 27th and the place as Leeds. The day was, in fact, the 17th. In 1989 she had been able to solve a murder in Peckham. After visiting the room where an old lady had been battered to death she ran into the street to tell officers that she could see the letters EARL and a red Ford Cortina with a rusty roof. In a nearby road there was a used car dealer trading as Earl Motors, and police enquiries showed the murderer had recently sold the dealer such a car.[5]

Croiset's involvement with the New York police went back to the early 1960s when he was able to predict that four-year-old Edith Kiercorius had not been taken by a woman to Chicago but rather had been killed by a 50-year-old weasel-faced man in New York after he had tried to assault her.

However, psychics are not always successful. In the case of the Mad Bomber, Gleason recalls he went to see 'A woman named Gloria. And that really didn't pan out – she was really fishing for me to tell her what she could tell me back.'

IV

It was time for what must have seemed an equally speculative but rather more structured approach. Gleason went to see a psychiatrist, Dr James A. Brussell.

Gennert had simply used common sense in his approach to Kürten. Now to this Brussell added contemporary psychological theory:

> The bomber appears to feel more and more
> strongly that the world has done him wrong.
> He suffers from paranoia, which doesn't fully
> erupt until the person is 35. He's been planting
> his devices for 16 years, so he's middle aged,
> between 40 and 50.

He also thought the choice of weapons, bombs and knives, was rooted historically in the Middle East and, based on the bomber's handwriting and because paranoiacs are often meticulous people, he made two additional deductions. He told Gleason:

He probably lives alone or lives with relatives, probably sisters. But also if you saw him he was probably wearing a suit, a dark suit, and it would be a double-breasted suit and more than likely a hat, a fedora.

Much of the bomber's correspondence was with the *New York Journal-American* and it was becoming more hysterical with one letter saying 'My days on earth are numbered!' Certainly his days at liberty were numbered. The paper printed an open letter to the bomber and he wrote back providing details of an injury, the outcome of his claim and some personal background. Con Edison was persuaded to search thousands of its old records and among them one of the secretaries, Alice Kelly, discovered that in the 1930s a man had unsuccessfully tried to claim compensation over an alleged injury incurred through escaping steam.

The records showed the injured man to be a mechanic of Slavic origin whose handwriting matched that of the bomber. He would now be 53 years old. His name was George Matesky, a man known for his precise manner, who lived with his two elderly sisters. He was traced to Waterbury, Conn., and there, on 21 January 1957, when detectives knocked on the door it was opened by Matesky in pyjamas. He was asked to get dressed and when he reappeared he was wearing a double-breasted suit. In all he had planted over 30 explosive devices of which 20 detonated.

Matesky had begun work for the power plant in December 1929 earning $37.50 a week. He had been injured on 5 September 1931. He would say there had been a gush of gas in his face and a horrific burning in his lungs. He had collapsed and coughed blood for two hours before he was able to go back to his rented room. But he had not filed a State Workmen's Compensation Board claim until 4 January 1934, well outside the year allowed by the Statute of Limitations, and his application was dismissed. A year later he was removed from the payroll.

In one of his last letters before his arrest he had written:

> When a motorist injures a dog, he must report it, not so with an injured workman. I tried to get my story to the press, I tried hundreds of others – no one cared. I was determined to make these dastardly acts known. I decided on bombs.[6]

Three months after his arrest, at his trial on 18 April Matesky was found to be an incurable paranoid schizophrenic. 'He's on his way out. He is an empty shell of a man,' said Dr Albert LaVerne. Matesky had suffered one serious coughing seizure in court and the noted New York judge, Samuel Leibowitz, committing him to the Mattawan Hospital for the Criminally Insane in Beacon, NY, said, 'One would be less than human not to be moved by the pitiful condition of this man, incurable both mentally and physically.'

For once Leibowitz was wrong in his judgment. Matesky survived and was cured. He was released in December 1973. One of his sisters, Ana, had died and the other was housebound. He devoted himself to caring for her for the remainder of his life and, on her death in 1982, he sold the house which in time became supervised apartments for the mentally ill. He died, aged 90, in Waterbury's Abbott Terrace Nursing Home on 23 May 1995 and was buried in the family grave at Calvary Cemetery.

James Brussell continued his career as a profiler, successfully assisting the police on at least five more occasions including the case of Albert de Salvo, the Boston Strangler, and inspiring a new generation of American police officers to take an interest in this branch of forensic science.

New York radio host, Barry Farber, recalls him:

> I don't know what it was that Dr Brussell had, but whenever he came into the room it came in with him. He was obviously special. He could see things where the rest of us would see nothing and he knew how to do his putting two and two together. He walked to a scene, looked around, spun around, spat out his instructions to the police – I don't think there's ever been one like him.

V

It was, however, over a decade after the capture of Matesky that the FBI, inspired by criminologist Howard Teten, started to teach profiling at its new Academy at Quantico, Virginia:

> Once the Academy opened in 1972 we started teaching the profiling course. Just an overview. And then we would focus in on the

psychological crime scene evaluation. We had a small class, all investigators and crime scene specialists and I had asked them when you look at a crime scene you basically say to yourself, what kind of person would do this? What is this person saying, either to the victim or to the people he expects to find the victim? What kind of job could you expect him to have? And from that point of view you're now getting to the point where you have investigative leads.

But how scientific was the FBI's work really? Howard Teten answers the question with another:

What is scientific? Science is the practice of trying to learn something about something. If you have no precedent you have to start with what you have and what you have available. Now, it might be said that wasn't scientific, but at the time it was about as scientific as you could get.

One of the earliest profiling successes for the FBI came in 1974 in Montana. In June the previous year a seven-year-old girl, Susan Jaeger, had been taken from her tent while the family was on a camping holiday. Her body was never discovered, nor was there any ransom note. In January 1974 the burned body of an 18-year-old girl was found in woodlands near the camp site. The local police were convinced that the same person was the killer of both girls but, unable to make further headway, they sought the help of the FBI.

A profile was developed suggesting that the murderer was a young white male who was a loner and who lived not far from the campsite. It suggested that he might also keep trophies from the killing. He was thought to be likely already to have come to the notice of the police. The name of David Meirhofer had already been put forward by an informant but he had successfully dealt with a lie-detector test as well as a truth serum. Now, sure that sooner or later the killer would contact her, Susan Jaeger's mother was instructed by the FBI to keep a tape-recorder by her telephone. He did make such a call and an identification was made of his voice. A search of his home revealed that he had indeed kept souvenirs of the killing. He later hanged himself in his cell before coming to trial.

VI

In Britain, from the 1960s psychiatrists and psychologists had been used on something of an ad hoc basis by the police. One success had come for Dr Patrick Tooley who profiled the killer of Susan Stevenson after she had had been attacked in Kent. His suggestion of the killer's age and social and criminal background and habits proved remarkably accurate when a Peter Stout was arrested and convicted.[7]

Then, beginning in 1982, came a series of rapes in the Notting Hill district of west London. In each case while the victim was out the rapist broke into her flat from adjacent communal gardens and lay in wait for her. Usually he would remove the light bulb and when the victim came in and found the light did not work he would attack her as she went into her room, putting a pillowcase over her head, and then ordering her to lie on the bed and assaulting her.

The police had a strong suspicion that the same rapist was also responsible for a series of attacks in Earls Court. Now for the first time the FBI was asked to help and supply a profile. Information was given on a total of 15 rapes in both areas but the deduction was not what was expected. The FBI profiler deduced there were two rapists at work. Part of the deduction stemmed from the fact that the more recent Notting Hill incidents involved both burglary and assault. The reasoning went that the prime motive was burglary and robbery, with sexual assault as a secondary but highly important motive. The conclusion was that the Notting Hill offender's previous criminal history would include crimes against property as well as minor assaults. It was also thought likely that he would be married.

So far as the Earls Court rapist was concerned the profiler noted that although the attacker used a weapon to threaten the victim he was neither physically nor verbally abusive. He would fondle, stroke and kiss the victims. It was reasoned that the primary motive was an attempt to prove himself sexually. The attacks were committed in an area where the offender felt at ease and it was thought likely that he worked or lived in or near the area of the first incident. He was thought to be a single man who had never married.

The senior investigating officer did not agree with the profile and remained convinced there was only one rapist. House to house searches failed to identify the rapist and now the psychologist Dr David Canter was asked for his views. He agreed with the FBI that there were, in fact, two rapists but he thought that the Notting Hill rapist might well be unmarried and dominated by his mother. A suspect who seemed to fit the profile was arrested but was later eliminated from the inquiry.

Two more rapes and three years later a 32-year-old 15 stone married bodybuilder and burglar, Tony Mclean, was convicted of the Notting Hill assaults. Mclean had led a charmed life and the fact that he had not been caught earlier had been due to a mistake over his prison release date. It had been thought that he was serving a sentence when one of the rapes took place. There was also a mistake when a DNA sample he had given wrongly eliminated him. Some five days before his arrest he had been caught in communal gardens at the rear of a block of flats with anti-crime paint on his hands but he had explained he had been taking a short-cut home and was released.

In fact his capture in July 1987 was largely due to the efforts of a local officer, PC Graham Hamilton, who knew Mclean as a burglar and was convinced he was also the rapist. When Mclean was arrested and questioned he dropped his trousers to reveal a 'scarred and shrivelled' penis. He could not be the rapist he said because 'I fell off my bike as a kid and cut my private parts. I've had trouble getting an erection since'. One of 13 children who originally came from Wales and who had changed his name, he had known his wife, Sharon, since she was 13. He was sentenced to life imprisonment. She said she was standing by him.[8]

The Earls Court rapist was never found.

David Canter recalls:

In those days people were making fairly
generalised judgements. What we've now
found with a lot of research is that one of the
most difficult things to actually say about any
offender is the details of their domestic
circumstances. It turns out that offenders often
come from very complex, rather dysfunctional
lives and therefore exactly whether they're in a
relationship or not is itself quite difficult even
to specify when you know all about the
individual.

Until 1985 Canter had only advised the police on
crowd behaviour in an investigation into emergencies
such as the fire at Bradford Town Football Club's
ground. He had made his reputation not as a criminal
psychologist but rather as an environmental one,
specialising in workplace design and industrial safety.
Then, following a series of up to 30 rapes at and near
railway stations in north London and the deaths of two
young women, Alison Day in Hackney Wick and
Maartje Tamboezer near Guildford, he was asked to
assist a combined operation between the Metropolitan
and Surrey police forces.

Canter believes that everyone has a mental map
which he or she uses to navigate their world: where
they live, work, shop and socialise as well as offend.
First time offenders commit a crime in a local area they
have mentally mapped and as they get more
experienced they may expand their horizons.

Canter worked out a 17-point profile showing that
the man sought was white in his mid to late twenties,
was probably living with a wife or girlfriend but had no

children. The man would have one or two very close male friends. He held a semi-skilled or skilled job and could possibly work on the railways. He also narrowed the area where the man lived to around Cricklewood in north-west London. When he was finally arrested John Duffy matched 15 of the 17 points on the profile. He was sentenced to seven terms of life imprisonment for rape and murder.[9]

VII

The Notting Hill case showed the need for more detailed profiles. One such approach was developed in Seattle stemming from the cases originally dubbed the Missing and Murdered Women's Cases. The first took place on 11 June 1974 when around midnight an undergraduate, Georgann Hawkins, was abducted from the campus at the University of Washington. A man on crutches had been seen earlier struggling to carry a briefcase. One girl had offered to help him but first she had to make a telephone call and when she returned the man had gone.

The next two abductions occurred on the same day when, on 14 July, Denise Naslund and Janice Ott disappeared within hours of each other. They had been out, independently of each other, sunbathing at Lake Sammamish Park. Denise had gone to the lavatory building at the lake; Janice had been seen wheeling her bicycle together with a man in tennis kit with his right arm in a sling. The remains found two months later in the Eastern Hills were identified as those of Janice and Denise.

This time there had been something of a clue. The police had, of course, already been investigating the disappearances and other girls had spoken of a man, Ted, who had approached them. One of them had volunteered to assist in carrying some surfboarding equipment and had seen his car, a Volkswagen Beetle.

The information sent to the police by the public was almost too much to handle. The artists impression produced a list of up to 3,500 names. There were 4,000 students at the University and 5,000 psychiatric patients in the area had been released that year. Even worse there were 41,000 Volkswagen Beetle owners in Washington State. Thirty lists produced a combined total of 300,000 names. The problem was to whittle it down.

Robert D. Keppel recalls:

> So the idea was, gee wouldn't it be nice to know if more than one person appeared on more than one list. So that's when we decided we would do the computer matching program.

In theory the idea was simple. Which names were common to the greatest number of lists? But there the difficulties began. Since the police had access only to old-style mainframe computers every name had to be entered on a punch card. It took the computer several weeks to come up with a total of 25 names which appeared on at least four of the lists. One of the most likely was a former university student who drove a Beetle and had been seen near one of the abduction sites. He also matched the artist's impression. His name was Ted Bundy.

In fact, the first victim of Bundy had survived his attack. Sharon Clarke shared a house with a number of other students, where she had a room in the basement. On 5 January 1974 when she had not appeared by mid-afternoon, her housemates went to see if she had overslept. She was unconscious with her face covered in blood. She had been hit over the head with a metal bar pulled from the bed frame. She had not been raped but the bar had been pushed into her vagina causing severe internal lacerations. She remained in a coma for a week before partially recovering. She could make no identification of her attacker and the police thought a man had been watching her undress and then come into the house through an unlocked door.

A psychology student at the State University, Lynda Ann Healy, was the first victim of Ted Bundy to die. She went missing from her rented accommodation in Seattle on 1 February 1974. She shared a basement apartment with four other young women. When her alarm sounded at 8.30 a.m. they went to investigate because she had an early morning job reading the snow forecasts on a local weather station for which she had to get up at 5.30 a.m. When they saw her bed neatly made up they thought she had left and had forgotten to switch off the alarm. It was not until her parents arrived in the evening for dinner that the sheets were pulled back and found to be covered in blood. Her nightdress, similarly stained, was on a hook in her wardrobe. Probably Bundy came in through an unlocked door and knocked her unconscious before kidnapping her.

After Lynda Healy's disappearance girls went missing on a regular basis in the states of Oregon,

Washington, Utah and Colorado. Between then and April 1975 attacks on some eighteen girls can be traced to Bundy. Later in 1974 he attacked Carol DaRonch when, posing as a policeman, he approached her in the centre of Salt Lake City and persuaded her to get in his car. He drove her to a quiet street but she survived the attack and managed to escape.

On 16 August 1975 in Salt Lake City, a police officer, Sgt Bob Hayward, was driving through the suburbs on patrol. In Brock Street he turned on his headlights catching a parked VW in the glare. That car was then driven off at high speed and Hayward followed. After a short chase, in which the VW jumped two sets of red lights, the driver turned into a garage. He got out of the vehicle and walked to the police officer. When asked for his driving licence he produced it. The name was Theodore Robert Bundy. At first he said he had not realised it was a police car behind him. He said he had been to see the film *The Towering Inferno* at a local cinema but the officer knew that the house was playing a triple bill of Westerns. He then asked Bundy if he could look inside the VW.

The passenger seat had been removed and in an open bag on the floor the officer found a brown knitted ski balaclava, a mask made out of ladies' stockings with holes cut for the eyes, a steel bar and a pair of handcuffs. He promptly arrested Bundy.[10]

Bundy was convicted in Utah and then extradited to Colorado where he escaped from prison on 7 June 1977 but was quickly recaptured. He remained in custody at Garfield County Jail until 30 December that year when, by cutting a hole in the ceiling of his cell with a hacksaw and climbing through, he again escaped. He spent some four hours searching for a car to steal before latching on to an elderly MG which soon broke down. He then hitched a lift into Vail and caught a bus to Denver. From there he took the 8.55 a.m. flight to Chicago, caught a train to Ann Arbour and checked into the YMCA. He stayed in the area for four days until on 4 January he stole a car which he dumped in Atlanta and then caught a bus to Tallahassee, Florida.

Now, using the name of Chris Hagen, he attacked six more young women, two of whom survived, until on 15 February 1978 he was arrested, again by chance after an officer noticed stolen number plates on a car near Pensacola Airport.

At first Bundy denied any involvement in the killings, claiming the police had made a terrible mistake. However a wax impression of his teeth matched marks on the buttocks of Lisa Levy, whom he had killed on 15 January 1978.

Bundy, a handsome man with abundant charm, had been awarded a scholarship in Chinese studies at Stanford, obtained a BSc in psychology and, for a time, was an assistant director of the local Seattle crime commission. He moved to Utah where he studied law at the University. During the time he was with the Seattle crime commission he worked with Ann Rule who later wrote *The Stranger Beside Me* on which Bundy collaborated. She was to say that he fitted no criminal type pattern:

I, along with everybody else who worked with him, was so busy denying and saying no, no way, not Ted Bundy, you don't know him, this man could not have done it. But of course I

lived to take back that statement. It took me
five years to be absolutely convinced that he
was guilty. It was not an easy conclusion.

Bundy was seen by one psychiatrist as being 'a man who has no problems, or is smart enough, or clever enough to appear close to the edge of "normal"'. Bundy himself claimed 'Sometimes I feel like a vampire.' It was his opinion that very few killers responded to voices and visions but that the majority were intelligent people who could make rational decisions so far as their crimes were concerned. The problem for law agencies was, he believed, that the serial killer would continue until stopped and that he would become more proficient at killing as time went by. Bundy may not have always been consistent because on another occasion he said that an entity resided within him and gradually took over his conscious mind.

His trial began in Florida in June 1979 and he was found guilty and sentenced to death on 23 July. He had been offered and declined a plea bargain which would have saved him from the electric chair. While in prison he married Carole Boone, a divorcee with a teenage son and, despite a second conviction for the murder of another girl in Florida, she firmly believed he was innocent.

It is not clear how many women he did kill. At one time he admitted to over 100 but later withdrew that confession. After a series of appeals which lasted some ten years he was electrocuted on 24 January 1989. Outside the prison a huge crowd cheered the announcement of his death.

The Bundy case encouraged Robert Keppel to

develop the use of computers in crime detection. In the 1980s he set up the Homicide Investigation Tracking System, known as HITS, a vast database which contains details of every solved and unsolved murder case in Washington State since 1981 and of every rape since 1991. This has a great benefit in that, with its wide-ranging material which also includes some robbery cases, the name of the actual offender may be in the file.

The theory is that most crimes are committed by a small number of people and that serious offenders will already be registered somewhere in the region's crime files which are brought together by HITS. Bob Lamoria, from the HITS in Seattle, gives an example of its benefits in the case of a serial rapist in the autumn of 1993:

> On our first cut we were able to narrow the field down from several million to 19,000 and that was just by physical description and type of crime. Then we said, okay now we only want those individuals out of that list that live within a six mile radius, that narrowed it down to 19. The third cut we asked the computer to limit it to those who had been convicted of rape and burglary. This cut it down to three. One of them was an exact match to the rapes that had been occurring during the last month. They set up 24 hour surveillance on the suspect. Within 24 hours they caught him breaking in trying to commit another one.

However the benefit of any computer system is limited when there is no description of the killer and when the location of the murder is unknown, as is the case in the so-called Green River murders.

In the Green River murder series during the 1980s at least 49 young women, most of them prostitutes, were found in and around the Green River near Seattle. The first victim was 16-year-old Wendy Lee Coffield whose body was found washed up on the shore close to the Peck bridge about 20 miles southeast of Seattle on 15 June 1982. The police had to resort to traditional psychological profiles during their investigation and one profile was actually offered by Bundy, probably in an effort to keep himself on death row and out of the electric chair for a few more weeks or months. The theory which Bundy advanced was:

> My initial impression was this guy is more or
> less in the same socio-economic kind of strata
> that the younger man can be associated with,
> lower middle class. I would say that he's
> between 20 and 30, probably closer to 20. My
> gut reaction is these girls are being approached
> by somebody that really puts them at ease. The
> last person they would expect to be the killer
> would be one of their own peers.

Keppel was impressed:

> Compared to all the other people that have done
> profiles he seemed to have more of a handle on
> the profile than anyone else did. He advised us
> that we should be looking for someone that
> might be on foot because that was his MO at the

time, where he went out and would park his car,
approach girls on foot and then take them to
where his car would be parked in a secluded area.
So he had assumed that the Green River killer
may be doing the same thing.

Bundy may not have provided great assistance in his
psychological profile of the Green River killer but at
least three days before his execution he did say what
had happened to Georgann Hawkins:

What happened was I knocked her
unconscious with a crow bar and handcuffed
her in the passenger side of the seat and drove
away. She was unconscious but she was very
much alive. Then went south on the freeway to
turn off at a floating bridge down the road and
up to the grass area and she's regained
consciousness at this time. And, gee, this is
probably the hardest part, I hope you
understand, it's not something I find easy to
talk about. I again knocked her unconscious
and strangled her.

What he would not admit was that he had *post-mortem*
sex with his victims. When asked he replied, 'Well, I
don't want to talk about that right now.' For his part
Keppel had no doubt of what had happened:

From what I know about Bundy's cases and
from Kürten's cases they were both sexually
motivated crimes. What we definitely knew
about him was that he was re-visiting his crime

scenes many, many times in the Seattle area. So
you can conclude that things were going on at
those crime scenes.

As for the FBI profile of the Green River killer, it read
remarkably like the profiles of other serial killers of
women suggesting that the man would be between 20
and 40 years of age, white, a heavy smoker who liked to
drink and who could have a background of sexual crime.
Five prime suspects were identified and eliminated.
Despite the expenditure of a staggering $15 million and
consultations with botanists, anthropologists,
psychologists and psychics no charges were ever brought.

In June 1984 the killings stopped. Keppel, asked if
he thought the killer would ever be found, was not
hopeful:

> Where I think the Green River killer is, well
> there's a number of things. He could be dead,
> could be hospitalised, could be in jail. Could be
> in another jurisdiction operating and we still
> don't know. We do not have a good suspect in
> the Green River case and there's 57,000
> suspects on the records. He may or may not be
> in that database of information. The rate things
> are going now, no, he'll never be discovered.
> Have to come forward himself.

VIII

By the end of the 1980s offender profiling in Britain
was regarded as a major breakthrough in police work

with a nationwide profiling bank due to open combining psychological and statistical analysis on child murders, rape and serial killers.[11]

Then came an almost crippling blow to offender profiling – the case of Colin Stagg, who was charged with the murder of Rachel Nichell but subsequently found not guilty. Ian Stephen, one of the psychologists responsible for the Development Unit at Barlinnie Prison, says:

> Ever since the film *The Silence of the Lambs*, profiling has become an almost magical process for both the press and the public, and it was inevitable that something would happen to puncture its image of infallibility.[12]

Even before the Stagg case there had been doubts thrown on the psychological profile and whether it was much more than applying old-fashioned common sense. There is also a tendency to attribute successful profiling to the catching of criminals such as Bundy and the so-called Clown Killer Wayne Gacey who murdered a series of young boys and hid the bodies in the house where he was living.[13] The reality is, however, that Bundy was caught because he tried to outrun a police officer who was looking for burglars and Gacey was caught because one of his victims, who was also an employee, failed to attend a birthday party and the boy's parents set out to look for him.

Dr Paul Britton, a renowned criminal psychologist, who had been involved in the Stagg case, had been asked to assist in the investigation into the kidnapping and murder of James Bulger, the two-year-old from Liverpool abducted from a shopping centre and killed on a railway line by two pre-teen boys. Dr Britton said that his 15 pointers included the suggestions about where they were likely to live, where the body might be found, the fact that the boys would not be high achievers and would be at ordinary schools and that, while one would be the more dominant personality, the other would not be a simple passenger. Another psychologist claimed, however, 'Common sense would tell you that the boys were truants, from a disturbed background. The video from the shopping centre gave the police an identification of how old the boys were.'

Professor David Canter and Ian Stephen believe that, rather as is the case when hypnosis is used, offender profiling should focus an investigation but that a conviction must be based on traditional forensic evidence.[14]

One of the founding fathers, James Brussell, wrote in connection with his successful profiling of the garishly named Christmas Eve Killer, George Metesky:

What proportion of my psychiatric deductions is science and what proportion is imagination? It's a hard question to answer. I can only say that I always start such a deduction with a solid base of science, but somewhere along the way intuition and imagination begin to take over. When you think about an unknown criminal long enough, when you've assembled all the known facts about him and poked at them and stirred them about in your mind you begin to see the man. You see him more and

more plainly. You picture his face, hear his
voice. As in the case of George Metesky, you
even see the clothes he wears.[15]

Stephen also believes that if judgment is clouded by the
Rachel Nickell case:

there is a real danger that not only will we
endanger any future murder investigations, but
that we will also jeopardise the treatment of
many serving offenders, for whom forensic
psychology represents a vital part of their
rehabilitation.

It is ironic that a death blow to the use of the offender
profile in the courtroom came shortly after John
Francis Duffy, the rapist and murderer whom Canter
had so accurately profiled, had given evidence leading
to the conviction of his close friend and fellow rapist
David Mulcahy in January 2000.

In 1992 Canter had advised in the case of 32-year-
old Paula Guilfoyle from the Wirral, West Merseyside in
which the prosecution's case had been that the heavily
pregnant woman had not hanged herself from a garage
beam but had been killed by her husband, Eddie, a
hospital theatre technician. Two suicide notes had been
left at the scene and the allegation was that Guilfoyle
had tricked his wife into writing them on the pretext
they were for a course he was attending on the causes
and effects of suicide. Guilfoyle lost his appeal against
his conviction but his case was referred back to the
court by the Criminal Cases Review Commission which
deals with unsatisfactory convictions.

Now the defence wanted to call an expert to cast light on Paula Guilfoyle's state of mind. The Court of Appeal would have none of it. Just as Mr Justice Ognall had rejected the prospect of Paul Britton giving evidence in the Stagg case so the court shut its face against this expert. First there was the question of the law against it; secondly, although the court accepted this was not necessarily fatal, he did not appear to have embarked on the task he had set himself in the present case. More importantly there was no criteria by reference to which the court could test the quality of his opinions; there was no real database comparing real and questionable suicides and there was no substantial body of academic writing approving his methodology. The court took the view that unstructured and speculative conclusions were not the stuff of which admissible expert evidence was made. Finally, if evidence of this kind could be given in relation to a deceased victim, there could be no difference in principle to evidence psychologically profiling a defendant.[16]

As Dr Eric Shepherd, who advises lawyers on pro-active defence in criminal cases, says, 'Everyone thought offender profiling was a silver bullet. But there are very few silver bullets.'

CHAPTER 4

Infiltrators and Surveillance

I

At the beginning of the programme *Surveillance*, in the BBC's series *Catching the Killers*, a covert operation targeting drug dealers is seen taking place on a Manchester housing estate. The investigators and infiltrators are not, however, police officers. Losing the battle against rising crime, local councils have resorted to using private surveillance companies to gather evidence against criminals. In this case the team is composed of former British soldiers and their technology was once only the province of the military and the police. To an extent the wheel has turned full circle over the last 100 years when agencies such as the Pinkertons regularly used extensive undercover operations, and infiltration of political and criminal enterprises was undertaken by the police very much more on an *ad hoc* basis.

In fact from the start the celebrated New York-based Pinkerton Detective Agency used undercover agents. One of the earliest and most remarkable police-cum-private detective infiltrators was the Irish-born James McParland, who in 1873 managed to infiltrate and, effectively single-handedly, destroy the Irish-American secret society the Molly Maguires, who were causing havoc in the coalfields of Eastern Pennsylvania. In a two-year operation he lived undetected in the community sending weekly messages back to the Pinkertons for whom he worked. His is a classic account of undercover work.

At the time the conditions in the Pennsylvania coalfields under which the mainly Irish immigrants worked were some of the worst in America. Apart from the relatively short period of the Civil War when coal was needed urgently, miners in Pennsylvania rarely worked a full week. Their hours at the pits may have totalled 14 a day but they were worked for half a dollar. The general conditions were dreadful with a shack in a 'patch', a 'cluster of a few dozen company houses along a crooked, unpaved street, built within the shadow of a towering colliery'. They were obliged to buy goods, usually on credit, at what was known as a 'pluck me', the company-owned store where goods had a 20 per cent mark up.

The Molly Maguires, no more than a loose association of interests at first, was probably founded by a Jeremiah Reilly. By the 1850s they were the only group prepared, or capable, of taking on the mine. In many ways the structure was the same as in the Irish land troubles of two decades earlier. The mine owners themselves were absent, as were the English from Ireland. In their place the oppressors were the Scots and the Welsh overseers.

From 1862 to 1865 there were some 142 unsolved murders and 212 serious assaults in Schuykill County, most of which went unpunished. The victims were mine superintendents, supervisors, foremen and those known to be disloyal to the Mollies. By 1873 their grip on the six Pennsylvania counties appeared invincible and it was the Molly-organised so-called Long Strike in 1874–75 which led the owners to determine to destroy them.

One of the people who stood to benefit most from the destruction of the Mollies was Franklin B. Gowen, a lawyer and former district attorney in Schuykill County. He was also President of the Philadelphia and Reading Railroad Company and, as such, was hostile to labour. There is a dramatic account of the meeting between Franklin B. Gowen and Allan Pinkerton, the head of the agency, which establishes the ground rules for an undercover agent then and now:

> He'll have to be Irish born, of course, and a Catholic – brave, cool-headed, just about as smart a lad as ever came over the seas. He'll need to work as a miner, and that takes a strong constitution. And he must have his eye peeled every minute to keep from betraying his purpose to the cunning rascals he's sent out to get.

Pinkerton continues:

> When the time comes for public prosecution, my operative must not be expected to give testimony in court – unless present circumstances are greatly altered.
> Keep no record of this meeting, or of any future dealings with me or the Agency. Avoid everything that even suggests 'detective' – for

at least one man's life, and the whole outcome
of our enterprise, will be staked upon absolute
secrecy. Whether my organisation is kept on
the job a week, a month, or a year or more,
this sort of caution must be maintained by us
all to the end.[1]

McParland's supply of cash was something to be
explained and he gave out that he was peddling
counterfeit Confederate money. His explanation
brought him entry to the Lawler household with whom
he lodged from the next month. He began work in the
mines late in February.

In the first week of March he crushed his hand in an
accident and was transferred to a shovelling job. Here
he met Frank McAndrew, a man whom he admired and
who was a rival of Mike Lawler for the position of
bodymaster. By the end of March 1874 men were being
laid off and McParland was advised to go to Wilkes-
Barre. He told Lawler and was persuaded to stay on the
promise of election into the Maguires in return for his
support in Lawler's re-election campaign. McParland
was also adroit at training fighting cocks and was in
charge of Lawler's stable. On 14 April 1874 he was
initiated into the Ancient Order of Hibernians.

McParland must have been a genuinely ingratiating
man because when the election came up in July and
was won by McAndrew, McParland became secretary to
the illiterate bodymaster. It had taken him just over
nine months since he had left Philadelphia to obtain
this position of power. It appears that McAndrew was
not the forceful person hoped for and there was a
campaign for McParland to become bodymaster. Before

he achieved that dubious honour he would certainly have had to carry out a beating, if not an actual killing. He continued his pretence that he was unreliable in drink, indulging so much that he broke his health with bad liquor. His hair fell out and he bought a wig. Now he was excluded from every decent hotel and bar. Later his eyesight began to fail.

On 18 November 1874 six people were killed as the Maguires stepped up their campaign of intimidation and took reprisals against strike-breaking miners. Throughout the winter McParland appears to have done what he could to dissuade the leaders from this escalating campaign of violence and in April 1875, on the pretext of attending his sister's wedding, he went to Chicago to see Pinkerton.

Part of McParland's undoubted charm seems to have been towards women and he had genuinely become involved with Mary Ann Higgins, whom he had met at a Polish wedding. She was the sister-in-law of James Kerrigan, the Mollies' bodymaster at Tamaqua. Now, in the summer of 1875 McParland's difficulties were compounded when Kerrigan ambushed and killed a policeman, Benjamin Yost, as he lit a street lamp. McParland was also coming under increasing pressure to arrange the assassination of Gomer James, a Welsh miner, who was believed to have killed an Irishman. McParland maintained he sent messages of warning to James and delayed nominating a killer together with a time and place by pretending to be drunk.

On 2 June the striking miners paraded and marched towards those collieries still open. They shut down, not re-opening until August. On 14 August the men received their first pay and James was shot and killed.

The real killer left the state but the reward money of $10 paid for the killing was claimed by Thomas Hurley, a Shenandoahan.

In early 1876 matters came to a head. On 18 January two Mollies, Michael J. Doyle and Edward Kelly, were indicted with the killing of a John P. Jones, a manager who had treated one of the Mollies badly. Supervising the killing had been Kerrigan and he now elected to turn States' evidence. His line was that he had been something of a reluctant bystander drawn into the brotherhood and afraid for his wife and family if he should try to leave. No, he had never taken part in any killing. As Doyle's trial proceeded to a guilty verdict Kerrigan began to sing loudly to the authorities. His statement ran to 210 pages.

According to Rowan:

> Pinkerton now had published lists of members of the Molly Maguires in local newspapers and rumour of a spy abounded in the organisation. Now was the time for McParland to be protected. His real identity was in danger of being revealed. He had been seen in Philadelphia and there was the possibility that a priest also betrayed him. Pinkerton's idea was not, however, to pull him out of the danger zone but was for him to be arrested so that, with suspicion diverted, he could continue his operations.

On 5 February, seven Mollies were arrested and charged with complicity in the murder of John P. Jones and that of patrolman Benjamin Yost. On 4 May 1876 the trial began of four Mollies charged with the murder of Yost. The next day Jack Kehoe, together with three Schuykill bodymasters and five other Mollies, was arrested. The organisation was broken.

McParland first gave evidence in the trial for the murder of Yost. It was, wrote William Linn, a spectator at the trial, a complete shock when he walked down the aisle of the court:[2]

> This was a complete surprise, not only to the Mollies, but to the public which had not hitherto known of his existence. This feeling of surprise deepened into one of wonder and amazement when, with perfect coolness and deliberation he told in detail the story of his career among the Mollies.
>
> When he told of being suspected as a detective and related his interviews with his intended assassins, his escapes, etc. judges, jury, counsel, and audience listened with breathless attention; and so completely spellbound were all these by his recital of things the existence of which had not been thought possible, that at anytime the falling of a pin might be heard in the densely crowded room.
>
> Much of this narrative which was not relevant was not objected to by counsel for the defendants because of the intense interest they evidently felt.

Eleven of the Maguires were hanged and a further 59 were convicted of various offences.[3]

II

There is little doubt that infiltrators have been used in Britain in political and religious intrigues since the time of the Tudors. The playwright, Christopher Marlowe, may well have begun his career as a spy by himself being the victim of an informer. His atheism had been reported to the authorities and he may have taken up the offer to work as a Government spy to avoid punishment.

Shortly before the establishment of the Metropolitan Police in 1832 there was another outstanding example of the use of the spy and a cover-up by the authorities of his operations. The history books may show that the Cato Street Conspiracy of 1820 was instigated by Arthur Thistlewood who had fallen under the spell of Tom Paine, the great Republican and, while he lived in France, of Robespierre. A closer examination will also show the crucial role played by a government spy to bring it to fruition and its disastrous conclusion.

Thistlewood had risen in the Army to the rank of Lieutenant and had married a lady of some wealth. She died and possibly he soon gambled away her fortune. Another account is that he lost his money by an injudicious loan to a friend. His great desire in life, it seems, became to assassinate the members of the Cabinet and then seize power. The attack was timed for Wednesday, 23 February 1820 when Lord Harrowby was entertaining the Cabinet in Grosvenor Square. The idea was that one of the members of the conspiracy should go to the house to deliver a parcel and then, when the door opened, the others were to rush the premises and kill the members of the Cabinet. The plan was to cut off the heads of Lord Castlereagh, the then Prime Minister, and Lord Sidmouth.

The plot had, however, been infiltrated by a government spy, George Edwards, who ran a shop near Eton school in which he sold models of the headmaster which the boys could use as targets. He was also employed by Sir Robert Birnie and the Bow Street magistrates.

Birnie himself led the disabling raid on the conspirators. One Bow Street Runner, Smithers, was stabbed by Thistlewood. The conspirators, excepting Edwards who, as is often the case with infiltrators, managed to disappear, were promptly arrested. He escaped, it is said, with Government assistance and fled first to the Channel Islands and then to the Cape.

There was never likely to be much chance of an acquittal on the charges laid of High Treason, but such as there was disappeared with Edwards. The defending lawyers argued that the jury should draw the conclusion from Edward's absence that the plot had no foundation in reality and that if it could be properly investigated the affair would be shown to be that of a spy and informer. It was said that the idea of attacking them at the Cabinet dinner was that of Edwards. In his speech before receiving the death sentence Thistlewood roundly denounced the absent Edwards whom he said had:

> a plan for blowing up the House of Commons. This was not my view: I wished to punish the guilty only, and therefore I declined it. He next proposed that we should attack the Ministers at the fete given by the Spanish Ambassador. This I resolutely opposed ... there were ladies invited

> to the entertainment – and I, who am shortly
> to ascend to the scaffold, shuddered with
> horror at the idea of that.[4]

If Thistlewood was right, and there is much to support his view, here was an *agent provocateur de luxe*.

When in the 1830s Sir Robert Peel's police marched forth it was never his intention that there should be such a thing as a police spy among them. The reason for their splendid military style uniform was so that a police officer could easily be recognised. Criminologist, Clive Norris comments:

> When the new police was set up there was a
> great reluctance to use undercover police work,
> and this was because it was seen to involve
> trickery and deception. It was seen to be
> Continental, it was seen to be based on the
> Napoleonic system of spies. What we wanted
> was a uniformed, recognised body of men, not
> people creeping around in corridors spying on
> the uninformed citizenry.[5]

Nevertheless spies there were from a very early stage and within a few years there was a disaster when the police clashed on open ground in an area between Holborn and Clerkenwell known as Coldbath Fields. One police officer, PC Culley, was killed and an inquest jury later returned a verdict of justifiable homicide. An inquiry followed swiftly.

And at the same time as the inquiry into the Coldbath Fields disaster another inquiry was set up. It stemmed from the behaviour of a former schoolmaster, Sergeant William Steward Popay, of both P division and latterly of the Walworth and Camberwell 'class' of the National Political Union. The Government was highly suspicious of the Union and Lord Melbourne instructed the police commissioners to keep him informed of its movements. In turn Popay had been instructed by his superintendent McLean to attend the meetings and, as it was found, had interpreted this to mean he should infiltrate the organisation. From 1831 to 1833, masquerading as a coalman put out of work by the Coal Act, Popay did just that.

His radical speeches soon ensured he was elected to office in the Union. In late April or early May 1833 his cover was blown when he was recognised by a Union member, John Fursey, at his station desk at Park House police station. For a time he managed to explain away his presence and indeed he marched with the members to Coldbath Fields but later, in the course of the defence of another rioter, George Fursey, Popay's behaviour came under scrutiny.

It was the end for Popay who protested, as well he might, that his plain clothes were for his own protection. It was found that:

> he complained to several members of the
> misery to which he and his family had been
> reduced; he paid frequent private visits to their
> leaders and never failed to address them as
> friends; arm in arm with another member he
> marched to a meeting to celebrate the French
> Revolution. More serious still he took part in
> discussions, supporting resolutions, sometimes

even proposing that their wording should be strengthened, and encouraged the establishment of an arms depot offering to give members of the Union sword practice.

His conduct was described as 'highly reprehensible' and he was dismissed from the force with ignominy. His superiors, who in turn argued that they had employed Popay at the request of the Home Office but only to watch the meetings of the Union, were criticised for not keeping him under closer control. While the Select Committee accepted the need for a plain clothes force it deprecated:

> any approach to the Employment of Spies, in the ordinary acceptance of the term, as a practice most abhorrent to the feelings of the People and most alien to the spirit of the Constitution.[6]

Looking backward there is little doubt that poor Popay was the sacrificial goat, but were there others like him who remained unmasked? Yes, said Frederick Young who had organised a petition to the House of Commons and maintained he and others had seen men:

> whom they knew to be policemen, disguised in clothing of various descriptions, sometimes in the garb of gentlemen, sometimes in that of tradesmen or artisans, sometimes in sailors' jackets.[7]

No, replied the police. Popay was a rogue, an original bad and sinful apple, not the tip of an iceberg.

Of course, it is now unbelievable that for two years Popay led this double life without the knowledge of any of his superiors. Did no single one of them ever ask how he came by his detailed information?

After the Popay affair, however, the Commissioners were keen to avoid a repetition and in 1839 a Metropolitan Standing Police Order prohibited officers from attending private meetings of any sort. Nor were officers encouraged to adopt a subterfuge to obtain evidence. Indeed policing in plain clothes was considered unsporting and with the exception of the small detective branch set up in 1842, all policing was done in uniform.

Over the years, however, there have been a number of instances which have come to light. On the tip of the iceberg principle it may be that, as with the special branch, there was a far greater number of occasions when a police officer had donned a disguise than the authorities would care to admit.

In 1845 a constable who had pretended to be a cobbler in order to arrest a counterfeiter was severely reprimanded, as was another who, six years later, hid behind a tree in Hyde Park to observe an 'indecent offence'. When these scandals broke the Home Office was at pains to play the matters down.[8]

The early police forces seem to have had only a rudimentary idea of undercover work. They did not learn from the salutary lesson of Sergeant Popay. In 1840 a PC Barnett of the Birmingham City police infiltrated the Chartists in the city. Unfortunately his superiors required him to work in uniform when he was not busy infiltrating. It was not long before he was seen in a theatre. His explanation that he was working in a private capacity for the theatre manager (an early example of police moonlighting if it was true) was not accepted.[9]

On the other hand once it had been created, Scotland Yard's detective force lead by Sergeant Field was happy to discuss its success and exploits in disguise. The novelist and social commentator Charles Dickens was told of an exploit concerning the arrest of silk thieves involving one of the young officers, Henry Smith, who disguised himself as a butcher's boy:

> Never, surely, was a faculty of observation better brought to bear upon a purpose, than that which picked out this officer for the part. Nothing in all creation could have suited him better. Even while he spoke, he became a greasy, sleepy, shy, good-natured, chuckle-headed, unsuspicious and confiding young butcher. His very hair seemed to have had suet in it, as he made it smooth upon his head, and his fresh complexion, to be lubricated by large quantities of animal food.

This facility was not altogether unsurprising. Dickens omitted to write that Smith (whom he cleverly disguised as Mith) had been a butcher before he joined the police.[10]

One of the earliest of police officers to put pen to paper, Chief Inspector Andrew Lansdowne, was at pains to correct the view of the newspaper-fed public that a policeman spent his days in donning and shedding disguises with the celerity of a quick-change artist:

> Now all this is fudge. During the Whitechapel
> business [the Jack the Ripper investigations] a
> zealous stripling certainly did put on women's
> attire one night, but he was not commended
> for his detective instinct in so doing.

Lansdowne did admit to two other occasions on which a disguise had been worn. One officer had enterprisingly dressed himself in a baize cloth to resemble a statue to catch a thief at the Great Exhibition of 1862. The second time was when an inspector he refers to as G. dressed as a clergyman to catch a shopkeeper selling indecent prints. Lansdowne was not pleased.

> It was scarcely a credit to the cloth that a
> clergyman's attire was considered the best
> disguise, but it was.[11]

Other officers were more prepared to admit to the use of disguise in run-of-the-mill criminal cases. Detective Inspector J.G. Littlechild maintained that a clergyman's outfit was a favourite with detectives. It was both easy to put on and it disarmed suspicion. In his time Littlechild had disguised himself as a surveyor and a sanitary inspector as well as a cab-man. Acting was clearly in his line. To win a private bet he had dressed as a minstrel and had been thrown out of a public house.

In the fight against some of the lesser known aspects of English criminal behaviour – arson, animal maiming and poaching in East Anglia in the nineteenth century – a Superintendent English was hired from the Metropolitan Police in 1844 for work in the West Suffolk area. He was clearly an example of medium-to-long-term infiltration. John Archer describes him as:

> the outstanding policeman of the period. He was the forerunner of the plain-clothes policeman, for he dressed and worked as a labourer in order to gain working people's confidence.

Archer was responsible for the trials of five principals and received an award of £100 and a watch for his effort.[12]

Much of the dislike of disguise can be traced to the attitude of the Commissioner of the time, Sir Charles Warren, who took over from Colonel Sir Edmond Henderson following rioting in Trafalgar Square in February 1886.

There is little doubt that the CID was having a really bad time in the latter part of the 1880s. According to the *Pall Mall Gazette*, whose gadfly-like editor W.T. Stead stung the authorities whenever possible, it had collapsed by October 1888. The reasons given were numerous. First, there was a rule that all officers had to be over 5ft 10in in height. All CID men had to serve two years in the uniform branch, so giving the criminals a chance to get a good look at them and, worse, by the time they did become detectives they could only walk with the characteristic Scotland Yard 'gait' and so were ever more readily recognisable. More serious were the limitations on payments to informers and the rule that an officer could not leave London on a case without the permission of the Chief Commissioner. 'Under these circumstances it is not surprising that our detectives do not detect,' chortled the *Gazette* in a display of good humour.[13]

As Bernard Porter says, Warren thought that:

> policing should be open, visible and by the book, rather like cricket, where everything was governed by the rules of fair play. Plain-clothes policing was like taking off the bails at the bowler's end without a warning whilst the batsman was backing up. It was also a constant temptation to corruption as history showed very well. This sort of attitude from a superior was clearly difficult for a dedicated detective like Monroe to live with. Detectives knew that life was not like cricket, and especially among the criminal fraternity. Corruption was the risk you had to run to be effective, and not half so dangerous as the stultifying effects of red tape. This was really the hoary old dilemma of the British police since its earliest days: how to reconcile purity with results.[14]

Nevertheless detectives still dressed themselves up, and down, and infiltrated the dens and stews of the East End to infiltrate criminal organisations.

III

The so-called golden age of a crime-free Britain of the 1930s may have been something of a myth but there is no doubt that the Second World War irrevocably changed the face of British crime. Before the outbreak the ordinary public eschewed crime. During the war while they probably saw their involvement as little more than fending for their families, new doors were opened for old and new criminals alike. Now, with bomb-damaged shops and buildings open to looting, all kinds of goods came on the black market and into receivers' hands. There was a steady trade in stolen ration books. Under the cover of the black-out the smash and grab raid proliferated and Billy Hill, the London gangleader, for one, found that small post offices were a profitable target for safe-breaking expeditions. By the end of the war it was estimated there were 20,000 deserters in London alone.

It was in this climate that on 31 December 1945 one of the more curious and relatively short lived of Scotland Yard's innovations, the Special Duty Squad, was created. Under the aegis of Sir Ronald Howe, then Assistant Commissioner (Crime), and Percy Worth, then head of Scotland Yard's CID, four young officers, John Capstick and Henry 'Nobby' Clark, both of whom were Detective Inspectors, and Detective Sergeants John Gosling and Matthew Brinn, were given the task to 'carry the war into the enemy's camp'. Each of the men had specialist knowledge of the criminals of a part of London and their brief was specific. They were to use their extensive knowledge of London's underworld and live among the criminal fraternity. Later they were joined by Detective Sergeant George Burton.

Neither you nor your men will give evidence in court. As far as the underworld is concerned,

> you will have no more material existence than
> ghosts. How you manage it is your affair but
> we want results – fast!

From those remarks of Worth the squad took its name. Its official title may have been Special Duty Squad but to everyone it was known as the Ghost Squad.

There were good reasons for the introduction of the Ghost Squad. Against the depleted ranks of the police was ranged a new type of criminal: cunning, ruthless and well informed. Many had served in the armed forces – some with distinction – and many more were deserters. They were younger, fitter, harder, more resourceful and more energetic than the pre-war criminals.

> All Britain was the province of these new
> criminals. Time, money and distance were no
> object if the pickings were good. They swooped
> almost every night. Lorry loads of tea, sugar,
> butter, clothes, cigarettes and whisky
> disappeared from the streets or were stolen
> from warehouses. Jewellery and cash vanished
> from private houses into the pockets of thieves
> who worked like phantoms. Fur and rings,
> clothing and petrol coupons, carpets, lipsticks,
> typewriters, razor blades, shoes – anything with
> a ready cash value was loot for the army of the
> underworld. The figures of stolen property rose
> to astronomical proportions.[15]

There had been at least one forerunner of the Ghost Squad, recalls Capstick. 'Squibs' Dance, along with his brother Alf, was a member of the Flying Squad:

A rough diamond, he always wore a cap and scarf, like a labouring man, and rolled his own cigarettes from a virulent brand of shag. He never took a cigarette out of his mouth once he had lit it. When the stub was an eighth of an inch long he spat it out, and he didn't care much where it landed. It was never a good idea to stand within a couple of yards of Squibs for that reason.

He more or less lived with thieves in the public-houses, and was usually accepted by them as a particularly cunning member of their own fraternity. He worked different areas in rotation, and was never tumbled. Drifting into a tavern in South London, cigarette dangling from his lower lip, he would be greeted: 'Blimey! Where have you been?' To which he would mumble, 'Well, I only came out of stir last week.' Then he would work in the far west of London and when asked 'Been having a lay down for six months?' replied shortly, 'Nah, four.' If somebody ventured to inquire which prison he had been in, and what he had done, Squibs would glare and mutter that he didn't talk. No wonder the underworld looked upon him as a real fly thief.[16]

Ghost Squad members effectively had a *carte blanche* to work as they wished. They would meet between 10.00 and 10.30 in the morning depending on when they had gone to bed the night before and at six o'clock they would telephone Capstick to tell him how their day had been spent. At first he sent a weekly report to the

Home Secretary but, with the Squad functioning more than satisfactorily, this requirement was dropped after three months.

The Squad had a spectacular success in February 1947. Information was received that a team from north London would raid the Midland Bank in Kentish Town. It was to be one of the earliest examples of kidnapping a manager, stealing his keys and then raiding the vault. The Ghost Squad could find out when but not where the manager was to be snatched. The information was passed to the then head of the Flying Squad, Bob Lee. It shows what dangers lie in undercover work even when precautions are taken.

Lee decided to substitute an officer for the bank manager and a DS William Davies took the part. Wearing spectacles and a bowler hat he left the office and travelled towards the manager's home near Woodside Park on the Northern Line. He was followed at a discreet distance by two other detectives. As he walked along a footpath by the then semi-rural station he was attacked and coshed. The officers saw him being bundled into a van. Once the gang had the keys, still bound and blindfolded, he was thrown out into the snow. Half the team began an unsuccessful search for him. Fortunately for him he was seen by a motorist who drove him to a doctor. The other half kept watch on the bank. Within an hour a man arrived and let himself in. The Ghost Squad swooped. Neil Darbyshire puts it delicately, 'The terrified robber, a window cleaner by day, was in no position to demur and immediately told the furious detectives all they wanted to know.'

At the Old Bailey the team received between three and five years. Davies received the King's Police Medal.[17]

A similar exercise took place the following year when a team of robbers were thwarted in their desire to steal some £250,000 from the BOAC warehouse at London airport. An informer tipped off the police and 14 detectives substituted themselves for the guards, mechanics and other staff in the warehouse. The arrangement had been for the guards to be given drugged tea but the warehouseman who had been approached had contacted the police. When the robbers arrived they found the guards apparently asleep. Fighting broke out and at the end some eight robbers including some of the most serious of East End criminals were captured.

By the late 1940s there were serious doubts about the wisdom of operating the Ghost Squad. There is no doubt that at the beginning it had great successes. In its first year it made 171 arrests and this had increased in 1948 to 252 criminals with 500 cases solved. The next year there was a drop to 180 arrests with 400 cases solved.

However, the money paid to informers was considerable and the law of diminishing returns was beginning to apply. Even more seriously, there were fears that accusations could be made that the police were acting as *agents provocateurs*. The original officers had become too well known to the criminals and officers from the Flying Squad were drafted in and out. Now, some officers were thought to be getting too close to their criminal counterparts for their and the Squad's good. There were suggestions that reward money was being shared by some officers and their informers.

In September 1949 the Ghost Squad was closed down by Sir Harold Scott. During the three years and nine months of its existence members had arrested a total of 789 criminals, solved 1,506 cases and recovered property worth more than a quarter of a million pounds. Despite this undoubted success the autonomy given to the officers, for the best of motives, can be seen as the beginning of the period when the Flying Squad began to operate 'a Firm within a Firm' which would lead to the great police corruption trials of the 1960s and '70s.

The Squad may have ceased officially to exist in 1949 but, according to the former Commissioner, Sir Harold Scott, in 1954 'a little group of officers continues to act in this way'.

Although ten years later officers were still being used to infiltrate gangs and carry out jobs with them, it was by no means common practice.

Says Leonard 'Nipper' Read, former National Co-Ordinator of the Regional Crime Squads:

> Before the Regional Crime Squads, there wasn't the money available and anyway there were considerable dangers for the officers. Without careful handling there is also the danger that the officer seeing money vastly in excess of his salary and pension may be turned.[18]

V

One of the first women to be used as an undercover agent on a regular basis was a Mrs Garner (or Gardiner) who, a florist before the First World War, developed a positive genius for detective work. She was loaned to

Commander Paget, then engaged in special intelligence work for the navy and some very important evidence on cocaine was obtained through her. She was the only woman on the staff of the Metropolitan Observations Service for the detection and location of enemy aircraft and the only woman who understood all the complicated machinery used for the purpose. In February 1920 Mrs Garner was awarded an MBE.

> In 1916 at the request of the Admiralty, we trained and supplied a selected policewoman for anti-espionage work, and to help tackle the problem of the drug traffic, which was then growing to very dangerous proportions amongst soldiers back on leave from the Front. Our unit disguised herself as a prostitute, got to know all her supposed colleagues, moved in circles where she was in constant danger from the drug runner, and obtained information of a most important kind, both in connection with drug-running and spying.[19]

In fact the First World War was a turning point in Britain in terms of infiltration and technical surveillance. Prior to the war pacifist and left-wing groups had been seen as part of the democratic process but after conscription in 1916 they were viewed at best as impeding the war effort and at worst as the enemy. Now they became the targets of Special Branch and MI5 attention. One of the earliest bugging devices, in the form of a microphone, was planted in 1917 and that year the telephone of a left-wing agitator and pacifist, Edmund Morel, was tapped and his mail intercepted.

Morel, branded as a revolutionary and probable German agent, was arrested in August 1917 and sentenced to six months' imprisonment. After the trial the War Office admitted that the real reason for his arrest was that Morel was trying to bring about strikes which would deprive the army of its supply of munitions and that although the authorities possessed enough evidence to this effect, this evidence was not sufficient to ensure a conviction in a court of law.

The microphone was planted at a meeting by a Captain Frederick de Valda, who in 1929 wrote an article under the pseudonym Major Frederick Douglas, in which he described how he ran agents in munitions factories in the north of England and was at the time investigating left-wing agitators – and by this he meant shop stewards' committees – in Sheffield, a city which in May 1917 would have a series of strikes.

> I discovered that certain premises known as a chapel were the headquarters of the Reds in the city. One night I managed to gain access to the chapel and secrete a hyper-sensitive transmitter behind the platform. Night after night several companions and myself listened into the plans of the Reds by means of the transmitter.

Later in the war he managed to bug the German Embassy in Madrid using what he called a 'super hypo-sensitive transmitter' by which he meant a microphone.

Two other instances of the success of women used in undercover work come from the 1930s and the time of the Second World War. In the first case Olga Gray was recruited by the celebrated spycatcher, Maxwell Knight, to infiltrate the Communist party in Great Britain. She was sufficiently highly regarded by the party to be asked to work at Headquarters and then by Percy Glading to run a safe house for them in Kensington. In 1938 she discovered that Glading had obtained blueprints from a worker at Woolwich Arsenal in order to smuggle them to Russia. Glading and his colleagues were tried and convicted but Olga Gray was obliged to give evidence and with that her undercover work ended. Heavy sentences were handed out by the Common Sergeant Sir Anthony Hawke who thought that, despite his known association with Communists, Glading, who received six years, had been motivated by greed.

In the second case in 1940 MI5 agent Joan Miller was able to infiltrate a Far Right club in which Tyler Kent was involved. Tyler, an American isolationist, desperate to keep America out of the Second World War stole confidential letters between Roosevelt and Churchill while he was working as a cypher clerk at the Embassy. The letters showed that Roosevelt privately wished America to intervene while publicly he was saying the opposite. The intention was that the letters be leaked in America where Roosevelt was seeking re-election on a non-interventionist platform.

VI

Women had been used by the police on a more or less casual basis over the years. In what amounted to an almost classic example of the *agent provocateur* one undercover woman, who was possibly the wife of a police officer (reports vary), was used to ask the advice of a chemist, Thomas Titley, about her pregnancy. He had long been suspected of being an abortionist but there was no evidence to put before the Grand Jury (the rough equivalent of examining magistrates). In 1880 an inspector wrote to Titley explaining that he had seduced a young woman who was now pregnant and wished to procure an abortion. Titley was asked to supply the necessary drugs. At first he seems to have been reluctant to do anything without, at least, seeing one, if not both of the parties. A police sergeant and the woman called at his house in the assumed characters of the seducer and the mother of the unfortunate girl. Medicines were supplied and so the evidence was now in place. The first problem to be overcome was that it was admitted that the story told to Titley had been baseless from beginning to end. There was no young man, no mother and no young woman. But in law the transaction was complete the moment the sale was effected. The Recorder had some strong things to say about the conduct of the police.

> What they did is to be justified only on the
> assumption that all means are fair which lead
> to the detection of crime. But even this is not a
> sufficient excuse for the means employed in
> the case before us. Thomas Titley was
> suspected, but no more than suspected, of
> having given his help in genuine cases before.
> What if the suspicion is unfounded? What if
> the temptation held out by the police had
> induced Thomas Titley to take his first criminal

step? The law knows nothing of suspicions. It presumes innocence until guilt has been produced. Is it the duty of the police to do all they can to lead innocent men into crime and then to turn around upon them and denounce them for the arranged offence?

There had to be a true bill against Titley but the Recorder also invited the jury to return one against the police and their witnesses for fraud and conspiracy, and this they did.

Two days later the police officers were discharged from the proceedings and Titley was sentenced to 18 months' hard labour. A series of memorials raised on his behalf were sent to the Home Secretary. One was from his wife, the second was signed by 286 neighbours and the third by 3,800 people from London and the provinces. They did the chemist no good either. Writing to Titley's solicitors, the Home Secretary said that he had examined the allegations and found there was no ground for interference in the man's sentence.[20]

Even by the late 1950s women were not used as undercover agents except in extreme cases, and their work following a series of sexual assaults in Croydon in the spring of 1955 earned two women officers, Kathleen Parrott, who actually had been one of the women originally attacked, and her Sergeant Ethel Bush, commendations.

Kathleen Parrott had been walking up a footpath to her home when she was attacked from behind:

All of a sudden I felt this arm go round my throat. He said to me 'Don't scream'. All I was

thinking of was my son, who was about ten at
the time. And I thought I'd never go and see
him again. And then I could feel his hand
going up the back of my skirt. But I had my
torch in my hand and I bashed him as hard as
I could. And all I could see was these glittering
eyes above a scarf. And I snatched that off. He
did eventually scarper. It shook me up for quite
a time afterwards.

The police now decided to mount an undercover and
surveillance operation using the women police officers
as decoys. Given the equipment today available for
even short-term and highly localised surveillance
operations, this seems to have been an extremely basic
one. Despite the attack, Kathleen Parrott volunteered
to act as bait while male officers watched and waited to
spring on the man. 'I mean, it wasn't very easy to go
up that path again. I know I had butterflies in my
tummy.' The man pursued her but when a police
officer stepped out he ran off for the time being, only
to return.

Ethel Bush was another of the decoys and she too
was attacked:

It was a peculiar feeling. You can sense
somebody there. I thought he perhaps might
grab me and pull me to the ground but I didn't
expect anything else. But he'd obviously got a
large chunk of wood, which he just bashed me
with over the head. And I thought I was going
to be protected.

Kathleen Parrott remembers, 'Everything happened too quickly. CID officers with a walkie-talkie were supposed to alert each other; so that they could help when it came to it.'

But, as Ethel Bush recalls, 'Everything went wrong. To start with the walkie-talkies didn't work. The dog came over the wall and the dog handler was injured with the glass on top of the wall.'

In the attack she received an eleven inch gash on the back of her head but as he fled her attacker dropped a pen. This, together with Kathleen Parrott's description, led one of the officers at the station to believe it was William George Barnett, a 29-year-old labourer, whom he knew from his beat. The pen was shown to Barnett's wife who said it was the one with which he did crosswords. He was picked out on a series of identification parades and when interviewed said, 'All I can say is I am sorry for the women, not for myself because I am no good in this world. I am a beast on God's earth.' At the Old Bailey in May 1955 the Common Sergeant, Sir Anthony Hawke, sentencing Barnett to ten years' imprisonment for attacks on six different women, told him, 'No woman is safe while you are at large.' He then praised the police officers Ethel Bush and Kathleen Parrott:

> I cannot personally imagine any higher
> courage being shown than when you went
> along that path with the full knowledge that
> you might be – as you were Sergeant Bush – the
> victim of a violent attack. I think this country
> is entitled to be very proud of you two officers.

Each received the George Medal.

VII

Although there had been elaborate undercover and surveillance operations conducted by the FBI and sanctioned by J. Edgar Hoover in America, these had been used for counter-espionage rather than organised crime. Clive Norris believes that this was because Hoover was worried that, as with the Ghost Squad in England:

> if his agents became too close to the underworld, they might become corrupt. And they'd become corrupt for one very good reason: the pay of an FBI agent is much less than the proceeds of drug or alcohol crime, all sorts of crime. And so the temptation for someone to actually go on the take is very, very strong.

It may, however, have been that J. Edgar Hoover was himself in thrall to organised crime. His long-standing homosexual relationship with Clyde Tolson was a fairly open secret. It was also thought that Meyer Lansky, the Mafia's financier who had a line in obtaining compromising material on prominent men, had information – said to be a photograph of Hoover in a woman's dress – which ensured he was kept at arm's length.[21]

It was not until after Hoover's death in 1972 that the FBI began using undercover operations in criminal cases and their prime targets increasingly became white collar crimes such as fraud and bribery. One of their largest was when, in 1978, an office was set up on Long

Island. It was a fake company run by fake directors who were in fact FBI agents. Known as Abdul Enterprises and run by a mythical sheik, the operation was called ABSCAM – Arab Scam. Later an undercover agent who was actually a sheik would appear and take part in some of the negotiations.

Word was put out that the sheik was game for false financial documents, stolen art and other shady deals. The conversations with those who came forward were secretly recorded. Then the emphasis shifted and the 'directors' put it about that they were representing rich Arabs who wished to invest in the American economy. What the FBI needed was someone with underworld contacts. They chose the overweight, bald and bearded, ebullient con artist Mel Weinberg who, in return for the dropping of a fraud indictment he was facing, was prepared to go undercover. A man who over the years had dealt with high-echelon organised crime figures, politicians and other conmen, he would be an ideal person to be able to connect and in the words of the FBI 'get something going'.

Weinberg sets out some of the essential requirements for the work:

> To be a good conman, you need a good line of
> bullshit and a big set of balls. You know what
> you're getting into and what you're doing and
> if it comes out good, you come out smelling
> like a rose, great, you know.

His conversations were audio-taped. Soon it was not simply conmen who fell into the web but politicians including Angelo Errichetti, the Mayor of the Borough

of Camden, New York who for a $25,000 bribe offered
to make introductions. According to Weinberg he also:

> offered us the Port of Camden for drugs. I
> mean, he was – he was a nice guy. I mean
> anything crooked he'd do.

Now came the introduction of videotaping and the
payoff to Errichetti meeting the 'Emir' at a party on a 62ft
yacht was captured on tape. Errichetti, who later served
three years, was the guest of honour and, naturally, he
and everyone there wished to be photographed with the
Emir who was happy to accommodate them. The pictures
were taken by FBI agents. The word spread through the
guests that since the Middle East was undergoing one of
its perennial crises the Emir wished to move to the United
States and was offering cash for a private immigration bill
to ensure his entry. Now the FBI moved part of its
operations to Washington, renting a two-storey house on
W Street to see who, if anyone, might be interested.
Florida Congressman Richard Kelly was one. Later Kelly
would complain of the tactics used by the FBI and protest
his innocence:

> I had a curiosity. You know how a moth is
> attracted to flame. I just felt as though that
> there was something going on, and I didn't
> know who was involved or why, and I was
> trying to find out.
> People come to a congressional office all the
> time asking for help with immigration and
> every other government agency. That's what
> congressmen do.

Kelly was offered $25,000 up front and then a further $75,000 when the bill was introduced:

> But they had to try to incriminate me. And that's all right, that's all right. If I was a crook. The FBI should have been protecting me not trying to entrap me. Why were they doing that? I think that is really the serious question. The government did not prove that there was any crime of this kind in progress until they started their investigation. The government has never proved that I've ever been involved in any kind of corruption or any kind of crime. Whatever these guys are doing is all right, but I've got no part in it.

On 2 February 1980 the FBI swooped and throughout the East Coast arrested Mayors, Congressmen, middlemen and even a Senator. The swoop pre-empted an article in the *New York Times* the next day reporting the sting, thought, though never confirmed, to have been leaked by the Justice Department.[22]

Kelly, the Senator and the five Congressmen pleaded entrapment. They were convicted but Kelly appealed and his conviction was overturned. Judge Bryant pointed out that placed in context the evidence against him was not black and white. At times he had appeared to reject the bribe. Nor was he keen on the methods used by the FBI, describing the operation as having 'an odour that is absolutely repulsive'.[23] That decision was, itself, later reversed and Kelly served a prison sentence.

Mel Weinberg was in no doubt about the legitimacy of the operation:

Entrapment is a two-way street. If I offer you a bribe, you'll have more obligation to get up and say, 'Sir you've asked me to do something dishonest' and walk out that door. We've paid him the money, shoved it in his pocket and he had a drink in one hand and a handful of cigars in the others, he's sitting there, he says 'If you'd know how poor I was, you'd cry for me'.

The first result of the scam was the promulgation of the Attorney General's Guidelines in 1981 but two committees delivered diverse reports on the operation. The Senate Select Committee, which issued its final report in 1983, found that the operations had substantially contributed to the 'detection, investigation and prosecution of criminal activity' but reached no conclusions about what safeguards should in future be in place. The CCR, the House subcommittee, was much more critical and when it published its report in 1984 suggested that its investigation had uncovered 'a pattern of widespread deviation from avowed standards with substantial harm to individuals and public institutions'. There had been a similar inquiry into *Operation Corkscrew* which had investigated alleged judicial bribery in Cleveland and the CCR concluded that 'the safeguards in practice were little more than rhetoric, offering at best limited constraints upon the investigators'.

Almost immediately after ABSCAM came a serious setback to infiltration cases. It was the trial of John DeLorean which began on 5 March 1984 in Los Angeles. The one-time millionaire car manufacturer was on a charge of plotting to import $24 million worth of cocaine into the United States. It had been done, said the prosecution, to try to raise money to save his ailing Belfast sports car factory. Time and again the television viewers in the United States had seen him reach into a suitcase of cocaine, lift a package and say 'It's better than gold. Gold weighs more for God's sake'.

His defence was that an FBI sting had been up and running to try to force DeLorean into buying the cocaine, something he had made every effort to avoid. A principal Government witness was convicted cocaine smuggler, James Hoffman, who, DeLorean claimed, had threatened him and the life of his six-year-old daughter when he tried to back out of the deal. On 16 August 1984 DeLorean was acquitted by a unanimous verdict of the jury who had deliberated for 28 and three-quarter hours. DeLorean who was by then a Born Again Christian, called out 'Praise the Lord'.

Howard Weitzman, the chief defence lawyer, said:

> The jurors are 12 citizens who have sent a message to the nation and the world that the type of conduct that was involved in the investigation, arrest, prosecution and ultimate vindication of John DeLorean will not be tolerated again.

Professor Alan Dershowitz commented:

> It was one of the great jury verdicts of all time. They stood up and said they were not going to cotton on to cops acting like a bunch of bums.

Eight jurors spoke at a press conference after the hearing. They did not wish to be identified as they said they feared themselves being entrapped by government agents.[24]

Times have changed again and similar sting operations have been highly successful in England, where the police in *Operation Bumblebee* set up a shop specifically designed to attract vendors of stolen goods, and in America and Canada. The difference would seem to be that ABSCAM went out looking to entrap people in criminal acts. For example, *Bumblebee* burglars were not encouraged to go out and burgle; the shop merely provided a place for them to dispose of the proceeds.

In June 1995, 43-year-old Montreal lawyer Joseph Lagana received 13 years following his arrest and charge on 241 counts of having laundered proceeds from drug sales. He was said to have conspired since 1993 to ship cocaine to Britain. Lagana had a very much hands-on approach, bringing sacks filled with small bills to the RCMP foreign exchange counter on the corner of Peel Street, Montreal. The raids were the result of a long-running sting by the RCMP begun in 1990. The money laundered through the RCMP front was wired into more than 200 bank accounts in Europe, South America and the United States. The operation had proved so popular that it was continued for four years. It was even thought to have made a profit.

VIII

There are few documented examples of English in-depth undercover infiltration work although there are now numerous accounts from America, often at high cost to the infiltrator. One example is of a northern Californian officer who went 'deep cover', riding for eighteen months with a group of Hell's Angels. The operation was a great success resulting, as it did, in a very large number of arrests of high-level drug dealers who had until then been regarded as almost untouchable. The officer was highly praised but the cost to him was a high one. He became personally involved in drugs and fighting and slid into alcoholism. His family life disintegrated and after resigning from the force he took part in a number of bank robberies and received a term of imprisonment. In another case a Chicago police officer, after posing as a pimp and infiltrating a prostitution ring, became so enamoured with the life that he took it up himself after the investigation. In a third, another officer, a member of an elite drug enforcement unit in Boston, became an addict.[25] Bob Leuci, the 'Prince of the City' in New York, also came close to collapse towards the end of his stint after he had posed as a corrupt police officer selling information.

What makes a good undercover officer? Joe Piscone, one of the most successful undercover agents of all time, is clear:

> You have to have a strong personality. Strong means disciplined, controlled, confident. It doesn't mean loud and abrasive or conspicuous. It means your personality can withstand the extraordinary challenges and temptations that routinely go with the work. It means you have an ego strong enough to

sustain you from within, when nobody but you knows what you're really doing and thinking.

You have to be street-smart, even cocky sometimes. Every good undercover agent I have known grew up on the street, like I did, and was a good street agent before becoming an undercover agent. On the street you learn what's what and who's who. You learn how to read situations and handle yourself. You can't fake the ability. It shows.

In Britain senior officers look to what Detective Chief Superintendent Roy Ramm calls natural attributes:

By natural attributes I mean their size, shape, colour, gender. Nobody too physically outstanding is selected, and we expect them to have some special skills that we think might be useful in their undercover role such as speaking a foreign language. We then take them on a training course for two weeks, which gives them a lot of basic about the law, making sure they know how to avoid overstepping the mark.

We are keen to make sure that the officers keep their feet on the ground, that they don't think they are part of *Miami Vice*, that they don't start to live their undercover role.[26]

There is now a thorough selection process followed by rigorous training. Even then officers who pass the course may not be used for weeks, months, indeed ever. Back in 1966, things were much more rough and ready.

The story of Bobbie James, an officer from a north country force, is one of the rare documented examples of undercover work of the period.[27]

James was deputed, almost at a moment's notice and certainly untrained, to infiltrate and report on a London gang of robbers. Married to a schoolteacher and with a young daughter, he had joined the police in Wales before coming to the north where he became a beat officer and then transferred to the CID after some six months. He was seconded to the Regional Crime Squad in April 1965 when, as he says, 'in those days they were still selling themselves to local forces'.

> I came to know a Hungarian, who was obviously a true villain with an English wife who was working as a prostitute. He'd been very active in London on smash and grab raids. He was giving me information. Money is the root of all evil. With a good class villain no matter what money he gets he gets rid of it easily, so the villain's wife went on the game in Hull. He was also working as a handyman ferrying other prostitutes. Some of his pals kept coming up to see him. Initially he tried to soft soap me and passed me information.
>
> Then one of his friends, another successful Hungarian, a smash and grab artist, came up to see him. My informant went back down to London with him and rang me and asked if he could see me. I met him at the station and he took me for a drink and five or six of the gang came in. I was passed off as a mate. I was never called by my name – just Taff. I stayed

overnight and saw him again the following day. It took a period of time for me to be accepted and gradually I let it be known that I was an escapee from Walton and was willing to assist in anything they did. I had no written guarantee from my superiors. It was never even mentioned. The prime object was to put them away as best you could.

The first job was a clothing shop in the Seven Sisters Road in north London. It was led by a Brian Scrivens. He was an absolute charmer, a man who could mix in any circles. He was also totally paranoid. He was speechless before a job – he did nothing but think about it. He'd been on the run for two years after escaping from a six-year sentence for armed robbery and was paying a detective in Fulham weekly rent for his freedom. He would go to the toilet with him to bung him. He used to say 'Here's another fucking payday for him'.

Another member of the team was another Brian also on the run after doing two out of four years. A third Hungarian had got out of Hungary at the time of the uprising and it was said amongst them that he was wanted for murder back there but I've no idea if it was true.

The Seven Sisters job was just because someone wanted clothes. We wore the suits for months afterwards but the basic jobs were smash and grab raids on furriers all over the south of England as far as Bournemouth. We would steal a Jaguar and then leave it in a car park for four or five days. There would be four of us on a job.

There would be the driver, the one who went for the window and two on either side would be on the pavement ready to fend off any spirited citizen who wanted to intervene. I would usually be one of those. The m.o. was to circle the place and do it any time of the day when we thought that it would be less busy. Early hours of the morning or mid-afternoon on half-day closing were really best. The men had no fear. If anyone was in our way they'd have no hesitation in carting them on the bonnet.

The gang was on the fringe of the Richardsons and things went in their direction. The firm got 25 per cent of the proceeds if they were lucky. There was a share out for those who were on the raid and we blew it all in a few days. If you were out of cash it was a treating situation. If you weren't on the job you got a backhander. It meant the man who was treated was now a 'friend' or a 'pal', someone who wouldn't squeal. It proved an affinity. If he was bunged then he was as near a trusted friend as he could become. Whoever was around when the job came up was invited. Work came to us rather than our going out looking. Someone had heard ... someone had suggested ... it was easy to do ... a lot of money ... jewellery somewhere. We would look at local newspapers to see who was appearing in court and for what.

Part of the time I lived with a man known as the Chinaman in N.11. He kept a collection of firearms in his place. Then I moved and I lived with Scrivens in the upstairs flat in Fulham Green. I drove the car for him on one occasion. We also did an electrical shop. Car radios were packed in oblong boxes. They were piled high along the wall. This was security money for a good Christmas. The women who lived with Scrivens were terrified.

One thing I'll never forget was watching a young girl procured for prostitution in Hull. This lass, she'd dyed jet black hair. She was married to a fisherman but separated. The fishing fraternity was then very localised. She was very pretty but common as muck. My Hungarians's wife, Tricia, befriended her. A Hungarian came up and took her out, gave her cash which she spent thinking it was a present. She got a good hiding when she couldn't repay and he took her to London and put her on the game. There was nothing I could do to stop it.

By the autumn things were getting difficult. My job was to get information back and not to be involved in a prosecution. There were always people being caught on or after the robberies and there were always people getting away but I began to think that I was getting away too much and someone would notice. In London my work had put seventeen people away in six months.

The end came in Hull in the December the Hungarian came back up and I'd been away from the team for a couple of weeks when his Hungarian friend came north. When he saw the jeweller's Carmichael's window he had eyes like organ stops. When we were all back in London the second one had been telling the group about Carmichaels. There was no problem he said about security. There really wasn't any. The difficulty would be getting out of the city. He'd got a local paper to read the crime and to see what the police were used to. Had they facilities to deal with robbery? The truth was they hadn't. There was another recce this time with Johnson and the second Hungarian and it was decided we would come up and do it.

I told them I knew the area because once I had been released from Hull prison and had to make my way home. I said I'd go and find a flat. I could then telephone and tell them where I was which was going to be in the east of the City. I was the first of the team to arrive and Johnson, Scrivens, and the third Hungarian all came up in a stolen Austin Cambridge. Some of us were going to get out of the city by train and so one had a ticket to Sheffield, one to Birmingham and so on. The second Hungarian was to be at the station.

The prime object was to put them away as best you could but the object of some officers in the Met at that time seemed to be to keep them out as long as they were paying. There was no question of my acting as an *agent provocateur*. That kind of person lived by committing crime.

In the meantime I'd told the powers that be and I had my left arm put in plaster to protect me against the police dogs when they arrived.

When the team asked what had happened I told them I'd had a long wait at Doncaster to get the connection and so I'd done a job. I told them I'd fallen off a wall whilst doing a screwing. When the police came round I was on my bike and away. They thought this was great. It was the beginning of December. In the flat in Williamson Street there was a provision for open fires. I got a couple of bags of pre-packed coal. I told the men I'd nicked it from a shop up the road. Nicking coal, in a strange sort of way, was as good as a high class burglary. What I was doing was copying the bravado they often showed.

We stayed in the flat six days. Every day we would case the place and we were also looking for a Jaguar as a getaway car. We went miles for the thing – as far as Harrogate. Then came the news that the higher ups thought it would be too dangerous to try and capture us as we did the robbery. On 6 December 1966 the flat was raided and we were all locked up. When we were nicked a nice fire was glowing. My cover went when I wasn't seen in the dock. It was only then that I learned two of them really were prison escapees.

Within the next year a man who had been serving a sentence for armed robbery was released six months after I had finished. He was a bouncer at the 51 Club and said 'How's your arm, Taff?' What had happened was Stocken was an escapee and he had spoken with the man who had put two and two

together. I said 'What are you on about?' and
he just shrugged. I never had any
repercussions. I saw my first Hungarian about
three years later. He was back with his wife in
Hull and now she had two children.

We put away about 17 people in six months
or so on my information which wasn't bad. As
for fear, I don't think I knew fear then. I was
young and the adrenalin was flowing.

On 12 December 1966 David Johnson, Brian Scriven
and the third Hungarian pleaded guilty to receiving a
car knowing it had been stolen. The Hull stipendiary
magistrate, committing them to the Quarter Sessions
for sentence, congratulated the officer in charge of the
case saying:

I regard this as an important case and it is
obvious that a great deal of thought, care,
intelligence and powers of observation went
into this operation.

Sadly, things did not go well for James in his
subsequent career in the police and he later resigned on
the grounds of ill health.

In rather more structured circumstances Metropolitan
officer, Frank, was able to infiltrate the team who planned
to rob the KLM warehouse at London airport. On 9
October 1992 Peter White and Carl Harrison were jailed
for 20 and 16 years respectively. White, who using false
references had obtained a job in the KLM warehouse, and
Harrison had planned to kidnap and torture Ann Blake
and daughter so forcing Ian Blake, a KLM cargo

supervisor, into opening the Heathrow strong-room which was said to contain up to £40 million in banknotes and diamonds. It was a thoroughly professional job with Blake's movements being watched and timed.

White contacted a former cellmate whom he wanted to fly his share of the proceeds from an airfield at Elstree to Switzerland for him. Unfortunately for him the cellmate had turned informer and a police *Operation Daedalus* was put into effect with Frank being introduced to White as a professional robber. He and Harrison were taken to pre-arranged venues such as Heston Service Station and Hounslow East tube station where up to 40 hours of incriminating tapes were recorded. Later a second officer was introduced as a driver.

On 8 December 1991, armed with handcuffs, wire ties, an imitation revolver and a CS gas canister, Harrison wearing a balaclava and with Frank in tow, went to Blake's home in Staines, Middlesex, to find more than 50 officers waiting for him. White was arrested later in the day. The surveillance operation had lasted five months.

Detective Chief Inspector Toby Child said of Frank:

> He put his life on the line in order to get us the
> result that we wanted. It is unusual for
> criminals in this type of offence to plead guilty.
> The operation was so successful that up until
> the arrest and even subsequent to the arrest,
> neither Harrison nor White suspected
> anything.

Commenting on his role as an undercover officer Frank said that the first fifteen minutes were the worst, 'I learned the background of the other person and I lived that during the course of the operation'.

Undercover work is recognised as extremely dangerous and stressful, and officers are now given an 'uncle' to whom they can speak freely without management barriers and paperwork. Although a number of officers have been seriously injured, such as Philip Etienne and Martin Maynard, both shot while working on a drugs case in Birmingham, fortunately in this country none has been killed.

One of the other problems an undercover officer faces is, as James did, having to stand by and watch the beating of another person rather than break that cover. In 1990 an undercover officer, posing as a customer, watched a fight in a Newcastle nightclub following which the late Newcastle hardman, Viv Graham, received three years for wounding Stuart Watson, the doorman of Hobo. At the end of the trial the doorman said he was sorry for what had happened and went on to accuse the Regional Crime Squad of using him as bait to get Graham and the others. Unsurprisingly the officer came under heavy fire from the defence lawyers and was asked whether, when he realised one of the men had a spiked weapon, he should have stepped in. 'No,' replied the officer, 'I had been briefed and instructed not to.'

Such instructions still apply. Martin Maynard recalls how he and his then undercover partner, Leroy, were unable to prevent a mugging on the estate on which they were operating:

We couldn't even risk going across the road and being good Samaritans by giving the man

first aid and comforting his wife. If one of the
targets saw us do that and we bumped into
them later, they'd be suspicious of us and
would never trust us. Your average criminal
won't do anything for anyone unless they
think they're going to benefit from it.[28]

One of the most successful long-term operations has
been *Operation Julie*, the codename – after one of the
women officers, 28-year-old Detective Sergeant Julie
Taylor – given to a drug surveillance in the late 1970s
which ended at the Bristol Crown Court in March 1978
and the jailing of Richard Kemp, a brilliant chemist
studying nuclear magnetic resonance for his doctorate,
who had started the operations with Dr Christine Bott,
daughter of an army officer and sister of a Scotland Yard
officer. They had met at Liverpool University and
according to her he 'turned her on to cannabis and
LSD'. Early in his career he produced LSD for an
American organisation in Paris.

Originally there had been one laboratory – the
Cambridge Connection – run by Kemp, Bott, the
American author David Solomon, a disciple of Timothy
Leary, the drug propagandist, and Henry Barclay Todd.
It had operated from 1970 to 1973 and then, when
Kemp and Todd fell out, one laboratory became two.
Kemp and Bott moved to Wales where among other
things she bred goats and he turned out LSD tablets.
The second, larger laboratory was in Hampton Wick
run by Todd with the assistance of a chemist and Brian
Cuthbertson a general assistant in charge of
distribution. Export was undertaken through
Amsterdam by a Chelsea restauranteur.

Julie became a worldwide operation with the American DEA running a simultaneous operation known as *Syntac 10*. It was discovered that Bott, alleged to be the group's banker, had a deposit box containing £45,000 in Switzerland and it was thought there was a supply route to West Germany where another of the defendants had a deposit box. There was also a supposition that supplies had percolated through the Iron Curtain.

In February 1976 *Operation Julie* was launched and from then on Kemp and Bott were under surveillance. A detective sergeant and a woman officer rented a cottage near the Kemp home for a two-week fishing holiday. The officer in charge Richard Lee posed as a London businessman recovering from a heart operation and was joined by another officer. Although they spent their time in the pubs they made no progress with the locals.

'I suddenly realised that they thought we were two homosexuals and that was why nobody would accept us,' said Lee. A young policewoman was hastily summoned as a live-in secretary and relations with the community improved dramatically.

Two officers, Eric Wright and Steve Bentley, spent eight months, part of the time camping in a van, living among the hippies in the village of Landdewi Brefi targeting Hughes who had been pushing drugs since the swinging sixties in the Kings Road. They met him in the local public house and became friends, losing £90 to him in a card game. At first Hughes was suspicious of them and accused them of being officers. Wright grabbed him by the throat and threatened to beat him up. Bentley increased their cover by rowing with the local constable about drinking after hours.

After four months they moved out of the van and began sending out messages on a radio transmitter from the loft of their cottage. This stopped abruptly when Hughes told them that when he could not sleep at night he liked to listen to ham radio wavelengths. As the months went by Wright drank and took drugs with Hughes, baby-sat his children and, he says, developed such a friendship that he came close to tipping him off that a raid was pending.

On 25 March 1977, 800 police made swoops in Wales and Seymour Road. In Wales they found nothing and it was not until shortly before Christmas that Kemp revealed his hiding place, beneath the quarry-tiled floor of the lounge at his home. The laboratory equipment had been hidden down a well.

Shortly before Christmas 1977 another raid produced a haul of 13 million tablets of LSD worth, it was said, £100 million. In a titillating sidebar to the raid it was made known that on a previous raid a hippy had been found having sexual intercourse with his girlfriend on the floor of an old caravan. The couple were on a 'trip' and the man had hammered a six inch nail through his nose 'for a new kick'.

Kemp received 13 years as did his rival Todd, Cuthbertson 11, Bott 9 and Hughes 8. To the annoyance of many of the officers involved in the surveillance, most of the defendants were paroled after serving half their sentences. Kemp and Bott returned to live together after their release.

The hope and belief of Richard Lee was that *Operation Julie* would lead to the formation of a National Drugs Squad. His hopes were misplaced and instead he soon found himself back in uniform. He resigned, wrote a book about the operation and bought a tobacconists in the north of England. Six others resigned almost immediately over various criticisms of the way they were treated when they went back to their forces and there were calls for a Home Office inquiry. Twenty-two members of the squad remained in the force.

Short-term undercover officers in *Operation Swordfish* were successful when they posed as the licensee, head barman and a barmaid for six weeks in 1989. The Cauliflower pub in Upminster Road, South Rainham had been going through managers at the rate of five within eighteen months before the police went behind the bar to flush out a protection team. In July 1990 the leaders, Donald Hoey and Leonard Sherwood, received six years apiece for counts of blackmail.

The dangers for an undercover officer are obvious as policewoman Elaine Manson discovered about the same time. In what the police described as the first serious outbreak of protection racketeering, Frank Salmon, a market trader from Dagenham, was jailed at the Old Bailey for seven and a half years. He had been convicted of blackmail, affray and an attack during which ammonia was squirted in a victim's face. Others in his team received up to four and a half years' imprisonment.

Salmon had reigned over a part of the East End and Essex for a little over a year, trying to obtain protection money from 23 winebars, clubs and saunas. He had shot up one bar and pressed a gun under the nose of a barman. In 1989 disc jockey Russell Holt, who played the East End pubs, had 42 stitches in his head and hand following an assault by four masked men. His ankle was

ABOVE *Alphonse Bertillon, French criminologist, 1853-1914. The police clerk turned Director of Police Identification initially had to battle with suspicion and ignorance in order to establish the first modern means of criminal identification. However his systems were later used throughout the world.*

'Thanks to a French genius, errors of identification will soon cease to exist not only in France, but also in the entire world. Hence judicial errors based upon false identification will likewise disappear. Long live Bertillonage! Long live Alphonse Bertillon!' Contemporary quote, from The Marks of Cain.

ABOVE *Detective Superintendent J Woodmancey, Chief Inspector John Capstick (also known as Artful Johnnie) and Detective Inspector John Campbell, May 1948, in the midst of the search for the Beast of Blackburn. It was Campbell who proposed that the entire male population of Blackburn be fingerprinted, a massive undertaking which ultimately identified the killer of the three-year-old girl.*

ABOVE *After willingly surrendering his fingerprints the Beast of Blackburn was identified and arrested, three months after the murder.*

© POPPERFOTO

LEFT *The nineteen year old Peter Griffiths who was found guilty of murdering the Blackburn born three-year-old. The jury took only 23 minutes to come to a decision. He was hung in November, 1948.*

OPPOSITE *Count Alfred de Marigny with his wife Nancy in the Bahamas, November 1943, after having been found not guilty of the murder of his father-in-law Sir Harry Oakes. The case remains one of the great unsolved murders of the twentieth century. De Marigny owed his life to his young wife who travelled to New York to hire Raymond Schindler, one of the most famous private detectives of his day.*

OPPOSITE *20 July 1982, London. Carcasses of the horses of the Household Cavalry lie in the road in Hyde Park after an IRA carbomb in which three people were killed, twenty-two injured. The conviction of Danny McNamee was later quashed and the case became an example of need to continually question the results and deductions of fingerprinting.*

ABOVE *A cheerful looking George P Metesky is arrested as the Mad Bomber of New York, January 1957. Metesky began his bombing career over sixteen years before, as protest at his failure to be awarded compensation for a mechanical accident at work. Both psychics and psychologists were consulted during the case.*

ABOVE *Ted Bundy, June 1977, having been recaptured after an escape attempt in Colorado. The perpetrator of an unknown number of attacks and murders, Ted Bundy at one point confessed to having killed over 100 women. He was electrocuted in 1989 after ten years of appeals. His case was influential in the developing use of computers in criminal detection.*

OPPOSITE *J. Edgar Hoover, FBI chief, with his long time companion Clyde Tolson in 1936.*

APRIL, 1935   FIFTEEN CENTS

THE
CRISIS

SHIELDS, ELLINGTON AND BROWN

(Escaped Mississippi noose, but Death trails them—See page 119)

THUMBS DOWN ON UNIONS!
BY J. WELLINGTON EVANS

THE GEORGE CRAWFORD CASE
A STATEMENT BY THE N. A. A. C. P.

UPON THIS ROCK

OPPOSITE *Lynch law at Marion, Indiana – two men were dragged from the local gaol by a crowd of five thousand townsfolk in order to inflict their own form of vigilante justice.*

ABOVE *Shield, Ellington and Brown, April 1935, who were beaten into false confessions of the murder of their employer Raymond Stuart. The night before his arrest Ellington had been attacked by local vigilantes : 'They got me out of bed and carried me to Mr Raymond's house. They tied me up with my hands to a tree and whipped me. They tied me up and whipped me good. Then they hung me, they pulled me up twice.' When Ellington was cut loose he confessed.*

ABOVE *The body of 60 year old kidnap victim Father Patrick E. Heslin is found buried on a beach near San Francisco, 1921. One William A. Hightower took the police to the body but claimed to have accidentally come across it whilst burying some liquor.*

OPPOSITE *The result of decades spent searching for a more scientific method of interrogation; Dr John Larson (right), Berkeley's Assistant Chief of Police, with an early version of what came to be known as the lie-detector.*

ABOVE *Larson put the lie-detector to the test in its first case and deduced that William A. Hightower, who continued to protest his innocence in the Father Heslin case, was in fact guilty. Shortly after Hightower did indeed confess to kidnapping and killing the Priest.*

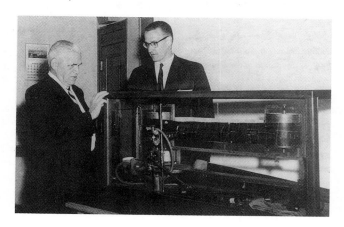

ABOVE *James Watson, who wrote* The Double Helix, *was awarded the Nobel Prize for his work in discovering DNA.*

RIGHT *Inside the nucleus of each human cell is a string of coded information in the form of a ribbon-like molecule of DNA which contains a genetic blueprint of that particular person's make-up.*

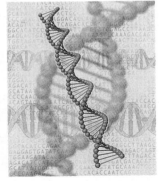

© POPPERFOTO

LEFT *OJ Simpson – the chief suspect in the infamous murder case which had a damaging effect on the practice of using DNA samples as convincing evidence.*

© POPPERFOTO

RIGHT *The bodies of Nicole, the former wife of Simpson, and a friend were found at her Los Angeles home in June 1994. Simpson's lawyers argued that police had contaminated the crime scene with drops of blood from OJ Simpson's sample.*

ABOVE *A Washington forensic scientist analyzes and compares DNA samples for identification in the OJ Simpson case.*

BELOW *Donato Bilancia is escorted to prison in Genoa by three Carabinieri having being arrested for the murder of six people, May 1998. DNA testing* methods had continued to spread through the world from the mid-nineties. The case of Bilancia, one of Italy's most notorious serial killers, further highlighted the potential DNA has in the fight against crime. It also caused a political debate about how the techniques could be used most effectively.

broken by a pool cue and he went to the police. He told detectives he had been asked to pay Salmon £1,500 from his earnings.

It was thought that Salmon, known as a womaniser, would be less suspicious if a female officer acted as a decoy and the police used Manson as the person to trap Salmon. Acting as the friend and business associate of Holt's wife, Denise Seaga, who ran a dress shop, she met Salmon on five occasions, paying out a total of £800.

On one meeting she was patted down by him for wires when he came to suspect she was a police officer. However, his antennae were sound. Another time he accused her of being a policewoman and she told the court, 'He started at me and flicked his fingers ... He shook his arm and a knife slid down inside his left palm'. On a third occasion when she was with him she noticed a bulge in the leg of his trousers and remarked it looked like the outline of a knife. 'Brains of Britain ...', he replied, 'In this business you get wankers who don't play ball.'

On 22 May 1989 she handed over £600 in marked notes and asked Salmon why he referred to the cash as a present. 'I am not going to shout out it is protection money, am I?' he replied. Shortly afterwards he was arrested.

Operation Motion, hailed as the way ahead in British policing and launched in October 1994 by West London Drugs Squad, involved three women police officers going undercover and posing as prostitutes in a brothel in Queensway.

> We were trying to create the image of tarty
> street girls. We didn't wash, we left our hair

dirty and matted and we deliberately chewed
our nails.

> We had an AIDS poster, packets of Durex
> lying around and bottles of water which
> addicts use to smoke. If you are playing the
> part of a prostitute you have to prepare for the
> worst. Some would grope you but you just had
> to grit your teeth. We had to be very careful
> not to ask for cocaine directly because that
> would have been entrapment and they could
> have got out of it in court.

The 35 dealers who were filmed on video pleaded guilty
and received sentences of between four and six years.[29]

Two years later in 1996 seven policemen joined the
client list of a high-class gay brothel which thrived for
two years 150 yards from Kensington Palace. An eighth
signed on as a rent boy. The owner was so keen to have
his premises in keeping with the exclusive area that the
exterior of the house was festooned with hanging
baskets of fuchsias and geraniums. Council officials
awarded him a prize for the best-kept hanging baskets
in the area. In-house sex at Image International cost
£65 and prostitutes sent to hotels cost an additional
£30. When the police officers were offered a menu of
boys available, in time-honoured tradition they
declined their services. The one assigned to be a rent
boy failed to turn up for work.

Their devotion to duty paid off. At Southwark
Crown Court a New Zealander, who was described as
'generous and kind', provided immaculate linen, fresh
condoms and required regular health checks of the
40–50 employees whom he sent on self-improvement

schemes, was sentenced to 18 months' imprisonment for living off the earnings of male prostitutes.[30]

Things may have come a long way since James was sent undercover but the psychological pressures on the infiltrator are still considerable. Former Transport Police officer David Corbett[31] worked undercover with the Northumbria police on *Operation Claymore* launched in 1996 to tackle the drugs problem which had led to 17 drugs-related deaths in and around the town of Blythe. For over four months he lived the life of a drug user and gathered information which led to the arrest of over 30 people and 20 convictions for heroin dealing and other drugs-related offences.

Corbett had grown up in the Gorbals area of Glasgow and as a teenager had known members of the infamous Cumbie gang which gave him the credibility to mix with the criminal fraternity. Unlike James an elaborate cover story was prepared. He was found a factory job from which he would resign in two weeks. He could tell dealers he was living off redundancy money from a previous employer and he wanted to buy drugs which he would sell back in Scotland. He was set up in a flat with an intercom system, a camera hidden in the kitchen cooker and a cupboard with a false bottom in which to hide the drugs. He also had a false passport, bank cards and a car with video equipment in the dashboard. He went to meetings wired up.

Operation Claymore was a great success but as the weeks went by Corbett, in his role, was spending more and more time in public houses and his alcohol consumption rose dramatically. He was swearing, drinking and becoming violent with little provocation. He requested that he be withdrawn from the operation.

On his return to the Strathclyde police he became sick and later left the force on the grounds of ill-health. Over all he had been undercover in various cities for some three years.[32]

Of course some undercover work is more successful than others. On the plus side has been the infiltration by Joe Pistone known as Donnie Brasco into the New York Families, as well as the less well known Frank Zaneth who was an undercover agent for the Royal Canadian Mounted Police for over 30 years from the conscription riots in Quebec in 1918 to the Cold War.[33] Criminals who became undercover agents included Cecil Kirby, a Mafia enforcer who also became an agent for the Mounties infiltrating the Montreal Mafia, and Billy Breen who worked for the FBI investigating the murder of Judge Wood, shot to prevent him sentencing a drug dealer to a long term of imprisonment.

On the minus side, in recent years, has been an undercover operation run by customs officers which allowed a bonded warehouse in London and other warehouses to sell drink for the home market rather than for export. The aim was to have provided a substantial number of convictions of senior players in the game. In the event a substantial amount of revenue, possibly over £1 billion, was lost.[34]

One of the problems with undercover and infiltration work is the likelihood of evidence obtained being excluded at a subsequent trial. In America there is a specific defence of entrapment but in Britain until recently the best that a defendant could have hoped is that when he or she had been inveigled into a criminal act by an undercover officer or a participating informant then the sentence would be reduced to reflect that. More recently, however, by virtue of the Police and Criminal Evidence Act 1984, a partial defence has arisen. The trial judge may, under ss 75 and 76, exclude evidence improperly obtained and the whole case may be dismissed. It is a power not used all that frequently. A number of people have found to their cost when attempting to have an unwanted spouse or lover disposed of, that the proposed hitman has been an undercover officer. The Court of Appeal has not been overly sympathetic to their plight.[35]

IX

In Britain at the time, sting operations such as ABSCAM were virtually unknown, but the police had been using the telephone intercept for some years. Its use in Britain in a straightforward criminal case really first came to light in the highly publicised 1956 case of the barrister Patrick Marrinan. He had been overheard talking to the London gangleader, Billy Hill, over the role he should play in going to Ireland to try to assist two men who had fled there after the slashing of Hill's rival, Jack Spot. Marrinan, who had broken the Code of Conduct of the Bar by talking directly to a client and making the journey to Ireland without proper instructions from a solicitor, was disbarred.[36]

In 1979 officer Peter Ware observed the Home Office guidelines and obtained a warrant so that a colleague could tap the telephone of a James Malone, suspected of dealing in stolen goods and exporting them to Italy. Malone was later arrested and charged. Under the then existing guidelines, officers had been instructed that they were never to reveal that a tap had taken place and so when he was asked this point blank in court he faced a dilemma. Ware recalls:

> We were told that we were to say, 'I can neither confirm nor deny'. If it's put to us, you know 'Was there a telephone tap in this case?' we were supposed to say, 'I can neither confirm nor deny that there was a telephone tap'.

Nor had James Malone any right to know whether his telephone had been tapped but during his first trial:

> We managed to get hold of a page from a policeman's notebook. And on the page there was a list of all my telephone calls from the previous day before I was arrested.

After a ten-week trial in June 1978 the jury at the Inner London Crown Court disagreed and when a second jury failed to reach a verdict the following year no further evidence was offered against him. The following year Malone brought a claim in the Queen's Bench Division of the High Court against the Metropolitan Police accusing them of illegally tapping his telephone. The case was dismissed but, undeterred, Malone went to Strasbourg where on 2 August 1984 the court ruled that the tapping had violated Malone's right to privacy because, since there was no clearly defined law in existence, it had not taken place within the law.

While Malone was conducting his campaign against telephone tapping in Britain phone tapping allegations were made during the Miners' Strike of 1984, the most pivotal industrial dispute of the post-war era. Had the miners been successful the Thatcher Government might well have fallen in the same way that a decade earlier strikes had done for Edward Heath.

One tactic of the National Union of Mineworkers was to send coachloads of pickets all over the country to enforce the strike, but it seemed that miraculously the police had prior knowledge of where the coaches were going and arrived first.

One of the coach operators, Clayton Jones, remembers the situation:

> You think that it a figment of your
> imagination. But because of the fact it was a
> repetitive situation, they were always about,
> always checking, always very noticeable when
> you went to the various areas.

The NUM would leave the decision about the destination of the pickets as late as possible and that information would be given to Jones over the telephone. He would then make arrangements and tell the drivers their destinations. As far as he was concerned the Union only communicated with him personally.

Jones's local MP, Ray Powell, became convinced that Jones's allegations that his phone was being tapped were true and accused the police of illegitimate telephone tapping in the House of Commons. Questioned on television, a senior police officer denied that any application had been made to the Home Secretary for the authorisation of any telephone tapping since the strike began, saying that the allegation that Clayton Jones's telephone was being tapped:

> is totally untrue. And if – let me go further and say that – if Mr Clayton Jones or Mr Raymond Powell have got any evidence whatsoever that phones are being tapped, that will be investigated rigorously by this police force and the appropriate steps taken. It is frankly, absolutely nonsense.

But other MPs apart from Ray Powell had their suspicions. Joe Aston, whose constituency was Bassethwaite, Nottingham, was one of them:

> It became very blatant in the Miners' Strike, you'd pick up the phone and you'd hear a faint click like a tape recorder going on. I'm not saying anybody was at the other end, listening. I think there was just an automatic tape recorder going like a faint whirr.

As a result of James Malone's success in Europe, the Interception of Communications Act was passed. Now the law required that all telephone taps had to be authorised by the Home Secretary. But the public still had no right to know whether a phone had been tapped. All they could do was to ask their Member of Parliament to take the matter up on their behalf but there was no obligation on the Government to tell them. If it was in the public interest to keep it secret then kept secret it was.

Even in the twenty-first century things have not improved. Madeleine Colvin, Secretary of JUSTICE, points out:

> It is very difficult to get an accurate figure on how many taps are done each year. Nor is there information on how effective the taps are. In the United States the authorities have to publish figures on the outcome of the tap. In the United Kingdom there are no such requirements. The government does not have a duty to notify an individual of a phone tap; again this is in contrast to the United States, and in many other countries where if someone's phone has been tapped the authorities have to notify them of this.[37]

X

In 1982 another Chicago-based case saw the FBI pitted not only against the constraints on surveillance but against an organisation which understood the art of counter-surveillance. Among the Puerto Rican community was a small cell of terrorists who wished to secure independence from the United States. Between 1973 and 1984 the terrorist group FALN detonated 120 bombs over the United States and, in so doing, became the most successful terrorist group in the history of the Union.

In the early years of the group, between June 1975 and November 1979, it claimed the credit for 19 bombings and six incendiary attacks, including the

Sears Tower and the City-County building in the Chicago area. They were coordinated with bombings in New York and with direct action on the island of Puerto Rico. Communiques called for a 'free and Socialist Puerto Rico' saying that 'if necessary ... written in red blood'. In late 1976 a bomb factory was discovery in Chicago but the terrorist actions continued and in January 1980 the FALN carried out an armed assault on the Oak Creek National Guard Armory in Wisconsin in an unsuccessful effort to obtain access to the weapons vault. In March that year the FALN temporarily took over the Carter-Mondale Presidential campaign headquarters, holding workers at gunpoint while the office was ransacked and spray painted.

On 4 April eleven members of the FALN were captured in Evanston, Illinois, as they were about to rob an armoured car. One relatively new recruit to FALN, Freddie Mendez, provided a good deal of information. Before being sentenced Mendez, although he could not identify any suspect still at large, explained the counter-surveillance techniques used by the group. So from December 1981 to January 1983 various Chicago law enforcement agencies began a long-term surveillance on a FALN suspect.

Agent Candice DeLong, who has herself written a book on undercover work, comments:

My role was to be on the street surveillance team. We were able to focus on one particular target that we thought might be going to a safe house. And, of course, our goal was to find that safe house. We focused on this one particular target, a married man unemployed with two children. We followed his activities and realised that every Tuesday night he was leaving his home and heading out for the subways and we would lose him. It was apparent that he was trying to be lost.

Eventually the FBI traced a safe house but as part of their counter-surveillance FALN members spoke in code so that when they talked about bananas and cherries and making a fruit cocktail they were talking about detonators and dynamite and about bomb-making.

There was legal provision for bugging a private home but the operation required more than that. Cameras were to be installed with the danger that the court might throw out the evidence. The risk was taken and a hole was drilled through the apartment's ceiling and a camera was installed overlooking the kitchen table.

Rick Hahn, of the operation, recalls what they saw:

There were guns on the table and we watched them that afternoon as they cleaned and loaded the guns and then they built firing circuits for explosive devices. From that point forward there is no argument to anyone as to what exactly is going on in that apartment. If you don't have the video you have no argument other than speculation to say that they're not talking about coconuts and plums and bananas and that they're talking about weapons.

Appropriately, 4 July was to be a special day for the FALN and they were targeting the US Army Reserve

Center at the North Side of Chicago to put down their counter-statement in the form of an explosive device. The FBI moved in.

The defence was, as anticipated, that there was no law which clearly stated that the Government had a right to put a video camera in a private home and the trial judge suppressed the evidence obtained by electronic surveillance. The FBI appealed the ruling and the Supreme Court was clear that there is no right to be left alone assembling bombs in safe houses. In exceptional circumstances a camera can be placed in a private home, but only after a warrant has been issued. The members of FALN were convicted.

It seemed now that the laws were in place to make the perceived abuses of ABSCAM and FALN surveillance a thing of the past. But in 1994, again in Chicago, another test was to come when Ray Frias, a local politician, was charged with accepting bribes in relation to obtaining a city permit for a rock-crushing plant. The evidence was videotaped but in a pre-trial motion, counsel for the FBI made the request that not all the tapes be played. These were the ones in which Ray Frias, following the global advice of Mel Weinberg in the ABSCAM case, had again and again told the undercover agent that he didn't want the money being offered. The judge rejected the motion and Frias was found Not Guilty.

The situation was not really that different in England. Patricia Hall, the mother of two young boys, disappeared from her home in Pudsey, Yorkshire, in January 1992. On 10 March 1994 her husband Keith was acquitted of her murder at Leeds Crown Court. The prosecution's case was that Hall, who ran a mobile grocery, had confessed to an undercover policewoman 'Liz' that he had strangled his wife and then incinerated the body. The policewoman had been planted on Hall after he replied to a lonely hearts advertisement in his local paper. All their meetings and telephone calls had been tape-recorded and when Liz was discussing marriage and expressed a worry that Patricia Hall might return, Hall was alleged to have said, 'I was sleeping downstairs, then I woke up. I strangled her. It wasn't as simple as that, there were voices in my head telling me to do it. I'm sorry. Does that change anything? Do you still want me?'

At that trial the judge, Mr Justice Waterhouse, refused to allow the jury to hear the tape, saying that the questioning by the policewoman had driven a coach and horses through the Police and Criminal Evidence Act 1984 which was designed to protect suspects in interviews. After the verdict he did, however, allow the publication of the contents of the tape. Hall has maintained his wife, who had had psychiatric treatment, had simply walked out on him after the marriage had deteriorated. He appealed to her to return so their relationship could be renewed.

Curiously enough, two days after the Hall decision a case at a Crown Court showed that the informer-*agent provocateur* is alive and well. A police informer, run by a Crime Squad officer, managed to persuade a gang to forge £18 million travellers' cheques. He is said to have netted around £100,000 by way of rewards.

In August 1990 the informer was arrested by the police in possession of £10,000 of counterfeit currency. He came under the wing of an officer and began to talk. At his trial in February 1991 a letter was sent by a ranking officer to the judge saying that this man could help to smash 'major criminals throughout the United

Kingdom and Europe...who are engaged in the large scale distribution of drugs and counterfeit currency'. It was also thought that he could expose paramilitary organisations in Northern Ireland who were using drugs sales to finance their activities. The informer, who had a string of relatively minor convictions going back to 1970, was sentenced to 18 months' imprisonment of which he served seven. As befitted a sensible policeman, the officer kept in touch with him during his sentence. By the end of the year and now relocated the man was being used in a target operation.

The target was Businessman 'A', who said that until he met the informer he was conducting a successful business in factoring and buying and selling end-of-range goods. An undercover operation was set up. First there was an attempt to persuade him to buy a container of drugs from Europe. The undercover police buyers said they would buy it from him. However he made no attempt to contact the 'sellers'.

This operation was not a success and in March 1992 a director of casework at the CPS headquarters, authorised the police to try to supply 'A' with fake travellers' cheques. Immunity would be given to the informer and an undercover officer for offences they might commit along the way to their target. In 1992 'A' and some friends were lured to a hotel on the M1 where there were £4 million fake cheques in the boot of a car. Seven men including 'A' were arrested. The informer received nearly £40,000 for his efforts.

Nor was the trial a success. Defence lawyers spent a considerable amount of time and effort in trying to get disclosure of documents from the prosecution including the amount paid to the informer as a reward.

In turn he disappeared. When it came to it the original officer did not attend the trial either. He had, said the police, suffered a nervous breakdown. The Judge dismissed the charges saying that the case was an abuse of process. He was particularly unhappy that the prosecution had not complied with his order for disclosure of documents.

What might have been disclosed if the documents had been produced is the sum of £50,000 also paid to the informer in 1993 for an earlier case. By now the informer had been resettled and was in contact with a printer, 'B', trying to persuade him to print forged Equity cards, MOT certificates and cheques. 'B', facing bankruptcy with the failure of his business, agreed to print the cards but not the other items. The informer brought pressure on Wilson to go ahead with the whole deal. 'B' claims that threats were made to ensure his full co-operation and, with £5,000 supplied to the police and handed on to the informer, the necessary equipment was bought. The police were tipped off and 'B' and seven others were arrested in the raids said to have uncovered a world record of $26.6 million forged cheques. The Judge, said the men arrested were victims of 'scandalous, corrupt incitement' which led them to being 'fitted up to commit crimes which none would have ever dreamed of committing otherwise'.[38]

XI

By the end of the twentieth century many were regarding video surveillance as the answer to the proliferating urban crime.

On 3 May 2000 a teenage girl was walking home near Egham from work late at night with friends. When they left her she was followed by a man across parkland and raped. He was caught because Egham, like so many towns in Britain, has streets lined with CCTV cameras linked to image databanks. The case demonstrates to what extent technology not only assists in surveillance work but how it impinges on daily life at the beginning of the twenty-first century.

The camera images were examined and showed her going towards Station Road and a car pulling up nearby. A man got out of the car and went towards a 24-hour shop. He then hesitated and went to a cash point and with the money he obtained went into the shop. The police were able to obtain authorisation to gain access to the cash point to see who used it and out of which account the money had been drawn.

It is clear from the video that the man had a keen interest in the girl and he can be seen going towards his victim. On the second day of his trial Kaleem Arshad pleaded guilty.

Nevertheless CCTV has voluble critics with claims that it infringes our civil liberties. Simon Davies says that:

> People view images of crime through the lens
> of a CCTV camera and then jump to the
> conclusion that CCTV is good for crime
> control. Now, this is a massive irony. The crime
> was never stopped by the camera. There are
> instances where, after the events, felons have
> been identified but that's not the point. Just
> because a technology is capable of resolving a

few crimes doesn't justify its existence. Nor
does it diminish the continuing problem we
have about the violation of people's
fundamental right to privacy.

In a typical day in central London, between, say, Liverpool Street Station and Paddington Station, a person will be surveyed by around 1,000 cameras. Five years ago the figure would have been around a third of that number. Davies believes that there will be a similar increase over the next five years to the point where virtually everyone in an urban area can expect to be captured on film at least several hundred times a day.

Detective Inspector Peter O'Sullivan, in charge of the Egham rape case, takes a different view:

I want the towns that I walk around and my
family and friends, people I know, to walk
around to be safe. This is one way of helping
make those places safe. The fact that people's
images are being captured all the time, well, as
long as they're not used for any purpose that is
inappropriate, I really don't see the problem.

The country which, a century ago, did not embrace undercover police work with anything approaching enthusiasm has, effectively, become one of the global capitals of surveillance.

Now, along with CCTV, the Regulation of Investigatory Powers Act 2000 has sanctioned the use of e-mail surveillance. In Britain although the text of an e-mail cannot be intercepted without a warrant, the police need no permission to discover with whom a person is communicating. Nor is there any right for a person to know if their e-mails are being intercepted even after an investigation has finished.

A refusal to surrender a computer decryption key to the police carries a sentence of up to eight years, with the authorities arguing that the power is needed to intercept the computer records of criminals. A similar measure foundered in America when it was blocked by Congress, fearing the damage it would do for the right to privacy.

Clive Norris takes a relatively sanguine view of things:

One of the major shifts with the development of a surveillance society has been to make us all become suspects.

Before, to become a suspect, the police needed reasonable suspicion to stop and search you, to enter your house, to gather information about you. But what the surveillance society does, it means we collect data in advance of anyone doing anything. So all of us become subject to having information stored about us, just in case we might be a criminal tomorrow.

Now this is a major shift. We have no idea how the information being collected about us now will be used by some future police force or some future government. In a sense, we just have to wait passively and see whether the future will turn out happily.

CHAPTER 5

Interrogation

I

The time-honoured method of obtaining a confession has been to exert physical or mental pressure on the suspect until he or she admits the offence. Whether the person has actually committed the crime is another matter. Whether the approach is a proper one is still another question.

Jose Sivuca Ferreira, State Deputy of Rio de Janeiro, Brazil where, it is alleged, the police still use extreme violence, has no doubt:

> Once violence sets in, it can only be countered with violence. There is no moral difference between us, the citizens of a country fighting an invading army and us fighting the army of criminals who try to invade our homes. There is no moral difference.[1]

He is supported in his beliefs by Maria Olimpia, a State Prosecutor:

> The police philosophy is to use the easiest way to investigate. They arrest a suspect and get him to confess. Then, they present it as a

solved case to the judicial system. In fact the
evidence for all this was initially obtained
through torture. This is generally the way that
the police operate even today.

It was ever so. In the Middle Ages in Britain a favourite
was the torture of *peine forte et dure* in which
increasingly heavy weights were placed on the suspect's
chest. The suspect died in any event but the benefit in
refusing to confess was that fortitude saved the man's
goods and chattels from being forfeit to the state.

Tony Collins, of the National Crime Faculty,
believes that times are changing:

Today the use of overbearing psychological
pressure, once common amongst the police, is
forbidden. The idea is to get a suspect to repeat
his story in minute detail, and then challenge
any inconsistencies.

The suspect is treated almost like a witness.
But invariably if somebody is lying they will be
caught out in their lies. And the interviewer's
role really is to try and get that person, if they
are lying, to more or less dig themselves a hole.
We will then challenge them on their lies.

Barry Irving of the Police Foundation agrees:

A good interview today means testing
everything that the suspect says. You need to
know the logical relationships between the bit
of evidence that you have and what's missing
so that you can't be fooled. And that sort of

preparation used to be very rare indeed. Now it's absolutely necessary.

Historically the heavy-handed methods once used by the British police to obtain confessions were never as ruthless as those used in America. There in 1931 a presidential report on common police practices shocked the Washington establishment. Written by some of America's leading lawyers the report detailed how, throughout the country, the police illegally relied on a form of torture known as the Third Degree.

In fact there was no reason to be shocked at all and the expressions of protest may well have been pharasaical. The Third Degree had been used on a regular basis for the previous fifty years and had been openly discussed on both sides of the Atlantic.

The corrupt New York police inspector Thomas Byrnes is credited with the invention of the Third Degree but he surely only refined and improved previous techniques. One of the refinements credited to him is the sweatbox in which a cell was heated until the prisoner, unable to endure it, would promise to give the required answers.

In the case of McGloin, the murderer from the Whyos street gang, Byrnes decided that he should not be allowed to sleep more than 15 minutes at a time and his meals were always late. He was put in a place where he could see the bloodstained dress of his victim carried by and he was allowed to see all the people who could have connected him with the murder coming and going around the prison.

Another murderer gave up when he was made to sleep in the bed of his victim and yet another when he was forced into the coffin in which the murdered man was to be buried.

'It was generally a case of the strain being too much for the human brain to stand,' said Lieutenant Edward F. Rayens when visiting London from the New York District Attorney's office. He took the opportunity to give an interview to the press explaining the Third Degree.

> The old Third Degree consisted chiefly of brutality. The suspects were not allowed to sleep. Whenever their cell door was opened a policeman or two would give them a couple of wallops with their fists or a blow or two with their clubs. Food was sometimes denied them.

But, as is always the case, things had changed.

> You can take it from me that the stories that float across the 'pond' regarding the brutality and unfairness of our methods are exaggerations, and frequently pure inventions, but it is true that a prisoner is treated differently in America from the way in which he is treated in this country.

If we have good grounds for suspecting anyone of a crime we try to make him confess. We tell him we 'have the goods' – to put it in English we make him believe that we can prove his guilt and that it will be easier for him to confess. If we know that a man is guilty but cannot prove it, what possible objection can be taken to persuading him to confess?

But things had indeed changed and, it was to be emphasised, kindness was the way to confession. As an example Rayens enthusiastically quoted the New York detective, George Dougherty, as plying the suspect with Havana cigars until he confessed.[2] Perhaps the gesture was not wholly altruistic and it was simply to make him sick.

Over the years the Third Degree was a favourite expression in the English courts. For example in the 1926 case of Henry Adams accused of killing a workmate, John Porter, it was alleged that Chief Inspector Gillan had used the technique to extract a confession. What was called a trial within a trial or *voir dire* was used to determine whether the judge should allow the confession in evidence. He had no hesitation in saying that the officer could not possibly have conducted himself in the way alleged. Adams maintained he had nothing to do with the killing at all but the jury returned a compromise verdict of manslaughter.[3]

In the case of Henry Julius Jacoby, an 18-year-old pantry boy accused of killing Lady White in her London hotel room which he had been trying to burgle, his lawyer Lucien Fior accused the police of Third Degree tactics to get him to confess. 'What is the first degree?' asked the judge acidly. Despite a recommendation for mercy by the jury because of his age, Jacoby was hanged.[4]

II

In theory, if not always in practice, since the end of the nineteenth century the British courts have imposed standards of behaviour for the police in their treatment and questioning of suspects.

The so-called Judges' Rules, which came into effect on an informal basis in the 1880s, were possibly devised by Sir Henry Hawkins in a fit of unusual good nature for he was known as 'Anging 'Awkins. The aim was to stop bullying and oppression and to provide a code of conduct which, if broken, would lead to the suppression of the confession obtained. Where the police had evidence to charge a man with a crime, suspects should be cautioned that they need say nothing more but that, if they did, it could be used in evidence. Not all judges accepted Hawkins's lead.

Indeed the Rules were not universally in operation by the early 1900s because a letter was written by the Chief Constable of Birmingham to the then Lord Chief Justice asking for clarification. One judge had censured a constable on his force for cautioning a prisoner while another judge had censured another constable for failing to do so. The first four of the Judges' Rules were approved in 1912 and a further five added in 1918. Now it was made clear that the police should not entrap a suspect nor should they actively discourage him from making a confession.[5]

Unfortunately the judiciary whether at magistrates' court level or in jury cases have not always provided the protection expected of them. Far too often over the years they turned a blind eye to cases of police brutality and oppressive questioning. It was only in a rare case that, if a defendant challenged the evidence of the police because of their conduct in questioning him in a police cell, he could hope to be believed.

Not even Lord Denning, hailed as the champion of the oppressed, has always been a shining light. Here he is commenting on the case of the Birmingham Six when they had tried to bring a civil action for damages:

> Just consider the course of events if this action is allowed to proceed to trial. If the six men fail, it will mean that much time and money will have been expended by many people for no good purpose. If the six men win, it will mean that the police were guilty of perjury, that they were guilty of violence and threats, that the confessions were involuntary and were improperly admitted in evidence and that the convictions were erroneous. That would mean the Home Secretary would either have to recommend they be pardoned or he would have to remit the case to the Court of Appeal. This is such an appalling vista that every sensible person in the land would say: It cannot be right these actions should go any further.
>
> This case shows what a civilised country we are. Here are six men who have been proved guilty of the most wicked murder of twenty-one innocent people. They have no money. Yet the state has lavished large sums on their defence. They were convicted of murder and sentenced to imprisonment for life. In their evidence they were guilty of gross perjury. Yet the state continued to lavish large sums on them in actions against the police. It is high time it stopped. It is

really an attempt to set aside the convictions on a side wind. It is a scandal that it should be allowed to continue.

In America interrogation laws are not as strict. The police, says Lieutenant Hunter of the San Francisco Police, 'are allowed to lie and cheat, so long as we do not shock the conscience'. Here the courts have been very snippy when it has been discovered that the police have lied to a suspect or more particularly to his solicitor.[6]

The widely read American police manual by Inban and Reid outlines 26 specific techniques to be used in interrogating a suspect. In an article on police trickery S. Welsh comments:

> most of these techniques will inevitably involve some sort of deception because they require an officer to make statements that he knows are untrue or play a role that is inconsistent with his actual feelings. The effectiveness of those techniques is amply documented by the authors as they recount case after case in which a strategic lie or timely false show of sympathy was instrumental in leading a suspect to confess.[7]

Welsh goes on to give a number of examples from American cases including the recital of the burial service to a deeply religious suspect, telling a suspect the victim was still alive (and therefore could make an identification), and the converse, telling him the victim was dead.

Of course what America could do so could the United Kingdom and there are a wealth of stories of officers, one of whom eventually reached the rank of Commissioner, who donned a white coat to act as the doctor called out for the suspect. The benefits of this were legion. There could be a denial that the suspect had called for a doctor. There would be no record of a doctor attending at the station. This would also tend to show that the defendant's wild accusations were now embracing the uniform branch as well as the CID and that if he was to be believed the court would have to find that there was a major conspiracy not simply between two or possibly three officers but one which embraced the whole police station.

Another story, which may be apocryphal, is of an officer who had a pet chimpanzee and brought it into the interrogation room where it appeared to be taking notes. When the suspect brought this up he was remanded for psychiatric reports. When the English courts did find the police had deliberately deceived the suspect's lawyer (as opposed to the suspect) they excluded the confession. In *Mason*, where the defendant was suspected of arson, during the course of an interview the defendant and his solicitor were told by the police deliberately and untruthfully that the defendant's fingerprints had been found on fragments of a bottle. The defendant then admitted he had handled the glass. On appeal the Court of Appeal excluded the confession saying that the judge should have considered the deception on the solicitor.[8]

But the American courts are becoming more concerned about the possibility of the false confession and now it is recommended that interrogations are videotaped, something which has happened in Canada for many years.[9] Alaska and Minnesota are two of the more progressive states in requiring the videotaping of all interviews while Texas requires only the video or audiotaping of confessions. Illinois began to reconsider the position after two boys aged 7 and 8 who had confessed to killing an 11-year-old girl in a quarrel over a bicycle were cleared by DNA evidence.

Fears that videotaping of interrogations would reduce the number of confessions appear unfounded. 'It hasn't hurt our cases to have juries observe how the police interrogate suspects,' says Amy Klobuchar, District Attorney of Minnesota's Hennepin County. 'It hasn't hurt our conviction rate in any way.'

There are occasional benefits. In one case in Minnesota the officers left the videotape running when they left the room. A suspect, who claimed to be blind, turned round a piece of paper to read it better.[10]

III

In the 1920s and 1930s interrogation in America's Deep South tended to be even more brutal than in the north. Beatings were the norm and a lynching was by no means out of the question. They also included a water torture and what was engagingly described as a 'mild use of the electric chair'. In an Arkansas case the judge ordered the destruction of the chair as an uncivilised instrument but, nevertheless, admitted the confession.[11]

In 1934 the small town of Scooba, in the heart of Mississippi, was the scene of a horrific murder case which would in time send ripples through the entire legal system.[12]

On 30 March a popular, white, unmarried, cotton farmer Raymond Stuart, was found dying in the living room of his farmhouse. A lamp had been smashed and part of his face and shoulder had been burned. His head and body had been struck with what appeared to have been an axe-like instrument. 'Mr Stuart's head was beaten almost to a pulp', reported the local paper.[13] The motive was thought to have been robbery.

One surviving witness, Henry Wallace, recalls the feeling among the local white population:

> The white men all got together in a kind of
> vigilante group and went right through the
> community, going to black men's houses and
> taking them out and trying to make them talk.
> At the time they were drag[ging] them out they
> didn't even know Mr Raymond Stuart was
> dead.

After questioning all the local black people three of Raymond Stuart's employees were identified as prime suspects – Henry Shields, Arthur 'Yank' Ellington and Ed Brown. They were taken into police custody where three days later they all confessed to murdering the farmer. A week later the three men were put on trial in the nearby town of De Kalb. In court, one of them, Ed Brown, claimed that he was innocent and that before he had confessed the deputy sheriff Cliff Dial had beaten him in the police station next to the jail. Giving evidence at the trial Brown said:

> Cliff Dial told me that he had heard that I
> killed Mr Raymond. I said: 'I declare I didn't
> kill Mr Raymond.' He said 'Come on in here
> and pull your clothes off, I am going to get
> you.' They bent me over a chair and I had to
> say yes, I couldn't help it.

Later he would tell his cousin that he had been beaten
so hard that blood had run into his boots. The other
defendants had similar stories to tell. Arthur Ellington,
who appeared in court with bruises on his neck, said his
troubles had begun the night that the vigilantes were
looking for Stuart's killers:

> They got me out of bed and carried me to Mr
> Raymond's house. They tied me up there with
> my hands to a tree and whipped me. They tied
> me and whipped me good. Then they hung
> me, they pulled me up twice.

Ellington was eventually cut loose and confessed. When
Dial was asked in cross-examination whether Ellington
had, in fact, been whipped he was quite open about the
situation replying, 'Not too much for a Negro, not as
much as I would have done if it was left to me'.

Despite this, Judge Sturdivant admitted the
confessions as evidence. Unsurprisingly, the three were
found guilty of murder and were sentenced to death.
The white population was really quite pleased with
itself. Justice had been seen to be done and a lynching
had been avoided. Gallows were built; the prisoners
spent their time praying and singing gospel songs and
became something of a tourist attraction.[14]

Then came an act of considerable bravery by a local lawyer, John Clark, who had been appointed to take the case only half an hour before the trial. He was convinced there had been a miscarriage of justice and appealed. His was a lone act in a small and hostile town where he had to make his living, and he received none of the support given to Samuel Leibowitz three years earlier when he had defended the Scottsboro' Boys.

On 25 March 1931 in one of America's worst cases, nine young black men were accused of the rape of two white women in a box car on a railroad between Tennessee and Alabama. They had certainly been in a fight with some white boys, one of whom was thrown from the train and went to the local sheriff. At the station at Paint Rock the nine black youths were arrested and accused of the rape of Victoria Price and Ruby Bates, charges which, at the time, carried the death penalty. There was neither medical evidence of rape nor were the girls distressed. The girls were portrayed as injured Southern petals, when they were, at best, semi-professional prostitutes. They were in effect forced to lie because in the manners of the time they could not admit consorting freely with one black let alone nine. Had they done so they would have faced vagrancy charges and imprisonment themselves. The boys' first trial was a farce. The trial judge assigned all the county's lawyers to the defence of the youths but six of the seven withdrew. Eight of the nine were convicted and the ninth, 13-year-old Roy Wright, was spared when only seven out of the twelve jurors voted for the death penalty. An appeal was allowed and retrial ordered.

Leibowitz at considerable personal risk – at the time a pamphlet 'Kill the Jew from New York' was being circulated – undertook their defence with exactly the same result. The Attorney General, Thomas E. Knight Jr, prosecuted in an entirely unbiased way, suggesting the jury should 'Show them that Alabama justice cannot be bought with Jew money from New York'. By now Ruby Bates accepted she had lied and neither she nor Victoria Price had been raped. Their story had been concocted to avoid the charges of vagrancy. Her confession did the boys no good and Leibowitz was obliged to return to the Supreme Court, which move brought another series of trials and the declaration that blacks must be allowed to serve on juries. Eventually Leibowitz withdrew from the case when it became apparent that the boys were now simply being used as political pawns.[15]

Clark had initially been convinced of the guilt of Brown, Shields and Ellington. He had also been ill when he was appointed and wanted to be recused, a request which Judge Sturdivant swiftly rejected. It was only after Clark learned of the beatings that he began to have some sympathy for his clients. Initially he said he had been 'simply going through the form of a trial'. Sturdivant also cut short any pre-trial discussions he and his colleagues were having with their clients.

Clark acted without further payment because, although Mississippi law required payment of $25 a client, Sturdivant, possibly fearing public reaction, refused to authorise it. Both Clark and his wife had political ambitions, which he was told would be severely jeopardised if he proceeded further with the case. He then took another unpopular step and notified the NAACP asking for financial help. They sent him a small cheque but took no further action pending the appeal.

A year later Mississippi's Supreme Court upheld the guilty verdict. Justice Anderson did, however, dissent in strong terms:

> Without the confession, the court would have
> been forced to direct a verdict of not guilty. Yet
> the appellants were driven to confess their guilt
> by the most brutal and unmerciful whippings.
> The Third Degree or its equivalent is still in
> use.

Clark may, at least, have avoided the crosses burned outside Leibowitz's room but his health was suffering and he was close to a mental and physical collapse. He was convinced it was becoming physically dangerous for him to continue. He wrote again to the NAACP and this time some notice was taken of him. The secretary, Walter White, and the board discussed the case with Chairman Louis Wright, concluding that any time a white lawyer in Mississippi says things are bad and he needs help, then we have to help.[16]

John Clark became too ill to continue his campaign and his wife wrote to Arthur Garfield Hays:

> He has been very unjustly criticised and has
> worried quite a bit because of the lack of help
> he has had in the hard fight he has waged. He
> has fought a good fight and kept the faith. I
> have encouraged him and helped in every way
> possible.[17]

Others, notably ex-Governor Earl Brewer, did take up his mantle and in 1936 the nine judges of the United States Supreme Court unanimously overturned the verdict.[18]

Of course, similar cases had been taking place throughout the South for years but, as Loren Miller wrote, the *Brown* case was a 'classic in the sphere of confessions as the first Scottsboro' case was in the right to counsel and time for preparation of a defence'.[19] It would provide a path to the decision that a suspect in custody must be informed of his right to the advice of a lawyer.[20]

Jerome Skolnick, Professor of Law at Berkeley, adds:

> The United States Supreme Court decision in
> *Brown v Mississippi* established that no
> confession in a criminal case can be admitted
> unless it was voluntary, and if it was not
> voluntary it's a violation of the due process.
> And that test is with us today.

IV

A decade earlier some American reformers had been turning their thoughts in the direction of a more scientific method of interrogation. It was the dream of Berkeley's Chief of Police, August Vollmer,[21] and his assistant John Larsen that modern science and technology would provide a foolproof way of getting at the truth.

One early device had been the well-received Sphygmomanometer.

Their latest crime detector is the Sphygmomanometer. It has reduced the duration of the Third Degree to approximately four minutes.

The Sphygmomanometer consists of three delicate machines linked together. The first records the suspect's breathing, the second the time between each breath and the third registers blood pressure.

It is based on the undeniable fact that no man, woman or child can tell a lie without affecting the blood pressure, no matter how calm the countenance or glib the statement.

The article went on to say that the device had been offered to Scotland Yard.[22]

In fact an early version of the lie-detector had been on offer since around 1915 promoted by a Harvard graduate, William M. Marston, when he modestly described it as 'the end of man's long futile striving for a means of distinguishing truth-telling from deception'.[23]

Marston had been involved in the celebrated case of a young black, James Alphonse Frye, convicted in Washington of murder in 1920. He had been accused of killing Dr Robert Brown, found shot dead in his office. Frye confessed to the murder and then withdrew the confession, saying curiously that he had been offered half the reward money had he been convicted. Frye's lawyers asked Marston to conduct a polygraph test and this had, according to the tester, shown Frye's innocence. The trial judge refused to admit the evidence and also refused to allow a second test to take place in the courtroom. The jury, seemingly impressed with the offer of a lie-detector test in open court, convicted Frye only of second degree murder. Three years into his sentence another man confessed to the killing. Meanwhile the Supreme Court had refused to allow the evidence of any such test.[24]

This does not mean to say, however, that courts will always exclude such evidence. David Lykken points out that across America both state and federal prosecutors with a weak case will offer a lie-detector test to the defendant. It is, however, a two-edged sword. If the test is passed the charges will be dropped but, if there is a failure, then the results may be used in evidence. 'Innocent suspects who, like most Americans, believe in the myth of the lie-detector, are inclined to accept such offers, often to their subsequent dismay.'[25]

Presently some 17 states admit the results of stipulated lie tests, undergone after prior agreement on both sides. The courts' attitude is one which has been the subject of criticism. The lawyer, Lee M. Burkey, puts the position succinctly:

> It is difficult to understand how the polygraph method is improved merely because the parties stipulate to be bound by it. Would the court approve a stipulation to be bound by the toss of a coin?[26]

The reverse of this is that in many states a District Attorney will not pursue a complaint of date-rape unless the complainant submits to and passes a lie-detector test.

Back in 1920 Larson had developed a much improved version of what came to be known as the lie-detector or polygraph and tests showed remarkable results, but would it work in a real criminal case? The opportunity to test it came with the kidnapping in August 1921 of a Roman Catholic priest, Father Patrick Heslin.

During the evening of 2 August, 60-year-old Father Patrick E. Heslin was kidnapped from the Holy Angels Church in Colma near San Francisco. A man wearing a long overcoat with motoring goggles covering much of his face knocked on the door and when Father Heslin's housekeeper, Marie Wendel, opened it said, in a foreign accent, that he would like to see the priest. The reason he gave was that his friend was dying following a motor accident. Later she described the man as small, dark and rather foreign-looking.

Heslin put on his coat and left with the man, taking with him equipment to administer the last rites. He never returned. The housekeeper did not raise any alarm until the next day. It was not, after all, unusual for the priest to stay overnight with a dying person. When he did not call the next day she telephoned the Archbishop of San Francisco, Edward J. Hanna. He decided to wait a little more time before he contacted the police and, meanwhile, a ransom note demanding a fairly modest $6,500 for the release of Father Heslin was delivered. The police were contacted and the press alerted. Massive hunts went on around the city but nothing was heard of the priest until eight days after his disappearance when a second ransom note was delivered. The same sum was asked for and the note seemed full of self-righteous pity. 'Fate has made me do this. Sickness and misery has compelled my action. I must have money. Please forgive this act if you can. The father is not dead YET.'

On 10 August a reporter for the *San Francisco Examiner* was due to interview the Archbishop when he heard a man who had also come to see the Archbishop explain that he was a William A. Hightower and could say where the missing priest could be found. In fact it was near a billboard advertising flapjacks.

He told a complicated story of two girlfriends having hidden some illegal liquor and that when he had gone to dig it up he had unearthed a black scarf. Eventually he led a police squad to the beach where Heslin's body was dug from the sand. The priest had been knocked unconscious, his skull crushed and two shots fired into his body. For some time Hightower stuck by the story of the buried liquor. One girl was found not to exist and the second denied anything to do with buried drink. The gun, which had been used to shoot the priest, had been pawned and was traced back to Hightower. Two tent pegs found near Heslin's body matched others found in Hightower's room.

Nevertheless he continued to protest his innocence and for the first time the lie-detector was used in a murder case. Larson was convinced that Hightower was lying and, shortly after, he confessed to kidnapping and killing the priest.

Despite considerable public opinion in favour of an execution, Hightower was sentenced to life imprisonment. In San Quentin he became a master chef specialising in patisseries.[27]

Eighty years later the polygraph is still one of America's favourite, if by no means wholly reliable, investigative tools.

One of its more celebrated failures was during the 1950s when Paul Joseph Altheide was accused of murdering a tailor in Phoenix, Arizona. He claimed to have been more than 500 miles away in Texas at the time. A lie-detector indicated that he was guilty but a reporter, Gene McLain of the *Arizona Republic*, went to Texas and found the witnesses who would go on to prove Altheide's innocence. On the other hand there have been countless examples of defendants who have passed a lie-detector test but who have been convicted on other evidence. They include Chester Weger, who was convicted of killing three women in Starved Rock State Park, Illinois in 1960. He claimed he had passed the test on two occasions by first swallowing aspirins and then washing them down with coca-cola. Leonarde Keeler, who succeeded Larson in the development of the detector, claimed he could defeat his own machine, while Gerald Thompson, later convicted of the murder of Mildred Hallmark, passed the test explaining later that when asked the specific question, 'Did you kill Mildred?' he concentrated on another Mildred.

Former FBI director, J. Edgar Hoover, was by no means a champion commenting:

> The name lie-detector is a complete misnomer. The machine used is not a lie-detector. The person who operates the machine is the lie-detector by reason of his interpretation. Whenever the human element enters into an interpretation of anything, there is always a possibility of error.[28]

By the 1970s the use of the lie-detector had increased exponentially. The modern, improved version monitors changes in breathing, blood pressure, perspiration and the heart rate during interrogation. Now the examiner will typically ask the subject a question unrelated to the case which he or she may find threatening and difficult to answer; for example he will be accused of a theft of money which has never taken place. This will, it is said, show that the innocent will react more strongly to threatening comparative questions about their lives while the guilty will react most strongly to questions about the crime they have actually committed.

But, as ever when there is a human input crucial to its effectiveness, things do not always work out correctly. In 1996 former FBI Special Agent Mark Mallah found himself on the wrong end of a lie-detector.

> I was a special agent in the FBI working in New York city in foreign counter-intelligence.
> United Nations is in New York so there are a lot of foreign officials that are assigned here. So in general terms our job was to identify which officials were intelligence officers, which were legitimate diplomats.

The Bureau was worried that there might be spies in its own ranks and among a number of agents in sensitive positions. Despite the former Chief's attitude to the lie-detector, tests were instigated and Mallah failed his.

> The examiner said, 'Well it looks to me like you're withholding information here. It's probably best if you just come forward, put this behind us. It's probably no big deal'. I said, 'Well I'm being truthful, I can't understand

how the charts are what you're saying they are
because I've had no unauthorised contacts, not
even close'. The examiner just looked at me
and said, 'Mark, you'll never convince me that
you're not guilty'. And he was absolutely right.
There was nothing I could have said, no
amount of logic or reason which was going to
convince him.

The FBI conducted a major investigation into his case.

I was under 24-hour surveillance. Cars were
parked outside my house in my
neighbourhood wherever I went. A plane
buzzed about our house every single morning
for a while. Then my friends started getting
interviewed, people I hadn't spoken to in 10
years were getting interviewed.

It was two years before he was cleared. His polygraph
test had shown what is known as a false positive.

It is now generally accepted that the lie-detector
measures emotionality, not lying, and that at best it is
only 90 per cent accurate so giving 10 per cent false
positives.

Jerome Skolnick believes:

The courts still have found even in the most
recent cases that it's not scientific. Let's say
that you give a thousand lie-detector tests
routinely as we do in our intelligence agencies.
If you say it's 90 per cent accurate you are
going to find that there a hundred who are

false positives. But among those hundred, let's
say, there are only two or three spies, all right?
So you're going to be labelling a lot of people
as spies who aren't spies.

Others regard the accuracy as nearer 70 per cent.

V

It has been in the field of military interrogation that
science has had its most devastating impact.

The Korean War was fought not only on the
battlefields but also symbolised the ideological conflict
between the Western Powers and the Eastern Bloc. In
this propaganda war the Communists tried to get
captured Allied soldiers to make public confessions
using the interrogation techniques now known as
brainwashing.[29]

Wallace Brown, an American airman shot down
over North Korea, recalls his ordeal:

We were picked up and taken to a Chinese
prison to make us say we had violated Chinese
territory and came down in China. But they
knew we hadn't and we knew we hadn't.

For seven months he was kept in solitary confinement,
forced to sit 24 hours a day:

You couldn't get up. You weren't allowed to
look at the window. So it was frustrating.
You're in a cell, so what are you going to do?

Well, you know I realised eventually what they were doing. They were breaking down your resistance. And with enough time it's effective.

When finally the questioning began:

The first time you really refused to answer anything, said 'I've said all I'm going to say', they say, 'Well stand to attention. Stand up. And you'll stand there until you answer'. Five or six hours, then 15. The most painful is the soles of your feet. Finally, it was a week, 154 hours of standing. They wanted the answer to one question and only one question and there was no way I was going to answer it. And I was told I was going to stand there until I answered it or died.

Wallace Brown was one of those who could not be coerced into making a false confession and when he returned to the Maxwell Airforce base in Alabama he was debriefed for another seven months.

The longest period of time was being interviewed by psychologists. They were better equipped to analyse and so they needed first hand from us what we had undergone so that they could then develop courses of instruction to counter this sort of thing for future military schools.

His experience would form part of the teaching of resistance techniques to brainwashing.

In fact the military did more than just search for counter-interrogation methods. To see whether Communist interrogation methods could be used not just to produce false confessions, but as a means of getting prisoners to provide truthful information, the Western military financed a series of bizarre scientific experiments. Volunteers such as student Michael Goymour were paid 92 cents an hour to see how long they could withstand the experiments.

Goymour wore a white mask, and sensory deprivation experiments reproduced the prison cell effect.

> We were placed in this small cubicle. There was
> a light diffusing visor and some sort of white
> noise going on all the while. All the meals were
> more or less the same. I was taken to the toilet
> sometimes. It was really disconnection with all
> ordinary sensory perceptions. There was a sort
> of increasing physical discomfort as it went on.

After four days be became confused thinking 'it was Wednesday afternoon when it was Thursday night'.

From experiments such as these the military learned how to speed up the sensory and perceptual deprivation of solitary confinement by applying a combination of techniques including hooding and white noise prior to interrogation.

Tim Shallice, Professor of Neurology at University College, London explains that part of the technique dates back sixty years:

> Some such as sleep deprivation are a standard
> part of secret police procedures throughout the

Second World War. Two of them, though, are fairly different: one is hooding, the second, the use of white noise machines. These two techniques are derived from scientific investigations into sensory and perceptual deprivations.

By the 1960s NATO countries had begun to subject some of their special forces and aircraft crews to these extreme methods of interrogation, to teach them how to resist. A declassified document on a resistance to interrogation exercise of the 1960s showed that, of a group of elite soldiers who endured up to eight hours in one interrogation centre, only 11 out of 75 managed to resist giving anything more than their name, rank, number and date of birth.

Counter-interrogation instructor at a NATO base in Germany, Fred Holroyd, recalls that the trainees were hooded, bombarded with white noise and then subjected to exhausting exercise:

You isolate the man, subject him to white noise, physically wear him down, whether it be leaning him against the wall with his fingertips and his legs apart stretched out or by making him do physical exercise. There is no doubt that most people within four and a half hours can be made to admit to anything really.[30]

It was a technique used at the height of the crisis in Northern Ireland. In 1971, hundreds of IRA supporters were interned without trial and 14, believed to be ringleaders, were singled out for special interrogation using methods similar to those on the military's resistance to interrogation courses. Again the suspects were subjected to white noise, hooding, little food and drink and being forced to stand in a fixed position. This time the men were subjected to the methods for six days and, since they were not IRA ringleaders and had little to offer up, they were sent back for more. Eight years later the European Court condemned the British government for human rights abuses.

There is little doubt that the techniques persuade people to talk. Whether it is effective is another matter.

VI

Even though one unnamed hypnotist boasted in 1931 that he could solve any crime,[31] hypnosis as a means of investigation is another method which has never had as much support in Britain as it has in America.

The history of the use of hypnosis in British criminal courts is riddled with gaps. One of the problems over the years has been that for long periods it has never been monitored and few have even known if and when it has been used in a case.

In America for a time in the 1960s and 1970s in what could be called its heyday, witnesses were even hypnotised in court to the fascination of the jury. But by 1982 the tide was turning slowly but surely and already Arizona and Minnesota had ruled that no witness who had been hypnotised should subsequently give evidence.

There seem to be four distinct stages in which hypnotism could be used in criminal cases. The first is in the initial investigation of a case where the police have little or nothing on which to act. They will therefore have a witness hypnotised in the hope that his memory will be improved and he will be able to supply some crucial detail. The second is to use hypnosis in the case of amnesia in, say, a victim of rape. The third would be to protect a witness from the rigours of cross-examination, and finally the suspect or accused could be hypnotised. At some time or another in some court or case somewhere each of these instances has been used.

Basically there are two techniques in use. The first is the so called 'age regression' in which the subject is taken back in time to the moment the incident occurred. The second is the television or crystal ball method in which the suspect is invited to describe, often in the third person, what is happening on an imaginary television screen. There is little doubt that both techniques produce heightened recall and awareness.

Unfortunately the downside is that the witness may be recalling events inaccurately. He or she may be lying either deliberately or inadvertently and, whichever is the case, the hypnotist is not able to distinguish whether what is being recalled is fact or fantasy. As Professor Bernard Diamond, who has campaigned against the use of hypnosis in courts, said, 'A witness cannot identify his true memories after hypnosis. Nor can any expert separate them.'[32]

In 1981 the Home Office organised a conference on the use of hypnosis at which the American professor, Dr Martin Orne, gave his views illustrated by some examples. One was of a murder by shooting in a main street on a dark night.

The witness had been seated in the cab of a truck near a street light. Under hypnosis he said he could not see clearly and was invited to 'wipe the windscreen' of his cab. Now things became clearer. He thought he could recognise someone who was ugly and who in fact had been a schoolmate. On the basis of this evidence a man, who could not be described as ugly and who, in fact, had not been at school with the witness, was arrested and charged. The defence instructed an expert witness who carried out forensic tests. He found that when the moon and street lights were similar to the night in question a man with good eyesight sitting in a truck could not give any description of two men who ran across the road nor could he distinguish their facial features at all. The truck had been parked in a pool of light from the street light and as a result the human eye could not distinguish features in the dark outside the pool. He could not have seen more than 25 feet.[33]

Dr Orne fell into the middle one of the three categories of American experts on the subject of hypnosis. At one extreme came Martin Reiser who believed that police officers could be trained to carry out interviews under hypnosis and indeed undertook their training. In turn they trained other officers. At the other end of the spectrum of thought was Dr Bernard Diamond who believed that hypnosis was indeed less than a boon and a blessing to men and spent a good deal of his time re-educating the courts to reject the evidence of hypnotised witnesses.

At the conference it emerged that Dr Lionel Hayward, from the University of Surrey, had hypnotised over 100 people for the police but no records had been kept which monitored whether the information obtained had been correct. It appeared that hypnosis had been used as a forensic tool from the 1950s but no one was quite sure how often and whether the witnesses had ended in court or whether the cases in which they appeared ended in conviction. Nor was it clear whether the defence or the judge knew of the hypnosis.

Deputy Assistant Commissioner John Thornton did, however, write that so far as the Metropolitan Police were concerned less than 20 people had been hypnotised between 1980 and 1982 and on only two occasions had it been used in cases which subsequently appeared before the courts.[34]

Some years later Eric C. Copperthwaite wrote that early in 1981 he had been asked by the Thames Valley police to help in the case of a cross-bow attack and since then 'I have become the most experienced and most used hypnotherapist in helping the police throughout Great Britain'.[35]

Following the conference, in 1983 the Home Office produced guidelines for the use of hypnosis which included certain minimum safeguards. The first was that it must be performed by a trained psychiatrist or psychologist independent of the police. It was put to good effect in 1984 when the Essex police used hypnosis in the case of an attack on an 11-year-old girl who had been so affected by the incident that she was unable to answer questions coherently.

Over the next few years came success stories including one from California where a witness recalled a registration number of a school bus in which 26 children had been kidnapped and another was instrumental, if that is the correct word, in the solving of the murder of a cellist at the Metropolitan Opera House in New York.

Meanwhile the American courts were swinging backwards and forwards, with the New York decision in *People v Hughes* [36] seeming to gain favour in a number of other jurisdictions. Basically this allowed a witness to give evidence to matters revealed in unaided pre-hypnotic interviews but not to give evidence relating to additional matters recalled during or after hypnosis.

The next well-publicised fiasco involving hypnotised witnesses in an English court came in 1987 when the Kent police had used a self-taught hypnotist who had acquired his knowledge from reading books in the local public library, as a result of which his technique was flawed. He hypnotised various witnesses of an affray and the trial judge at Maidstone Crown Court, Judge Felix Waley, ruled that:

> It is plain from the evidence and reports I have read that a witness who has been hypnotised is going to be in a condition where that which arises apparently from memory is as fixed as a film screen and therefore there can be no useful test. [37]

In 1988 following consultation with the British Medical Association and the National Council of Civil Liberties, the Home Office produced a further set of guidelines but to what extent these were actually published was another matter. In 1994 neither the police desk at the Home Office nor *Liberty* (to which the NCCL had changed its name) seemed to know of them. [38]

There had in the meantime been the case of Eddie Browning, a former nightclub bouncer convicted of killing Marie Wilks. On 18 June 1988 she was brutally murdered after her car broke down on the M50 near Bushley, Hereford. Her body was found three days later. She had bled to death after her throat had been cut.

The evidence against Browning was thin. The abductor was said to have spiky blonde hair which Browning did have and witnesses said that she had been driven away in a silver Renault. Browning had one of those. There were no traces of blood in Mr Browning's car although Marie Wilks must have bled profusely.

An off-duty police inspector who had driven past the scene had been hypnotised and, correctly, his evidence had been videotaped. He had recalled a car pulling on to the hard shoulder and, during the session under hypnosis to try to help him recall further details, he recalled a non-hatchback Renault with a completely different number plate from that of Mr Browning. The videotape was not considered to be relevant to the case and was not disclosed to the defence.

Unfortunately the Court of Appeal, when quashing Mr Browning's conviction, did not feel it necessary to make a decision whether a court should ever accept the evidence of a previously hypnotised witness. In fact the Home Office soon cleared things up. Replying to a question in the House of Commons, Charles Wardle of the Home Department, said:

In 1988 the Home Office issued guidelines to the police discouraging the use of hypnosis in the investigation of offences on the grounds that evidence obtained by this method would be likely to be both unreliable and inadmissible in court as well as carrying a risk of harm to the witness.[39]

It was not proposed that further guidelines be issued. And there, it seems, the matter has ended so far as the British courts are concerned. In France the wrangle continued until the end of 2000 when the appellate court, the *Cour de Cassation,* ruled that evidence gathered while a witness is under hypnosis cannot be used in court.

The case involved a police officer who witnessed an armed robbery during which a woman officer was taken hostage and a colleague seriously injured. His only memory of the incident was seeing the robbers escape in an Audi 800. Under hypnosis from Alban de Jong, a Paris-based hypnotherapist, he had recalled part of the registration number and, as a result, the robbers had been arrested and convicted.

De Jong, a former police officer, was understandably unhappy with the decision, protesting that he did not do Black Masses and nor was he a sorcerer. He had, he said, been asked by more than 20 examining magistrates to work on between three and five cases a year. In one instance he hypnotised a man who had been suspected of murdering a child. He could recall nothing of his movements on the night in question but under hypnosis was able to provide an alibi. 'If people see nothing, they will continue to see nothing,' he said.[40]

Nor was the matter wholly resolved in America. In March 1999 the Governor of Mississippi, Mel Carnaham, was under pressure to reprieve Roy 'Hog'

Roberts convicted of killing Thomas Jackson, a guard, in a prison riot at the Moberly Training Centre for men, midway between Kansas City and St Louis, in 1983. Three other guards had only identified him after undergoing hypnosis. They had not previously identified the 337lbs 'Hog' Roberts who, in the words of another guard, 'stood out like a red rose in the Sahara Desert'.

In turn Roberts had undergone a lie-detector test administered by an examiner regarded as 'not defence prone' and had passed it. There was no physical evidence against Roberts who was alleged to have held the guard while two other prisoners stabbed him in the eye and the heart. Their clothes were covered in blood but his were not. They had not been sentenced to death but Roberts was executed on 10 March 1999.[41]

VII

On 22 April 1972, after a fire broke out in a house in Doggett Road near the railway station in Catford, south-east London, in a room on the first floor firemen discovered the body of Maxwell Confait, a transvestite prostitute. That weekend there were further outbreaks of arson in the area and the police believed they might be connected to the murder. One target was a shed near a sports ground and three local youths were spotted running away from the fire.

Colin Lattimore, Ronnie Leighton and Ahmet Salih were arrested and confessed to setting fire to the shed but, at least initially, denied committing the murder of Confait or setting fire to the house. Colin Lattimore was the first to crack. At the time he was 18 but was said to have a mental age of eight. He had been diagnosed as educationally subnormal and, later, psychiatrists were to say he was highly suggestible 'so that the slightest indication of the expected answer will produce it'. He confessed saying that he and his two friends had committed the murder.

Leighton was 15, and although considerably brighter than his friend Colin, he was described as 'borderline subnormal' and 'really an immature, inadequate, simple dullard'. Salih was described as reasonably intelligent. He was just 14. After their confessions their parents were called to the police station.

The crucial question for the prosecution was the time Confait died. Lattimore, who had allegedly admitted strangling Confait, had a watertight alibi for the night of his death. Independent witnesses could trace his movements from 6pm to 11.40pm. Another had seen him at home at 11.45pm and his father could place him in the house at 12.35am.

The doctors at the committal proceedings put the time of death between 6.30 and 10.00pm, basing their conclusions on the onset of rigor mortis. Once the case was committed, under the provisions of the Criminal Justice Act 1967, the boys were obliged to give details of any alibis they had.

> [It] was never contemplated when this change
> went through that it would also favour the
> prosecution in providing a chance to blur the
> edges of its evidence when that was found to
> be in conflict with a disclosed alibi. Colin,

Ronnie and Ahmet were caught by this
disclosure, which alerted the prosecution to its
only chance of a guilty verdict. If the alibi had
not been disclosed, the evidence about the
time of death would have remained as clear
and unequivocal as it was at Woolwich
Magistrates Court.[42]

The boys were convicted in November 1972. Lattimore
was convicted of manslaughter on the grounds of
diminished responsibility, Leighton of murder and
Salih of arson. Lattimore was ordered to be detained
under the Mental Health Act without limit of time,
Leighton during Her Majesty's pleasure and Salih to
four years' detention. Their appeals were dismissed.

Their families did not accept the verdicts and with
the assistance of their MP, Christopher Price, they set
about obtaining a referral of the case to the Court of
Appeal. In June 1975 the Confait case was indeed
referred by Roy Jenkins, then Home Secretary, back to
the Court. Jenkins, in his letter referring the case, had
written that if Confait's death took place:

some appreciable time before midnight, it
appears that the evidence of the boys'
whereabouts would assume greater importance
and that doubt would be thrown on the
accuracy of their statements of admission to
the police, the truth of which they denied at
the trial.

Over the years the Court of Appeal has been
something of a graveyard for the hopes of appellants.

For example when the case of the Birmingham Six, jailed for life in 1974 for bombings in Birmingham, went before the court, the then Lord Chief Justice pronounced that the longer the case continued the more convinced he and his colleagues were of the men's guilt.

On this occasion, however, when the case came before the Court of Appeal in October 1975 it was established by further medical evidence that Confait's death had in fact taken place 'some appreciable time before midnight'. Lord Justice Scarman said the effect of this fresh medical evidence was to destroy the lynchpin of the Crown's case and to demonstrate that the version of events contained in the admissions relied upon by the Crown could not be true. The boys' convictions were quashed.

He accepted, however, that it was still possible that their confessions to the arson at 27 Doggett Road could be correct but added their statements could not be regarded as sufficiently reliable evidence standing as they did, alone, to justify the convictions for arson which were based solely upon them.

Recriminations followed swiftly upon the boys' release. How could the boys have confessed to a killing they never committed and, moreover, how could the Director of Public Prosecutions, Sir Norman Skelhorn, have authorised the prosecution? Sir Henry Fisher, a former High Court Judge, was appointed to hold an inquiry. It was held in private and in his report published at the end of 1977 he found that Detective Superintendent Graham Stockwell, one of the interviewing officers:

gave his evidence [to the inquiry] convincingly
and made a favourable impression on me. He
has a frank and open manner; he seemed calm,
steady, careful and intelligent (as his posting to
the Fraud Squad indicates); I judged him to be
wholly trustworthy.

Not so Ronnie Leighton who had had a quick spat with
Donald, later Lord Justice, Farquarson who represented
the police.

Early in his cross-examination by Mr Farquarson
when Leighton was asked why he started fires, he
replied, 'I tell you I don't know. If you keep on, mate, I
will knock you one'. He then left the room saying, 'I
have fucking had enough of this.'

Sir Henry Fisher's findings went as follows:

(a) Lattimore's alibi was genuine and that he
could have taken no part in the killing;
(b) Leighton and Salih could have taken part in
the killing; and
(c) all three could have set light to 27 Doggett
Road.

He could not accept that the confessions could have
been made without at least one of the boys having been
involved in the killing and arson. In January 1980 the
then Director of Public Prosecutions, Sir Thomas
Hetherington, received 'new information' about the
case and Sir Michael Havers, the Attorney General, told
the House of Commons eight months later that he was
satisfied that Confait had died even earlier: before
midnight a day earlier, on 21 April.

I am also satisfied that if the evidence now available had been before Sir Henry Fisher he would not have come to the conclusion that any of the three young men was responsible for the death of Confait or the arson at 27 Doggett Road. Counsel has advised, and the Director of Public Prosecutions and I agree, that there is insufficient evidence to prosecute any other person.

The new information had came through an Inspector Eddie Ellison who investigated the story of a man who claimed he was being blackmailed for a murder he had committed. There had been two men, each of whom maintained he had seen the other kill Confait but had not been involved himself. It was not thought there was sufficient evidence to prosecute either man.

What Sir Henry did correctly identify, however, was the need for changes in the way suspects were interviewed, as well as the need for an analysis and evaluation of a case by a legally qualified person at as early a stage as possible.

He found there had been breaches of the so-called Judges Rules which governed police interrogation of suspects. He also found that the questioning of Lattimore was unfair and oppressive. Lattimore was mentally handicapped and he should have waited until someone, a parent or friend, could attend the interview.

As for the lawyers, and in particular the DPP's officer in the case Dorian Williams, Sir Henry had this to say:

I believe he did as much as under prevailing practice was expected of him. Sir Norman Skelhorn did not criticise him ... The scrutiny which Mr Williams provided in this case fell short of the scrutiny which I believe is required and which (in theory at least) the procurator fiscal would carry out under the Scottish system ... If I am right in thinking that Mr Williams did as much as under the prevailing system was expected of him, then I am driven to the conclusion that the practice was unsatisfactory.

The purpose of such evaluation should be not only to judge the narrow question of whether there is evidence to support the prosecution's case, but to look into the strength and weakness of the prosecution's case in an objective way to determine whether continued prosecution is justifiable.

In his memoirs Sir Norman Skelhorn had little to say on one of the major controversies his career:

In view ... of the developments that have now taken place, resulting from fresh evidence having come to light – which was apparently not available either at the time of the prosecution or at the time of Sir Henry's inquiry – I do not think that any useful purpose would be served by now dealing with these matters. Sir Henry's report was of course published appreciably later than my retirement, but in so far as he suggested revision of procedures, both by the department and by the police, I feel sure that they will have received careful consideration.[44]

It was the start of the road which led to the Police and Criminal Evidence Act 1984 (PACE) and the Prosecution of Offences Act 1985, the second of which saw the foundation of the Crown Prosecution Service as well as the end of a considerable amount of the autonomy the Metropolitan Police had to prosecute their own cases without qualified legal assistance unless they specifically requested it. By providing very considerable safeguards for suspects both in the form questioning may take, the recording of interviews and the provision of legal representation, PACE substantially curtailed the way in which the police throughout the country could conduct their enquiries.

The next step along the road to these reforms came on 23 June 1977 when the Government announced its intention to set up a Royal Commission on Criminal Procedure under the chairmanship of the Vice Chancellor of the University of London and Professor of Oriental History, Sir Cyril Phillips. The Commission was under way by February 1978 and reported in January 1981.

As a result, three years later came the Police and Criminal Evidence Act accompanied by a series of Codes of Practice, which have regularly been strengthened and amended, establishing the required police behaviour in all aspects of an investigation – stop and search, arrest, interrogation, and general behaviour at the police station.

Of course PACE was there to be circumvented, and circumvented it was. During the latter part of 1988 and in 1989 when the squad was disbanded, there was growing concern about the activities of the West Midlands Serious Crime Squad. The whisper against it was that certain officers had consistently flouted the requirements of PACE and its Codes of Practice in their investigation into crime and their interrogation of suspects.

In 1987 a man was arrested and held as a Category A prisoner at Winson Green prison in Birmingham. During his detention, which lasted ten months, he attempted to commit suicide. In November 1987 all charges against him were dropped because his solicitor had obtained forensic evidence which he believed demonstrated that his confession – on which the charge against him was based – was not genuine. So said Clare Short, MP for Birmingham Ladywood, raising the man's case in the House of Commons on 25 January 1989 when she requested that the Home Secretary set up an inquiry into the Squad by HM Inspectorate of Constabulary.

On 22 June 1989 another man, who had been two years on remand at Winson Green prison, was acquitted at Birmingham Crown Court of two bank robberies at city banks. The jury had heard defence allegations that interview records as well as forensic evidence had been fabricated. The trial judge Richard Curtis QC described some of the police evidence as 'unattractive' and 'totally misleading'. From his remarks in court it seems that prosecuting counsel also accepted that all was not well with the police evidence.

A 12th victim was cleared on 22 June 1992. His first appeal had been rejected in 1988. This time the Crown did not oppose the appeal of a man who had served four years of a seven-year jail sentence for a reprisal gangland shooting. Notes of his interviews with the squad had disappeared from the court file. Lord Justice Taylor commented that the explanation that the officers had sought the notes to answer a Criminal Injuries Compensation Board inquiry was highly unlikely to have been sound and truthful.

The cases continued to be heard by the Court of Appeal throughout the 1990s. In the case of Binham the Crown conceded that it could not support the conviction. Eight statements had disappeared from five different places. The Crown did not believe this was sheer coincidence. One statement had disappeared from the files of the Crown Prosecution Service although there was no suggestion of impropriety on their behalf.

In 1984 the Police and Criminal Evidence Act together with its attendant Codes of Practice set out in detail how interviews with suspects were to be conducted. Sections 76 and 78 gave the trial judge, or magistrate, power to exclude evidence which had been obtained unfairly.[45]

In theory now there should be no problems with obtaining proper 'voluntary confessions' which would be admissible in evidence. In practice it has been very different. After PACE things were meant to have improved. With the presence of the custody officer, the independent policeman to supervise matters and protect the suspect against brutality and oppression; with the opportunity for the suspect to communicate with a solicitor and have him present at the station before any questioning could take place; here surely was enough to ensure that confessions would truly be voluntary and that roughing up suspects would be a thing of the past.

As with most things in this best of all possible worlds, it has not quite worked out like that. Lawyers have spent some of the happiest, and most profitable, days of their lives arguing in the Crown Court and in the Court of Appeal over the admissibility of confessions allegedly made in breach of the Code of Practice.

On 10 December 1992 the Lord Chief Justice presiding over the Court of Appeal quashed the convictions, at Swansea Crown Court in November 1990, of three men, Stephen Miller, Tony Paris and Yusef Abdullahi, for the murder of Cardiff prostitute, Lynette White. She had been found hacked to death on St Valentine's Day 1988 in her 'punter's room', a seedy flat in James Street, Cardiff, where she charged £10 a time. She had been stabbed over 50 times and her throat had been cut through to the spine. She had been due to give evidence at the trial of a woman accused of trying to kill a prostitute. Witnesses saw a dark-haired white man with cut hands and wearing blood-stained clothes outside the flat and the police duly issued a photofit. Ten months later, although the white man had not been eliminated from the enquiries, five black men including Stephen Miller, White's boyfriend, were charged.

With the shades of the Confait case hovering over the police station, Miller, who had an IQ of 75, was repeatedly questioned. He denied the offence on no less than 300 occasions during his 19-hour questioning which reduced him to tears.

Said Lord Justice Taylor:

> If you go on asking somebody questions, and tell him he is going to sit there until he says what you want, there will come a time when most people will crack. Oppression may be of the obvious, crude variety or it may be just by relentlessness.

The Crown conceded that if the tapes of the interview should not have been admitted at the trial then they could not seek to uphold the convictions. In giving judgement the Lord Chief Justice spoke harshly about the oppressive conduct of the investigating officers and was critical of the solicitor who had sat in on the interviews. Apparently at the trial the crucial (No. 7) had not been played. Had this happened there was no doubt, thought His Lordship, that the trial judge would have excluded the confession. It was never satisfactorily explained why that tape had not been not heard.[46]

Another recent case before the Court of Appeal, this time in Belfast shows the modern attitude of judges to what they see as oppressive questioning. On 20 December 2000 fifty years after his conviction for the murder of Patricia Curran, the daughter of a Northern Ireland judge, Iain Hay Gordon cleared his name. Patricia Curran had been killed in 1952 and Iain Hay Gordon had been found guilty but insane. At the time he had been serving in the RAF at a base near the Curran home where Patricia had been stabbed repeatedly in the grounds. He had maintained he had signed a confession only after he was exhausted by the questioning and after the police had threatened to tell his mother about an alleged homosexual liaison.

In his autobiography Detective Superintendent John Capstick had described the interrogation:

> I had to make that boy tell me the truth about his private life and most secret thoughts. Only then could I begin to believe him when he began to tell the truth about the death of Patricia Curran. I hated to use what might well seem to some like ruthless methods. I was never sorrier for any criminal than for that unhappy, maladjusted youngster. But his mask had to be broken.[47]

Now the Lord Chief Justice of Northern Ireland, Sir Robert Carswell, said of the confession that Capstick, the senior Scotland Yard officer sent over to conduct the investigation, had set out to achieve a 'sapping of the appellant's will'.

The circumvention of PACE has mirrored the circumvention of the *Miranda* decision in the United States. Ernesto Miranda was arrested in Phoenix, Arizona and taken to the police station where a victim of rape and kidnapping identified him as the perpetrator. The police then brought Miranda into the interrogation room, questioned him for two hours and obtained a signed confession. He had never been advised of his right to a lawyer or that anything he said would be used in a court of law. The Supreme Court held that:

The defendant's confession was inadmissible
because he was not in any way [informed] of
his right to counsel nor was his privilege
against self-incrimination effectively protected
in any other manner.

Now, Miranda-ising is something of an art form. Some officers will play things strictly according to the book but others will give the caution in a way that it appears, to the less intelligent or practised suspect, that it doesn't matter at all and the words are meaningless. Nevertheless, a quarter of a century after the decision many authorities believed that, as with later proponents of videotaping, the cautioning of a suspect has had no effect on the conviction rate, something feared by Justice White in his dissenting decision in the original case:

In some unknown number of cases the Court's
rule will return a killer, a rapist or other
criminal to the streets and to the environment
which produced him, to repeat his crime
whenever it pleases him.[48]

VIII

Even where there is no attempt to force a confession or to fabricate one there is still the problem of the voluntary false confession made without any inducement whatsoever.[49]

One of the earliest recorded false confessions which had a significant effect on English law is the so-called Camden Wonder, a case in which three people were executed following false confessions.

In 1660 William Harrison, the 70-year-old steward of the Dowager Lady Camden in the market town of Chipping Camden in the Cotswold hills, set out to collect rents from her tenants and never returned. A search was carried out over the next days but there was no trace of either him or his body. The searchers did, however, find a hat, neck band and comb which were recognised as Harrison's. The hat and comb had been cut and the neck band was bloody. The worst was feared. One of the searchers was a John Perry and, as is often the case where people take an interest in a crime, suspicion fell on him. He was arrested and appeared before magistrates on at least two occasions. On the second he said that Harrison's murder had been carried out not by him but by his mother and brother. He did, however, admit that he, along with the other two, had committed a robbery at Harrison's home the previous year. The three were found guilty and hanged.

Two years later Harrison reappeared in the village with a far-fetched story that he had been kidnapped and sold into slavery to a Turkish pasha. When his master fell ill he had escaped taking with him a silver drinking bowl which he had used as payment for a passage to Lisbon. He had then travelled on to Dover, London and finally back home.

The best view of the whole affair is that John Perry was 'subject to chronic mental derangement' as Lord Maugham, a former Lord Chancellor, put it. Perry's body was still hanging in chains when Harrison returned. It was promptly cut down and buried. As for Harrison it is thought that he had embezzled money from the Dowager Lady Camden and had hidden until he could be pardoned under the Act of Indemnity 1660. His wife hanged herself soon after his return. Out of the case grew the belief – espoused with joy until they found it to be incorrect, by New York *mafiosi* and others – that where there was no *corpus delictus* – no body – there could be no conviction. In fact it was not until the case of Onufrejczyk in 1954 that a conviction without a body took place in England. The Polish farmer was convicted of killing his partner with whom he farmed. Even then the death penalty was respited because of the lingering fear that the victim might just be living behind the Iron Curtain and would re-appear as did Harrison to the embarrassment of everybody.[50]

Some people simply like the notoriety of a confession. In the celebrated murder of Elizabeth Short, the Black Dahlia case, in Los Angeles in 1947, somewhere over 60 people confessed to her murder. The confessors included several women and people who had not been born at the time of her death. In the 1990s confessions were still being received. Professor Keith Simpson recalls an unpublicised case in Hertfordshire in 1956 in which he was called to a police station by which time three false confessions had already been logged. Before that, in the case of the

Lindbergh baby kidnap, some 200 innocent people confessed.

It is to eliminate these nuisances that the police, when giving details of a victim, hold back a secret clue so that although they may announce there was a baseball cap lying by the body they will not say whether it was a New York Yankees or a Detroit Tigers cap. If the caller does not know the logo then he or she can, in all probability, be easily eliminated.

One of the most dangerous as well as tiresome of false confessors in modern times has been Henry Lee Lucas. The problem for investigators is that he confessed to some 600 murders in 19 states, a great number of which he could not possibly have committed. He was eventually sentenced to death for one he almost certainly did not commit, the murder of a woman known only as Orange Socks, because that was all the unidentified person was wearing when her body was discovered in a culvert in Williamson County in Central Texas.

At his trial he repudiated his confession and called an alibi which showed that he had been some 1,200 miles away working as a roofer. After his conviction he admitted several more murders but reporters from the Dallas *Times Herald* had been making enquiries and had discovered that a number of his confessions had to be false.[51] In June 1998 Lucas was eventually reprieved for the Orange Socks murder alone after a lie-detector test was in his favour.

He maintained that he had confessed because 'I wanted to open up people's eyes to what was going on in law enforcement, how they didn't care if they got the right person or not. I don't think anybody, a human being anyway, could kill 600 people'.[52]

Others more cynically inclined think that he enjoyed being a celebrity. With his increasing number of confessions creating a valuable clear-up rate as far as detectives were concerned, he had reached a point where he wore his own clothes in his cell, was given painting materials and cigarettes, and had Cable TV.

Times have changed yet again in England and Wales. In the belief that because of the right to silence there were not sufficient convictions forthcoming, the rules were changed. In exchange for the guarantee of a lawyer being present during questioning, now if a defendant exercises that right to silence, the prosecution and judge can comment adversely, asking the jury to consider why an innocent man should not provide an explanation of his conduct. It is too early to see whether the change will have the desired effect and improve the conviction rate.

CHAPTER 6

DNA: The Way Forward

In 1989 22-year-old Chris Ochoa was convicted of rape on his own confession after he had been interrogated without a lawyer for 12 hours. Ochoa, who had no previous convictions, was told he should 'fess up' because otherwise he was 'going to get the needle' – after all, he had raped the girl at the Pizza Hut during the course of a robbery. In October 1988 the manageress, Nancy Lena DePriest, of a Pizza Hut in Austin, Texas, had been found tied and shot in the lavatory. Richard Danziger, Ochoa's 18-year-old co-accused, was at the time on parole following a conviction for forgery. They each received life imprisonment. Then on 25 February 1998 the office of the former Governor of Texas, George W. Bush, received a handwritten letter headed: RE: Murder Confession.

In the letter Achim Josef Marino, himself serving life for aggravated robbery with a deadly weapon, wrote how he and not Ochoa and Danziger had killed Nancy DePriest. He went on to say that his family still had the bags in which he had taken cash from the restaurant. He had, apparently, written to various people including a newspaper editor and the Austin Police Department as early as 1996 claiming that he had committed the rape and murder, but the confession had been ignored. The reason for his first confession was that he had heard that Ochoa and Danziger were serving life sentences and that, fearing he was about to be killed in prison, he wanted them off his conscience. Now he was writing again. He no longer feared being killed but he had turned to religion and had been 'led to Jesus Christ, His Father or Creator, the Holy Spirit and, of course, this confession'.

It would eventually turn on DNA evidence whether his confession was genuine and if Ochoa and Danziger should go free.

I

On 21 November 1984 a 15-year-old girl, left her home in The Coppice, Enderby in Leicestershire to visit a friend. At about 7 a.m. the next morning her body was discovered by a hospital porter on the Black Pad, a pathway in Narborough near the M1, on his way to work at the nearby Carlton Hayes psychiatric hospital. There were traces of semen in her pubic hair and tests revealed a high sperm count indicating that, in all probability, the killer was a young man. Two days later a post-mortem was conducted at Leicester Royal Infirmary when Chief Superintendent David Baker of the Leicestershire Constabulary learned that the blood test showed that the offender was an A-group secretor with a PGM of 1+, the same as 80 per cent of the population.

On 22 January the next year, PC Neil Burney called on the home of Colin Pitchfork in Haybarn Close, as part of a routine check. Pitchfork and his wife had moved into the village two months after the murder and the only reason for a visit was that he had two convictions for indecent exposure prior to his marriage in 1981 and one after. He had been told that he would 'grow out of the urge'. Pitchfork was able to provide an account of his movements at the time of the murder. He had driven his wife to her evening class with the baby in a carrycot. He had returned home and then, again with the baby, he had collected her at the end of her sociology class – she was hoping to become a probation officer. She confirmed his story and, although technically he may have been without an alibi, he had no history of violence and it was thought highly unlikely that he would leave the baby to go and commit a murder.

By the summer of 1984 there were no really positive leads. The enquiry was run down and by the autumn there was a list of 30 possible suspects, a number which was eventually reduced to eight, but there were no probable ones.

Then in November 1984 Dr Alec Jeffreys discussed publicly the discovery of the genetic fingerprint and, in March 1985, published an article in which he claimed that the chances of two people having the same genetic fingerprint were, for all practical purposes, practically zero. But what was a genetic fingerprint?

In 1983 Dr Jeffreys, rather than looking at blood groups, had begun to look at deoxyribonucleic acid (DNA). Every human is made up of a vast number of different types of living cells. Inside the nucleus of every cell there is a string of coded information in the form of a ribbon-like molecule of DNA which contains a genetic blueprint of that particular person's make-up.

The amount of information contained in the codes is enormous. Each human cell contains a string of 23 pairs of chromosomes, each of which contains almost 100,000 genes and DNA chains made up of 100 million base pairs. The complete human genetic code involves three billion base pairs controlling everything from height and build to the colour of the hair and eyes.

Since human beings share many basic characteristics, large sections of the genetic code are common to all individuals. But because everyone's make-up is unique – except for twins – the coded information is as individual as a perfect set of fingerprints. Furthermore, as Dr Jeffreys' explains:

> Within our DNA there are bits of DNA that
> have stuttered – a bit of DNA repeated over and
> over again. And these stuttered bits often vary
> a lot from person to person. So imagine an
> ordinary bit of DNA reading say 'Mary had a
> little lamb' one of these bits of DNA would
> read 'Mary had AAAAA little lamb', and the
> number of As varies from person to person in a
> really quite spectacular fashion.

Dr Jeffreys' discovery would not only have a great impact on the murder investigation but also on criminal cases throughout the world. Things would never quite be the same again.

Meanwhile in October 1985 a 16-year-old hairdresser was attacked and forced to fellate a man in Wigston near Narborough. She told her employer the next day and the police were contacted. Nothing came of the enquiry.

Then on 31 July 1986 a second girl left her local newsagents in Enderby, where she had a part-time job, to visit friends in Narborough. The quickest route was along Ten Pound Lane near the M1. The friends were out and she was last seen alive walking back to Ten Pound Lane. At 9.30 that evening her parents informed the police that she was missing.

Two days later, on 3 August, her body was found off Ten Pound Lane. She had been raped and she too had semen in her pubic hair which suggested that in both cases the attacker had ejaculated prematurely. It was now highly probable that he was a local man.

One of those seen in the neighbourhood on his motorbike was a kitchen porter who worked at a local hospital and who had been seen in the area. He had a history of sexual disturbance and liked to talk about deviant sex. He referred to girls in derogatory terms and a former girlfriend said he liked rough and often anal sex. He fitted the psychological profile of the killer. He was arrested and questioned. He had, he said, seen the second girl while out on his motorbike and gave a detailed confession saying he had probably gone mad. He was able to give a number of very accurate details of the killing but was wrong in others. He was arrested and charged. Nevertheless DCS Peter Baker, who was officer in charge of the case, was unhappy. The man was regarded as unstable and false confessions in high-profile cases are regular.

When Dr Alec Jeffreys was asked to test material from the youth and the semen samples found on the bodies of the girls, he said unequivocally that they did not match. On 21 November 1986 the youth was released after he had spent three months in custody.

So began a second enquiry. The *Leicester Mercury* printed a four-page special feature containing every fact and photograph which might be thought to help. A £20,000 reward for information was put up by local businessmen and the case was featured on *Crimewatch*.

Now Baker decided to try to obtain samples from all men in the neighbourhood aged between 17 and 34. This ambitious and expensive project was highly reminiscent of a number of fingerprint cases, notably the one when all men in Blackburn had been fingerprinted after the killing by Peter Griffiths of a female child in Queen's Park Hospital, Blackburn on 15 May 1948.[1]

A letter was sent to every man within the age group inviting them to give a blood sample. There could be no compulsion for a man to give a sample but, naturally, those who refused would be subject to special scrutiny. The men were asked to bring some form of identification such as a passport or driving licence. Testing sites were set up with three, two-hour evening sessions taking place each week. By the end of January one thousand men had been tested but only a quarter eliminated. The problem was that while those who were not blood group A could be eliminated immediately that only accounted for 20 per cent of the population and the laboratory was swamped. It was also a very expensive process costing £120 a time. There was a further flaw. The actual killer was most unlikely to volunteer to give a sample. By May 1987, 3,653 had given samples but only some 2,000 had been eliminated.

Once again the murderer was caught, not by fancy new techniques but by simple old-fashioned policing. On 1 August a bakery worker was drinking in a public house in Leicester with friends who also worked at the bakery, including the manageress of one of their shops. The mass sample was discussed and a worker volunteered that he had taken the test on behalf of a friend, Colin, from Littlethorpe who also worked at the bakery. Since the worker was not the rapist there was no question that his sample would have matched so he was never in danger.

It was six weeks before the manageress reported the conversation. She had wanted to tell the son of the owner of the public house who was himself a policeman but she had to wait for him to return from leave.

A check was run on Colin Pitchfork at the Criminal Records Office at Scotland Yard and showed that after his third conviction he had been sent to Carlton Hayes for psychiatric counselling. Given that he had been questioned over his whereabouts for the murder of the first girl it was a simple matter to check his signature on that statement with the one on the form signed at the blood sample-taking. Unsurprisingly they did not match. Enquiries began at the bakery and it was found that Pitchfork had been asking around for someone to take the test for him. He had received his request letter in January and had told his wife he was afraid to attend because of his record as an indecent exposer. Finally he had persuaded his friend, the bakery worker to take the test saying that he, Pitchfork, had already given a sample on behalf of another man. He had driven his friend, sworn to secrecy, to the testing centre and had substituted his own photograph in his friends passport.

Once they had heard of the deception it took the police less than 24 hours to arrest Pitchfork. At 5.45 on 19 September the police arrived at his home and he confessed there and then to the murders in front of his wife. Asked why he had killed the second girl he replied, 'Opportunity. She was there and I was there'. His more detailed explanation was that in both cases he had initially intended merely to expose himself to the girls but they had seen who he was and so could identify him if they saw him in the village. They had effectively backed him into a corner. It was, he explained, their fault. 'There's rules to how I play that game [flashing]. They always have room. No matter where I exposed myself. They always have room to walk by me. It's the easiest way. You shock them. They walk by you and then you get your exit route clear.'

He claimed that the second murdered girl had not given him his required space. She had apparently not walked by but had run into a field. He had followed her and she had seen his motorcycle jacket. He had felt that if she reported the matter to the police then there might be more enquiries into the killing of the first girl. 'The same feelings were coming back. That I was in a trap again.' After raping the second girl he decided to kill her reasoning, 'One murder or two – the sentence is the same.' The psychiatric treatment he had received had clearly not benefited him. He claimed he had exposed himself to 1,000 women.

On the day he killed the first girl he explained that at 7 p.m. he had indeed taken his wife to the evening class and had collected her at 9 p.m. as she had confirmed. Their baby had been in a carrycot on the back seat of the car when he had stopped, raped and killed the young girl. During his marriage he had had an affair with a young girl student at the college where he had been studying cake decorating and had also acquired another mistress who had a stillborn child by him.

He pleaded guilty at Leicester Crown Court on 22 January 1988 and was sentenced to life imprisonment for each of the killings together with two ten-year sentences for the rapes and three years for two sexual assaults as well as three years for perverting the course of justice. His stand-in at the blood test was given a sentence of 18 months suspended for two years.[2]

That same year on 9 February 22-year-old computer operator Helen McCourt simply vanished. She stepped off a bus at 5.15 p.m. some 300 yards from her home in Billinge near St Helens, Merseyside and disappeared. It would be DNA evidence that led to the conviction of her killer despite the fact that her body was never discovered. During the investigation into her disappearance a witness said that she had heard a high-pitched scream which seemed to come from the direction of the George and Dragon Public House in the village.

The landlord, Ian Simms, was one of the prime suspects. His name was in Helen's diary and he had been heard to say he hated her. She had been barred from the public house two days before she had vanished. Simms was however able to provide an alibi. He had been with someone else at the time Helen had disappeared.

There was some physical evidence. An earring identified as belonging to Helen was found in Simms's car and the missing clip to the earring was found in a bedroom in the pub. Blood was found on the stairs and floor and on Simms's jeans and shirt. The problem was that Helen had never given blood so her type was not known. Blood samples were taken from her mother and father and a genetic fingerprint was taken. This was then compared with the blood on Simms's clothing and the conclusion was that it was 16,000 times more likely that it belonged to the offspring of Helen's parents than a random member of the population. On 14 March 1989 Simms was sentenced to life imprisonment after the jury had found him guilty of murder. It was the first murder conviction reached by genetic fingerprinting 'by proxy'.

The dubious distinction of being the first person overall who was convicted by the use of Dr Jeffreys' technique came in November 1987 when Robert Melias broke into a house in Avonmouth, Bristol and raped a 45-year-old disabled woman before taking her jewellery. Melias was picked out on an identification parade and semen stains from the clothing of the victim were subjected to the 'bar-code' test and matched. On 13 November 1987 Melias was sentenced to eight years for rape and five for the robbery.

In America 24-year-old Tommy Lee Andrews was convicted of a string of rapes between May 1986 and March 1987 in and around Orlando, Florida. Only two of his victims had been able to make a tentative identification and, while his blood type matched that of semen recovered from the victims, it belonged to 30 per cent of American males. In the first rape trial on 27 October 1987 he called an alibi supported by his sister and girlfriend. The prosecution had difficulties explaining the statistics of the DNA evidence and how they claimed there was only a one in 10 billion chance that another man was the rapist. The judge declared a mistrial but Andrews was convicted of a subsequent rape on fingerprint evidence and was sentenced to a term of 22 years. Then the Assistant State Attorney, Tim Berry, read about the Pitchfork case and sought the help of a New York laboratory, the Lifecodes Corporation. Samples were sent and the genetic profiles provided a perfect match. Andrews was sentenced to a further 65 years imprisonment and Michael Baird, a director of Lifecodes, announced, 'If you're a criminal, it's like leaving your name, address and social security number at the scene of the crime'.

The first person to be convicted of murder in America by the use of DNA evidence came after 35-year-old Debbie Davis was found raped and strangled in her flat in Richmond, Virginia on 17 September 1987. Two weeks later 32-year-old neurosurgeon Dr Susan Hellams was attacked in her flat on 3 October and when her law student husband returned home he found her body pushed into a bedroom cupboard. The third victim of the man the press dubbed 'The Southside Slayer' was 15-year-old Diane Cho whose partially clothed and bound body was found in the cupboard of the bedroom of her home near Richmond, Virginia on 22 November.

In December the body of 44-year-old Susan Tucker was discovered in her flat in Arlington. She had been raped and strangled a week earlier. The officer in the case noticed the tidy way in which the murderer had left the flat and linked it to the behaviour of Timothy W. Spencer, from Washington DC, whose *modus operandi* was breaking into houses while the occupants were asleep. He had no convictions for sexual offences but he had been at liberty, living in a halfway house, when the killings occurred. He was questioned initially as a routine suspect but, when asked to give a blood sample, asked if it had anything to do with rape. At the time he had only been told he was being questioned in connection with burglaries.

The match came from a semen sample removed from Susan Tucker's body and again the team at the Lifecodes laboratory was consulted. They gave the chance of a second match as 135 million to one. There were also matches with samples from Debbie Davis and Susan Hellams but it had not been possible to obtain sufficient material in the case of Diane Cho.

In July 1988 Spencer stood trial for the murder of Susan Tucker. The defence argument was to be that since Spencer shared the same genetic make-up as his relatives, they were just as capable of committing the murder as he. The trial judge ruled that if this line of defence continued he would allow evidence of the other murders to be introduced. On 17 July Spencer was convicted of first degree murder and sentenced to life imprisonment. On 22 September 1988 he was convicted of the murders of Debbie Davis and Susan Hellams and was sentenced to death. The same day the jury voted he should be executed.

II

On 5 February 1987, a man, who has been referred to in subsequent reports as David Rivera, returned to his apartment in the Bronx where he lived with his partner Vilma Ponce, who was expecting their second child, and their two-year-old daughter Natasha.[3] Normally she would open the door for him. That afternoon, however, the door was locked against him from the inside.

Thinking she might be asleep he went to the local grocery store and telephoned. There was no reply. He then telephoned his mother who said she had last spoken to Vilma at 2 p.m. In a conversation about cooking the girl had said that she did not know what she was getting for supper that night. He asked his mother to call the police and returned to the apartment. He stood on the pavement and whistled up at the window. As he did so a man came out of the building. Rivera would recall him as Hispanic, with medium length hair and a moustache. He was aged about 30. He was also covered in blood. The man passed Rivera, smiled, and walked across the street.

Rivera went into the building and this time was able to get into the apartment. There was blood everywhere and when the police arrived they found Vilma half naked. She had not been raped but she had been stabbed 58 times. Natasha had also been stabbed 16 times in the chest. Both were dead.

Two days later Rivera, who had been staying at his mother's, accompanied by two police officers, went back to his flat to get some clothes. After he had picked them up the police drove off and then outside the block Rivera saw again the man who had passed him on the day of the murder. He approached him and asked him to smile. The man did so and Rivera went straight to the local precinct where he identified Joseph Castro from photographs shown to him. Then a friend of Vilma's, Barbara Troy, told of how she had been with Vilma when they had both seen Castro in the street and Vilma had said how the man had tried to get fresh with her even though she was heavily pregnant. It was also learned that Castro had re-fitted a defective lock in the Rivera apartment.

After the murder the police had found a brown bag containing unfrozen chicken and steak in the apartment and deduced that Castro had followed Vilma back to the apartment after she had been out shopping for supper. He had surprised her at the door and with the defective lock she had not had time to throw a second working bolt.

The case was not, however, foolproof. Husbands are regularly the first suspect and it was thought that Castro might try to suggest that he had fitted the lock perfectly but that Rivera had tampered with it to throw suspicion on the handyman.

During the time between Castro's initial interview and his arrest he had been seen by a detective from the 48th precinct in the Bronx who had noticed what appeared to be a blood stain on the band of Castro's watch. He had taken it as possible evidence and the strap was now sent to Lifecodes for a DNA examination.

The results were positive with blood on the watchband matching the DNA pattern of Vilma Ponce at three different locations on the DNA ladder. The frequency was said to be one in one million of the Hispanic population.

Before the trial began the judge had ordered that all forensic witnesses appear before him to give evidence, after which he would decide whether to admit the DNA results under the decision in *Frye*. Had DNA gained sufficient acceptance among scientists to be admissible?

So far so good for the prosecution. Their first witness, Dr Richard Roberts had worked closely with James Watson who had written *The Double Helix* and who had been awarded the Nobel Prize for his work in discovering DNA. Later Roberts would also be awarded the Nobel Prize. It was not possible, he said, for DNA analysis to result in a false positive. He gave evidence that he had examined the X-ray films of the DNA results and, although he had initially been bothered over the clarity of one of the films, the second and third had given a clean interpretation. He did not, however, say, nor was he asked, whether there was a DNA match.

In fact there had been something of a joint conference of experts on the use of DNA in the criminal field some time earlier when, in February 1989, Dr Michael Baird had provided a presentation of the work undertaken by his Lifecodes laboratory. The conference had been held at Dr Roberts's laboratory and one of the delegates was former Rhodes scholar, Dr Eric Lander. He had been disturbed by what he saw as the possible inadequacy of Lifecode's controls and he had questioned one of the speakers.

Also in the invitation-only audience was Peter Neufeld, along with Barry Scheck, one of the lawyers appointed by the court to defend Castro during the pre-trail hearings.[4] During one of the breaks in the conference Neufeld asked Lander to look at the scientific evidence in the case. He was unimpressed and said so. Invited to join the defence team in challenging the DNA evidence Lander finally agreed, if not to appear as a witness, at least to provide an education for the lawyers by advising on the daily transcripts of the courtroom evidence. He found fault with the evidence adduced by Michael Baird of Lifecode and finally agreed to appear as a witness himself. He did so for six days.

Then, in April, at another conference he met with Roberts and gave him a copy of his 50-page-long report.

Roberts was disturbed by what he read, and a conference of the scientific witnesses in the Castro case was called, not to be attended by the lawyers. The result was a jointly prepared document that the DNA results were not sufficiently conclusive to determine whether there was or was not a match. The statement said that the tests neither implicated Castro nor cleared him. Lifecode however persisted with the view that the tests implicated Castro.

The stumbling point was the appearance of two extra bands on Vilma Ponce's DNA. Lifecode said that it was bacterial contamination. Lander believed the bands were human DNA and they certainly did not match. Justice Gerald Sheindlin declined to allow the DNA evidence to go before the jury but he ruled that the jurors could be told that the blood on the watchstrap was not that of Castro.[5]

What was left against Castro was mainly the evidence of Rivera. The DNA evidence excluded, Neufeld and Scheck had dropped out, their task done, and at another pre-trial hearing Rivera proved a most positive witness. The prosecutrix, not however convinced that a Bronx jury would necessarily convict, offered a plea bargain. Castro would receive 20 years to life. He accepted and admitted that the blood on the watch did come from Vilma Ponce, something Lifecode saw as their vindication.

III

There is little doubt, however, that the fallout from the Castro case was prolonged and heavy. There had in fact been earlier problems when in 1987 a man from the Bronx, charged with rape on the basis of the victim's identification of him, hired a commercial DNA testing laboratory to compare his blood with semen samples from the attacker. The laboratory then declared a mismatch. The prosecution obtained an order from the trial judge requiring him to submit a second sample and this time the laboratory suggested that the two samples had come from different people. The prosecution then asked for the man's bail to be revoked and contemplated charging him with conspiracy to pervert the course of justice. A third sample was provided and then, according to the assistant district attorney, the laboratory admitted that a mistake had been made. The original mismatch was confirmed. The following year another prosecutor refused to allow a laboratory to undertake the testing because 'their testing has been inaccurate and therefore unreliable'.[6]

Now, after Castro, the debate concerning the acceptability of DNA evidence in American courts reached a pitch. A study was undertaken by the National Research Council of the National Academy of Sciences and three years later, in 1992, its report was published. The *New York Times* carried an article, 'Judges are asked to bar genetic "Fingerprinting" until basis of science is stronger'.[7] The next day a news conference was called to refute the newspaper's claim.

In England at the end of the year a judge at the Central Criminal Court ruled in the case of *Hammond* that in the particular circumstances DNA evidence was inadmissible. In January 1993 the Metropolitan Police Forensic Science Laboratory called a meeting on 'The use of DNA statistics in criminal cases' and that same year a report, 'The ability to Challenge DNA Evidence', was commissioned by the Royal Commission on Criminal Justice. It recommended that DNA evidence should only be admissible when all the DNA evidence had been disclosed to the defence and when an expert had been made available to the defence.

In April 1995 the world's first DNA database opened at the Home Office's Forensic Science Laboratory in Birmingham. Now every person accused or convicted of a recordable offence is on it and the DNA is only removed if the suspect turns out to be innocent and then not always. The first match occurred within a matter of months when a suspected burglar in Derbyshire was arrested on an unrelated offence and a DNA sample matched a sample left at the scene of the burglary.

There are now over one million people in the database which has resulted in some 10,000 arrests. In Manchester it has been used for what is known as mass crime, notably burglary. But, particularly in its early years, the database has not been without its critics. At the time it was opened Professor Dennis Lindley commented:

> DNA evidence – like any evidence – can never
> be looked at in isolation. In many cases DNA
> evidence has been wrongly presented. The
> trouble is that it is very difficult to persuade
> people to change their minds.[8]

As technology has progressed juries in America have begun to demand DNA evidence which links the accused to the crime. Peter Neufeld is sceptical. 'Juries will say, "C'mon! the guy must have left behind some DNA." As if they could tell DNA from doughnuts.'

His view is echoed in a report by the staff members of the Institute of Law and Justice, Alexandria, Virginia:

> Juries begin to question cases where the prosecutor does not offer 'conclusive' DNA test results if the evidence is available for testing.[9]

Neufeld believed that with the rising tide of cases laboratories were under pressure and false tests were relatively frequent. Dr Jerry Coyne of the University of Chicago believed that private forensic laboratories were producing false tests with a frequency of between one in a thousand and one in a hundred. 'Tell a jury that there is only a 1 in 50 million chance OJ was not the man but a 1 in 100 chance the lab screwed up and you have an acquittal.'

It was in fact the OJ Simpson case which for a time did even further harm to DNA samples as convincing evidence. Peter Neufeld, one of his lawyers, who dealt with the DNA evidence, commented:

> There was a mismatch between OJ's samples and the evidence because of sloppiness in the tests. Far too many private toxicology labs are under enormous pressure from thousands of police departments. Some cut corners.[10]

In 1994 the bodies of Nicole, the wife of former American Football superstar, OJ Simpson, and a male friend were found at her Los Angeles home. The chief suspect was Simpson whose volatile relationship with his wife was well known.

Barry Scheck, who had appeared in the Castro case, now appeared in the DNA phase of the Simpson trial along with his colleague Peter Neufeld, arguing that the police had contaminated the crime scene with drops of blood from OJ Simpson's sample. They also argued, something which was hotly contested, that the Los Angeles laboratory had made serious errors and that DNA from one test had found its way into another. Scheck is insistent that he is a great believer in DNA:

> I never challenged the science, but the way the police conducted its investigation. If you do it right, you will convict the guilty.[11]

Nor has testing always been without its problems in the United Kingdom. In 1998 Raymond Easton from Swindon was arrested in connection with a burglary 200 miles away in Bolton. He had appeared on the database following a domestic incident. He recalls:

> I was arrested. I told them I had Parkinson's disease and that I couldn't walk very well. I've never driven a car in my life and I've never been to Bolton.

He had, he said, been looking after his daughter at home at the time of the burglary but nevertheless he remained the prime suspect for eight months. The DNA match had been based on a six-point test which looked at the DNA profile of six loci on the genetic ladder. Its reliability is enormous – one to 34 million. However, some calculations suggest that if there are between 700,000 and one million DNA profiles in the database there is roughly a one in fifty chance that there can be a mismatch. In the end Raymond Easton's solicitor arranged a ten-point test and he was eliminated. The six-point scale was abandoned in June 1999. The ten-point tests, which offer a far higher reliability rate, are now routine.

But even in the early 1990s the technique was being accepted more readily by the courts. In 1990 Andrew Deen, dubbed in the press as 'The Bedsit Rapist', had been convicted on genetic fingerprint evidence at Liverpool Crown Court when experts gave evidence that there was only a one in three million chance that he had not raped three young women in Manchester. The Court of Appeal had doubts about the profiling evidence and, quashing his conviction, ordered a retrial. Now Howard Bentham, for the Crown told the court that techniques had improved and there was only a one in 500 billion chance that Deen was not the rapist in one of the cases. Deen changed his plea to guilty. The other two charges of rape were left on the file. He received a sentence of 11 years.

The next year a second case came before the courts in which the Court of Appeal had ordered a retrial. It had shades of the New York fingerprint case of Caesar Cella, some ninety years earlier.[12] Denis Adams was convicted solely on DNA evidence despite the fact he had claimed to have a cast-iron alibi and his victim was unable to identify him. He had, he said, been in bed with a woman when the attack in Hemel Hempstead took place and she gave evidence confirming this. The jury did not know that he had been convicted of indecent assault on a previous occasion when he had run the same defence.

That same year the police asked 800 men in the one-time mining community in Ansley Common, near Nuneaton to provide samples. Fifteen-year-old Naomi Smith had been assaulted and stabbed to death before her body was dumped under a slide in a children's park on 14 September. People were also asked to watch for and report on young men who suddenly disappeared from their homes. The usual rules prevailed. The men could not be forced to give a ten-second swab sample from inside the mouth but, of course, particular attention would be paid to any who declined. In February 1997 Edwin Douglas Hopkins was convicted of her murder. Bite marks on her breast were said by the prosecution to have been 'better than an autograph'. Hopkins was one of the youths who had given a saliva swab. He claimed he had been visiting his sister at the time. The court was told that in effect the chances of another match was five times the population of England and Wales.

A similar operation had been carried out in Cardiff following the death of Claire Hood in which over 2,000 men were tested without any initial success. Then, in January 1996, 19-year-old computer studies student was arrested and charged. He lived only 100 yards from Claire.

Mass testing was put into operation again in 1995 when 120 men, possible suspects in the rape of a woman in Regent's Park, London, were asked to provide samples. They would have a lawyer provided free and be given £10 expenses. Again, if they declined they could expect to be investigated.

It is unlikely that such dragnet operations could take place in the United States where constitutional protections against self-incrimination and unreasonable search and seizure, as well as the American's zealous protection of privacy rights, would militate against the procedure.

In fact, three detective sergeants in the Gloucestershire police force claimed that their human rights had been breached when they were moved to desk jobs after they refused to give DNA samples in October 2000. It was all part of a campaign introduced the previous February to tackle the complications of contamination of crimes scenes. The Association of Chief Police Officers said that the fears of some officers that their DNA profiles would be used other than for elimination purposes were wholly unfounded.[13]

By the end of the 1990s the doubts about the validity of DNA evidence focused not on the science itself but on the techniques used to interpret the statistics and presentation of the evidence. There have even been suggestions of fraudulent practices. Writing in *Nature*, Zakaria Erinclioglu argued that unregulated forensic science practices in the United Kingdom could lead to a spate of wrongful convictions.[14] His complaint is an old one. Scientists are obliged to appear not as independent experts but for the defence or prosecution. He maintains this means they are dependant on the goodwill of their clients and the less scrupulous may be influenced by a desire to please them. He also pointed out that with the exception of pathologists there is nothing to stop anyone, qualified or not, from advertising themselves as specialists in DNA testing.

Juries can also be wrongly influenced by the way evidence is given. In a study cited by Jonathan Koehler of the University of Texas at Austin, one jury was told the probability of a match was 0.1 per cent. Seventy-five per cent of the jurors thought the accused was likely to be guilty. When another jury was told the match was one in a thousand, less than half thought the same way.[15]

IV

Since the mid 1990s the DNA testing methods have spread throughout the world and the case of one of Italy's most notorious serial killers of recent years, Donato Bilancia, has highlighted the enormous potential that DNA has in the fight against crime. It also caused a political debate about how the techniques could be used most effectively.

In 1997 Maurizio Parenti ran a number of illegal gambling clubs, known as *bisce*, from villas on the coast near Genoa. That summer was a particularly successful one for him. His illegal clubs were bringing in serious money and he was also engaged to a 22-year-old society beauty, Carla Scotto. They married in August and went on honeymoon. In October, the morning after returning to their flat in Genoa, they failed to answer their telephone. The pair were found covered in sheets on the floor of their bedroom.

The police initially suspected a Mafia connection. The killings had all the hallmarks of a gangland execution with Parenti handcuffed behind his back having been shot once in the back of the head. It was known that he had connections to a prominent Sicilian crime family and it was thought he had run foul of the

Mafia. But the safe had been burgled and in any event that line of investigation got nowhere.

Three days later there was another dual killing when two elderly jewellers, Bruno Solari and Maria Pitto, were killed in their flat. There was, however, seemingly no connection between the victims, but ballistic tests showed that the same bullets, of a rare Finnish make manufactured between 1972 and 1981, had been used in the killings.

The next killing came in the November when a moneychanger who ran a bureau in Ventimiglia was shot so ruthlessly it appeared at first that two men had been involved. But again tests showed the bullets were of the same Finnish make. The season was rounded off by the murder of a night security guard in Genoa.

With the next spring, however, came a series of murders of prostitutes. On 3 February the body of an Italian prostitute, Silvana Bazzoni, was discovered, to be followed on 9 March by that of an Albanian prostitute, Stela Truya, whose body was found near a lay-by at Vaerze near Savona. Nine days later a Ukranian girl, Ludmyla Zuskowa, was found shot dead at Pietra Ligure. Another girl, this time a Nigerian, Tessy Edoghaye, was shot on 29 March and on 14 April a Macedonian, Christina Walla, was also killed. Both had been forced to kneel before being killed and Edoghaye had actually been knee-capped. In the early stages of the investigation it was thought the girls had been killed as a result of warfare between the various ethnic gangs, particularly Albanians, who used hundreds of women and controlled the £20 million prostitution rings along the Riviera.

One victim, however, had escaped when on 27 March an Ecuadorean transvestite, Julio Castro, who traded as Lorena, had been picked up in Novi Ligure, a well-known prostitution zone north of Genoa. Castro had been made to undress but, before he could have sex with his attacker, two security guards approached them. The attacker opened fire and shot both guards in the chest. He then began to fire on Castro as he escaped into the woods. Castro was hit in the side and the hand but he survived. He was able to provide a description for a photofit and said he had been picked up in a dark Mercedes 190. He was also able to provide a partial identification of the number plate. Now the focus of the investigation changed and it was thought the killer might be a man seeking revenge for having contracted the AIDS virus.

Then the killer also changed direction. On 12 April he killed a nurse, Elisabetta Zoppetti, on an inter-city train between Genoa and Milan. He had noticed her sitting alone, followed her to a lavatory and opened the door with a pass key he had bought locally. He shot her in the head after she had screamed. Then, on 18 April, he repeated the exercise on the Ventimiglia train. This time he shot his victim with a .38 revolver in the back of the head. This second woman was Maria Angelo Rubino, the 32-year-old fiancée of a local police officer.

Now, for the first time in the case links were made; efforts were co-ordinated and five local state forces joined with the *carabinieri* in Genoa under the direction of Major Filippo Ricciarelli. The ballistics unit in Parma identified the bullets as identical with the ones used to kill the prostitutes and also the murders in the autumn and early winter of 1997. Another photofit was put together with the help of the ticket-conductor who had seen the killer get off the Ventimiglia train and a taxi driver who had driven him to San Remo.

Soon after, the police were contacted by a small-time businessman, Pino Monello, who said that he had sold a Donata Bilancia his dark blue Mercedes. The police checked out Bilancia and found that as a young man he had stolen a lorry load of *panettone*. It had not been a successful effort. He had tried to sell it outside a department store and had promptly been arrested. More significantly, in 1990 he had also been accused of the attempted robbery at gunpoint of a prostitute but the charge had been dismissed.

Monello recalls:

> I had sold my old dark Mercedes to a man
> called Bilancia. I had met him in a gambling
> joint. Bilancia had never registered the car and
> I kept getting tickets for not paying the
> motorway fee. I contacted the police and it was
> decided that I could arrange a meeting with the
> man.

He met Bilancia in a bar in the Foce and it was arranged that a second meeting should take place. Afraid that he also might be killed, Monello declined to give Bilancia a lift to the outskirts of Palermo. After the meeting the police took Bilancia's coffee cup and sent it to the police laboratory. In case the owner of the bar was a friend of Bilancia, the officer collecting the cup said he was a gypsy fortune-teller who could see from the coffee grounds that the bar had just attracted the Evil Eye. DNA tests were carried out and Bilancia's DNA from the coffee cup matched the semen from one of the crime scenes.

The police had also been following Bilancia around Genoa trying to pick up a discarded cigarette end so they could use the saliva for DNA testing. They finally collected one and it matched a DNA sample taken from the clothing of the Nigerian girl, Tessy Edoghaye.

On 4 May a warrant was issued and as Bilancia walked out of a hospital where he had been for a routine check-up he was arrested. Initially he denied any involvement, saying the police had the wrong man and that he did not resemble the photofit but then the gun and remaining bullets were found hidden behind a sofa in his flat. Ten days later he made a full confession.

For two days he hardly stopped talking. In fact, Parenti and his wife had not been his first killings. He maintained that he had been cheated in a gambling club by Parenti and his partner Giorgio Centenaro and had heard them discussing how they had taken him for over 400 million lire. He had determined on revenge and had mugged Centenaro outside his flat in early October. He had put adhesive tape round his mouth and Centenaro had promptly had a fatal heart attack. The official verdict had been death from natural causes but, said Bilancia, he had telephoned the examining magistrate and told him he was wrong.

He had then dealt with Parenti and his wife. He had waited until Parenti had said good night to his bodyguards and had then entered the flat. He had first killed the club owner after telling him how he believed he had been cheated. Then, as Parenti's wife came into the room he shot her. The killing of the jewellers had been because they had screamed. He had only intended to rob them but had panicked. After that he had clearly developed a taste.

As for the prostitutes he said he had decided to kill one of every nationality. His last killing had been during the robbery of a San Remo petrol station on 21 April.

Before he had taken to killing he had been a professional burglar and safebreaker. He would identify his targets in the casinos along the French and Italian Rivieras and would follow them. He had worked in Switzerland and Britain. Apart from a short spell in prison in France in his adult life he had managed to avoid conviction.

As for his criminal profile, he was a middle-aged white man living alone. As a child he had been something of a joke in the neighbourhood pretending to be far tougher than he in fact was. School friends would say 'Don't do a Bilancia'. He had had, he said, a traumatic childhood and his brother had committed suicide, throwing himself in front of a train after custody of his son had been awarded to his wife. Apparently Bilancia had chosen killing as his way of dealing with his history. He had wanted to kill himself but had lacked the courage to do so. His parents could not believe their son had been arrested. 'He's always been kind and truthful,' said his mother.

The length of time during which Bilancia was able to operate caused serious political repercussions with calls for a National Database. The Italian forensic scientist who carried out the tests on the cigarette believes that to be the way forward with DNA taken from known criminals:

Bilancia was a convicted burglar before he
started to kill. He might have been on the

database and might have been caught after the second or third crime. If he hadn't been on the database it still could have been used to match DNA from crime scenes that don't appear to have any connection. In Bilancia's case the murder of the newlyweds would have been linked to the killing of the first prostitute.

V

The number of prisoners released following DNA testing after wrongful convictions has continued to grow. Barry Scheck and Peter Neufeld have established the *Innocence Project* aimed at assisting wrongfully convicted men to clear their names through methods like DNA testing. So far around 100 long-term prisoners have been found to be innocent after testing.

In February 2001 Earl Washington, a 40-year-old man with a mental age of ten, was released in Virginia. He had spent 18 years in prison including nine on Death Row. In 1985 he was within nine days of being executed before being reprieved. He had been convicted in 1982 of rape and murder mainly on the strength of his confession but an analysis of the transcript showed that he had been led into the confession with the police supplying him with the facts. In 1993 genetic evidence cast doubt on the validity of his conviction but the best Washington obtained at the time was a commutation of the death sentence. In 2000 new DNA evidence linked two other men to the crime.[16]

In America there are, however, serious problems standing in the way of clearing the prisoners. Many states allow only a very short time for the filing of new evidence. In some the limit is as short as 21 days. Some states also allow law enforcement agencies to destroy evidence after a conviction. Some prosecutors also fight against allowing testing arguing that the courts are already clogged with hopeless appeals. A Bill introduced to standardise the rules governing DNA evidence based on the New York testing laws foundered in the summer of 2000. However there are some encouraging signs, not least in Ohio where Attorney General Betty D. Montgomery says firmly, 'We are here to find the truth'. Under a new programme the state will pay the $1,500 cost of DNA testing for a death row inmate requesting it.[17]

Just as DNA is being used to release innocent men so it is being used to trap killers who have believed that for many years they have literally got away with murder. In one of Britain's longest murder investigations Ian Lowther was convicted at the end of September 2000 of the 1977 killing of Mary Gregson as she walked by the canal in Shipley, Yorkshire. Early DNA techniques were not sufficiently advanced to provide a profile but in December 1998 police scientists were eventually able to obtain a DNA profile of the murderer taken from her clothing. Oral swabbing began of over 3,000 men who had lived in the area at the time she was assaulted and killed. Lowther, now divorced and a grandfather of four, was the 532nd swab to be taken. He admitted to the murder saying he had been drinking at lunchtime and had attacked her on the way back to work.[18]

Another long-running case was the 1970 murder of the pregnant teenager Rita Sawyer who was found stabbed in a field in Leamington Spa. It was only in 1988 that a DNA profile matched a sample taken at the time of a mass screening. The suspect died and was never named.

In 2000 David Frediani, long suspected of the killing of DNA scientist Helena Greenwood in San Diego, California, was convicted of her murder 15 years after she had been found battered and strangled to death in her front garden. A year before he killed Dr Greenwood, Frediani had pleaded no contest to attacking her at her former home in San Francisco. She had given evidence against him. Now particles of his skin found under her fingernails gave 15 markers against his DNA. 'That kind of evidence makes it kind of hard for him to explain,' said Detective Laura Heilig who arrested Frediani.

VI

The prospect of routine DNA screening of the whole population of the United Kingdom came a step closer when in January 2001 a Bill was drafted which would allow the police to retain indefinitely samples taken from innocent people.[19] It followed the decision of the House of Lords in the autumn of the previous year that, where the police had improperly failed to destroy fingerprints and DNA samples taken and then used them in a later case, the evidence should not be excluded.

One case involved the rape of a 68-year-old woman. Wendall Baker had been arrested for an unrelated offence of burglary and the sample should have been destroyed after his acquittal on that charge. The allegation was that he had attacked her while she was in bed, binding her arms with flex from her alarm clock and then beating her, breaking a rib. He had then bundled her into a cupboard from which he had removed her vacuum cleaner to make space.

Their Lordships said the exclusion of critical DNA evidence was was contrary to good sense and that it had to be borne in mind that respect for the privacy of defendants was not the only value at stake:

> The purpose of the criminal law is to permit
> everyone to go about their daily lives without
> fear of harm to person or property. And it was
> in the interests of everyone that serious crime
> should be effectively investigated and
> prosecuted.

Now it seems that for around 600 killers, living in Britain and leading ordinary lives with family and friends, their days at liberty may be numbered. The Forensic Science Service boasts a 40 per cent chance of a stain found at a crime scene being matched with a name already on the database whose million plus names is expected to triple within ten years. An example of its effectiveness comes from Eastbourne where in a recent blitz by Sussex police 80 arrests were made and where in the six months to February 2001 the Force identified 426 suspects from DNA matches, double that of the previous year.[21]

Liberty, formerly the National Council for Civil Liberties, has consistently argued against a National Database. In 1988 a spokesman commented:

> While a balance needs to be struck between individual privacy and law enforcement we believe that the proposal for a national database goes way beyond what is acceptable or necessary in a democratic society.[22]

It remains concerned that the courts are becoming blinded by science and that, despite FSS insistence that DNA evidence must never be the sole evidence, positive DNA identification will equate to a guilty verdict.

On 16 January 2001 Chris Ochoa walked free from prison where he had served over 12 years. He had, he said, confessed to the crime under duress. His release was due to a non-match of semen found at the crime scene and his DNA. His co-accused was not so fortunate. Richard Danziger though released soon after Ochoa had been so badly beaten by another prisoner that he suffered severe brain damage and may require full time care for the rest of his life

Notes

1. Fingerprints

1. Adolphe Quetelet also developed a theory that crime was cyclical. So, for example, applying this in very basic terms to modern times, people having spent their money at Christmas would have to steal to recoup immediately afterwards; burglaries would be more prevalent during the dark hours of winter; with people leaving for their holidays there would be more crime at seaside resorts; the dark nights and burglaries would return and as Christmas again approached and easily saleable goods such as lorryloads of whisky and cigarettes were available there would be more thefts. These would dry up as Christmas actually approached as no-one wished to be separated from their families and theft would recommence after Christmas.

2. Macé was regarded as a brilliant detective who in 1869 had solved the Voirbo murder case which had shocked and entertained *le tout Paris*. Part of a corpse, sewn in calico, had been found in a well and Macé had traced it back to a tailor Voirbo. He was convinced that the killing and dismemberment must have produced a great deal of blood and although the shop floor had been well cleaned the wood was uneven. Macé poured water through the cracks and then had the floorboards torn up. Underneath was a quantity of coagulated blood. Voirbo confessed that he had killed a friend, Bodasse. For a detailed account of the case see Colin Wilson, *Written in Blood* (1995).

3. Pierre Brullard quoted in Jurgen Thorwald, *The Marks of Cain* (1965), p. 43.

4. Library of Congress, Washington; Pinkerton Archives, Case Binder 33 Crimes and Associates of Sophie Lyons. For a time there was an erroneous belief that Bertillon had, in fact, discovered fingerprints. Ironically, in 1902 through fingerprinting he identified Henri-Léon Scheffer as the murderer of Joseph Reibel on 17 October at 157 rue du Faubourg. This may have contributed to the myth.

5. A sergeant was very much like the Queen's Counsel of today. Champerty was the criminal practice of financing a case in which one had no interest on the basis that the financier would receive a share of the winnings. Maintenance, the financing of another's case with no reward, was also illegal.

6. *Nature*, 28 October 1880.

7. A genuine scientific dilettante, Galton also tried to discover the source of the Nile and then took up ballooning before he set sail for South Africa where he studied and measured the native tribes. After the booth at the International Fair he established a permanent measurement laboratory in South Kensington where it was fashionable to have one's measurements taken by his assistant. Despite frequent breakdowns in his health he lived until the age of 90. His home at 42 Rutland Gate became a meeting place for scientists; see Sir Francis Galton, *My Life* (1908) London.

8. For an account of the gang and Lepine's efforts to destroy them see James Morton, *Gangland International* (1999), Chapter 30. Lepine was a much loved and respected Prefect who invariably wore a bowler hat. During a strike by the porters in the central market he led the gendarmerie to a confrontation and then called out 'I forbid you to attack these honest men'. This broke the strike which ended in Lepine being carried in triumph by the porters. For a partial account of his career see Jean Belin, *My Work at the Sûreté* (1950).

9. In fact in the late 1880s Dr Wilhelm Eber had arrived at fingerprinting via a very similar, if coarser, route to Fauld's. He had seen the impressions made by the blood-stained hands of slaughterhouse workers and had started taking 'hand-pictures'. In 1888 his report had been discarded on the basis that no officer knew of traces on doors and other surfaces which would permit adequate reconstruction.

10. Tighe Hopkins, 'Tracked by fingerprints' in *Penny Magazine*, c. 1903. Or, in a rather more modern case when a Patrick O'Connor spent four and a half days in an Army guardroom because he had the same name as a known deserter. The two men had the same National Insurance number, the same birthday, the same dental fillings and the same abdominal scars from appendix operations. But they did not have the same fingerprints. C.H. Rolph, 'Fingerprint everybody at birth' in *Daily Mail*, 21 April 1966, when he also wrote that research at the Cambridge Institute of Criminology forecast that on present figures 29 per cent of men then living in England and Wales would at some time in their lives be convicted of an indictable offence.

11. Vucetich in a letter to a friend quoted in Jurgen Thorwald, *The Marks of Cain* (1965), p. 82.

12. Sir Melville Macnaghten, *Days of My Years* (1914).

13. Muir began his working life as a bank clerk and then an agent for a sugar company before reading for the Bar. His many notable cases included the defence of Eddie Guerin who had escaped from the French penal colony of Devil's Island and whom the French wished to be extradited, and the prosecution of Harvey Hawley Crippen. He was noted for his rousting of police officers into providing the necessary evidence to perfect their cases and in that of Crippen forced a strangely lethargic Inspector Walter Dew into finding the shop which sold the pyjamas in which Crippen had wrapped his wife's body. He was then able to show the pyjamas were only sold after Crippen had bought Hilldrop Crescent, so defeating his argument that the body, which he said was not that of his wife, had been in the cellar prior to his arrival. See S.T. Felstead, *Sir Richard Muir*.

14. *The Times*, 15 September 1902.

15. S.T. Felstead, *Sir Richard Muir*, p. 191. In *The Referee* the journalist George R. Sims wrote 'his words rang out as though it was the execution bell at Newgate prison tolling, so deadly was his condemnation of the brutal crime'.

16. The brothers were hanged together by John Billington at Wandsworth prison on 23 May 1905. Collins retired as a Superintendent in 1925. He died in 1932. His superior, C.H. Stedman, had retired to Gorleston-on-Sea in 1908 when given only a few years to live by his doctor. In fact he survived to write a congratulatory letter to the Fingerprint Bureau when it held its 50th anniversary dinner in 1951. See Fred Cherrill, *Cherrill of the Yard*. The first time a palm as opposed to a fingerprint was accepted in evidence was in 1931 when William Egan was sentenced at the Old Bailey. It was claimed that the first conviction in British, and possibly world, criminal history on the basis of a glove print was when a 26-year-old man pleaded guilty to office breaking at Inner London Sessions. On 29 January 1971 an alarm went off at the premises of a surveyors in Wilton Road, Victoria. The man was found nearby in possession of a pair of gloves and, said Colin Hart-Leverton prosecuting, police laboratory tests showed that 'the chances of finding matching gloves were the same as one man's fingerprints matching another and that, as is well known, is virtually nil', *Daily Telegraph*, 7 May 1971.

17. Sir Melville Macnaghten, *Days of My Years* (1914), p. 106.

18. Bertillon had at least one further major sin marked against his name. He had consented to appear in the Dreyfus Affair as a handwriting expert in the highly political and anti-Semitic trial of 1895 when the French army officer Captain Dreyfus was convicted of being a German spy and sent to the French penal colony of Devil's Island. It was in part the esteem in which Bertillon was held, even though handwriting was not his speciality, that led to Dreyfus' conviction. Following a long campaign to prove his innocence, to which the author Emile Zola contributed the celebrated pamphlet *J'Accuse*, Dreyfus was released in 1906. Restored to the army and promoted, Dreyfus served in the First World War and died in 1935. Bertillon, even on his deathbed, could not be persuaded to admit his mistake. A member of the reserved affairs section of the Foreign Office, Maurice Paleologue, who was involved in the Dreyfus affair from the beginning, described Bertillon as 'a madman, a maniac, armed with the crafty, obstinate and powerful dialectic which is the characteristic of interpretative psychosis'. Bertillon was also considered to be anti-semitic. See Rayner Heppenstall, *A Little Pattern of French Crime*, pp. 40-41. For an account of the recovery of the Mona Lisa see René Cassellari, *Dramas of French Crime*, Chapter 2.

19. Faurot was regarded as very much the father of American fingerprinting. After his success in 1911 he went on to establish the police department's fingerprint bureau. He retired in 1930 with the rank of deputy commissioner and three years later set up a company to provide 'clean fingerprinting' instead of messy inkprinting. It did not catch on. See *Time*, 23 April 1933. He died in 1942.

20. *New York Times*, 11, 12, 13 and 20 May 1911.

21. During the Second World War Cherrill and Sidney Birch went to Edinburgh to prove the identity of a palmprint left by a gap in the glove worn by George Harold Rollet.

22. 'Pretty', 'Handsome' or 'Big' Jack Klutas, who had attended the University of Illinois, was one of the more educated bandits who roamed the mid-West. He was a leading member of a gang, the College Kidnappers, which specialised in the kidnapping and blackmailing of Underworld characters who had recently staged a successful robbery, and who for obvious reasons, could not report the matter to the police. He was betrayed to the police by a gang member, Julius 'Babe' Jones.

23. Perhaps the most famous of gangsters' doctors was Joseph Patrick Moran, no relation of 'Bugsy', but on whose payroll he appeared for a time. Moran had started life well enough, qualifying with honours from Tufts Medical School. Convicted twice of performing illegal abortions, he then worked as the quasi-resident house physician for Al Capone. Another version of his death is that after the Battle of Little Bohemia in April 1934 he refused to treat John 'Red' Hamilton who died at a Barker-Karpis hideout in Aurora, Illinois. This, together with his unreliability in drink, caused him to be shot after Dillinger's death. The third version is that while in drink he was boasting in the Casino Club near Toledo, where he was last seen, that 'I have you guys in the palms of my hands'.

24. Now techniques have improved. In February 1997, 68-year-old Dr Jose Castillo was convicted of harbouring a fugitive and obstructing justice. He had been the confidante of Philadelphia drug lord, Richie Ramos, whose face he had successfully altered after he disappeared in 1990. He also sliced fifty pounds of fat from his waist and cheeks and turned his fingerprints upside down. Ramos was not found until 1992 when he was offered the chance of thirty years instead of life without parole if he agreed to give evidence against Castillo. Ramos did what he could for his doctor by failing to recognise him in a courtroom identification where the choices were Castillo, a 39-year-old lawyer and a young woman, but the damage had been done.

25. The belief has persisted. In 1941 an unknown man, allegedly wealthy, poisoned himself and then cut his throat in a Mayfair hotel after he had burned off the papillary ridges from his fingers in a scaldingly hot bath. The experts skinned his fingers and photographed the skin the wrong way round. The base of the papillary ridges revealed in the photograph showed the man to be Thomas Gray Newbould, a three times convicted fraudster. *Daily Express*, 28 March 1972.

26. Quoted in Carl Sifakis, *The Encyclopedia of American Crime*, p. 250.

27. Vucetich died from cancer of the stomach on 28 July 1925. He had already been suffering from tuberculosis for some years.

28. It would not have been without precedent. On 25 February 1924 the body of 11-year-old Vera Hilda Emma Hoad was found in a field near Chichester, Sussex. The probability is that she was killed by Earl(e) Leonard Nelson, also known as Earle Ferrell and Virgil Wilson, who was hanged in Winnipeg, Canada, on 13 January 1928. He was suspected of the deaths of over twenty women in the United States and Canada in cities as far apart as San Francisco, Detroit and Portland. He was finally arrested and hanged after killing Emily Patterson in Winnipeg on 9 June 1927. In his possessions were found clippings of the killing of Vera Hoad and also of another young girl, Nellie Clarke, in similar circumstances in Birkenhead. It was known that he had been in England between 1919 and 1925 and that he had been in both the Sussex and Liverpool areas. The British authorities hoped that there might be a stay of execution to enable him to be questioned over the English murders but none was given.

29. *Daily Herald,* 8 August 1959. Another case involving the printing of the male population of a town was at Potters Bar, then in Middlesex. On 29 April 1955 Elizabeth Currell was killed near the 17th tee at Potters Bar Golf Club. She had been beaten to death with an iron tee marker. 15,000 prints of local men were taken and it was matched to a 17-year-old local government clerk.

30. *Punch*, 25 May 1966.

31. C.H. Rolph, 'Fingerprints from all', *New Statesman*, 20 May 1966.

32. *Sunday Mirror*, 8 April 1973.

33. *Police Review*, 2 January 1979 and *Daily Telegraph*, 5 January 1979.

34. See J. Lacey Reynolds, 'About fingerprints', *New York Times Magazine*, 12 January 1958.

35. Stephen Grey, 'Yard in fingerprint blunder', *Sunday Times*, 6 April 1997.

36. Jon Robins, 'Fingerprints system that needs a helping hand', *The Times*, 7 November 2000.

37. Stewart Tendler, 'Court quashes IRA bombing conviction', *The Times*, 18 December 1998.

38. *The Scotsman*, 15 May 1999.

39. David Ekins, 'Fingerprint forgery', *Crime and Detection*, November 1966.

40. 'Warder's finger-print planted', *Empire News*, 23 January 1938.

41. See for example Kirk Wilson, *Investigating Murder;* Daniel Cohen, *The Encyclopedia of Unsolved Crimes*.

42. 'Lifting' was usually done by developing the print with powder and then lifting with adhesive tape and mounting to preserve it. It was a common practice in America but banned in Britain until 1970 when Scotland Yard adopted it as an economy measure.

43. For theories and solutions see e.g. Alfred de Marigny, *A Conspiracy of Crowns;* Marshall Houts, *King's X: Common Law and the Death of Sir Harry Oakes;* Michael Pye, *The King over the Water;* James Leasor, *Who Killed Sir Harry Oakes?* 'Murder in Paradise' in Murder Casebook, No 34 provides a good account of the case with a number of pictures and a review of the theories.

44. See Disciplinary Proceedings, *New York Law Journal*, 27 July 1992; *New York Times*, 17 November 1992, 4 February 1997.

2. Ballistics

1. *The Times*, 10 and 21 December 1860. This may have been the first but it was by no means the last time that a murder was solved by matching pieces of newspaper. In the case of the 1935 murder of Isabella Ruxton, whose body was found in Scotland, a piece of newspaper with the body showed that the edition had come from the Lancaster area where her husband, Buck Ruxton, was a doctor.

2. For a full account of the case see Belton Cobb, *Murdered on Duty*.

3. A.Lacassagne, 'La Deformation Des Balles de Revolver' in Volume 5, *Archives de l'Antropologie Criminelle et Des Sciences Pénales*.

4. Albert Llewellyn Hall, 'The missile and the weapon', *The Buffalo Medical Journal*, June 1900.

5. Hans Gross (adapted J.C. Adam), *Criminal Investigation*, pp. 423–4. Gross also commented that although in the present case it appeared to be clearly murder there was no great significance in no weapon being found at first. A weapon was, he said, usually stolen by the person discovering the body because a suicide had 'superstitious effects'.

6. 'Study of the Fired Bullets and Shells in Brownsville, Texas, Riot', Annual Report of the Chief of Ordnance, US Army (1907).

7. See Francis Russell, *Tragedy in Dedham*; Jurgen Thorwald, *The Marks of Cain*. It has been suggested that the South Braintree robbery was staged by the Morelli gang. On 18 November 1925, robber Celestino

Maderios confessed to the crime but declined to name his colleagues. His claim was rejected and he was executed for another murder on 23 August 1927, the same night as Sacco and Vanzetti. According to the, by no means necessarily reliable, Mafia defector Vinnie Teresa, Frank Morelli told him in the 1950s 'We whacked them out, we killed those guys in the robbery. Those two greaseballs took it on the chin'. See Vinnie Teresa, *My Life in the Mafia*. Tresca was shot dead, probably by the mobster Carmine Galante, on 11 January 1943 on the orders of Vito Genovese, a long-time supporter of Benito Mussolini whose regime Tresca vigorously opposed.

8. Sir Sydney Smith, *Mostly Murder*, Chapter 7.

9. For one of many accounts of the case see Gordon Honeycombe, *The Murders of the Black Museum 1870–1970*.

10. For a full account of the events leading up to the massacre see Laurence Bergreen, *Capone*; James Morton, *Gangland International*.

11. *New York Times*, 27 March 1931.

12. On 15 February Jack McGurn was shot while bowling in Kafora's Bowling and Billiards Parlor at 805 Milwaukee Avenue, Chicago. A comic Valentine card was left by his body.

13. Jurgen Thorwald, *The Marks of Cain*, p. 218.

14. In March 1971, following a burglary at an FBI office in Media, Pennsylvania, documents were strategically released to the press and interested parties. One sent to the Panthers showed that their headquarters in Philadelphia had been the subject of a wiretap. The Black Panther Party was founded by Huey Newton and Bobby Seale in 1966 in Oakland,

California and was probably the most extreme example of Black Power in action. The group had a ten-point programme which began '1. We want freedom'. Initially reformist rather than revolutionary, by the end of the decade it had adopted a Marxist-Leninist stance. By the early 1970s its leaders were dead, in prison or, in the case of Eldridge Cleaver, the Panthers' Minister of Information, in exile abroad.

15. The raid took place with the help of an undercover FBI mole who had been with the Panthers for just over a year. In 1966 Bill O'Neal had been charged with stealing a car. It was his first offence and Roy Mitchell, an FBI agent, offered to square the charge if O'Neal would work for him. He was sent to join the Panthers as part of the FBI's counter-intelligence programme COINTELPRO in 1968 and his first job was as a handyman and doorman at the Chicago headquarters. He found the movement extremely disorganised and rose through the ranks until he became the armourer. He provided the floor plans of the headquarters and was extremely annoyed that he had not been warned of the raid. Nevertheless he stayed with the now thoroughly disorganised Panthers for a time and then worked with a police officer, Sgt Stanley Robinson who killed two drug dealers. In 1973 he gave evidence which led to Robinson's conviction after which he entered the witness protection programme. 'Panther Infiltrator still in hiding' in *Chicago Tribune*, 24 July 1984.

3. Offender Profiling

1. The quotations throughout this chapter from Robert D. Keppel, Barry Farber, Dr David Canter and Anne Rule are taken from the BBC's *Catching the Killers*

2. The ages and details from Kurten's confession are taken from Karl Berg's *The Sadist*. Other accounts of how he was captured vary slightly in content.

3. *New York Journal-American,* 10 January 1957.

4. For an account of the case see Colin Wilson and Patricia Pitman, *Encyclopaedia of Murder*.

5. Dela Jones with Mandy Bruce, *A Psychic Eye.*

6. See *Republican-American*, 1 September 1995.

7. For an account of the case see Tom Tullett, *Clues to Murder*.

8. Michael Fidler and James Lethwaite, 'I'm standing by my rape beast', *Sun*, 14 April 1989. A psychic, Zak Martin, was thought at one time to be about to be called in but after a disagreement between his sponsors, a women's organisation, he withdrew. He had, he said, been successful in solving two murders in Ireland and had been used in the hunt for Shergar, the kidnapped Derby winner. He had however believed there was only one man involved in both sets of rapes. See *Observer*, 2 September 1984.

9. Tim Bouquet, 'Professor Canter: policing's secret weapon', *Readers Digest*, February 1994.

10. The arrest of Bundy closely resembled that of the Yorkshire Ripper, Peter Sutcliffe, on 2 January 1981 when he was questioned after the police were suspicious of a car parked in a dimly lit driveway.

When it came to it offender profiling had nothing to do with his capture; it was down to old-fashioned police work.

11. See for example Adam Sage, 'Find the killer by looking inside his head', *Independent*, 2 August 1991; Maurice Weaver, 'Psycho-fit: the pieces to catch a kidnapper', *Daily Telegraph*, 5 February 1992.

12. John Crace, 'When you ask why, you know who', *Guardian*, 26 November 1994.

13. In C.B. Meyer, 'Eine Einfuhrung in die Kunst der "Profiler"', *Basel University Law Journal*, January 2000.

14. John Crac, 'When you ask why, you know who', *Guardian*, 26 November 1994.

15. James A. Brussell, *Casebook of a Crime Psychiatrist*, Chapter 2.

16. Gilfoyle (2001) *The Times*, 13 February.

4. Infiltrators and Surveillance

1. Richard W. Rowan, *The Pinkertons*, pp. 203–4.

2. Quoted in Arthur H. Lewis, *A Lament for the Molly Maguires*, p. 240.

3. After the trial McParland travelled west to Colorado where he became head of the Denver branch of the Pinkerton agency. His work in infiltrating the Mollies was acclaimed throughout America and formed the basis of the first Sherlock Holmes novel, *The Valley of Fear*. For criticism of McParland and the Pinkertons see Patrick Campbell, *A Molly Maguire Story* and for McParland's subsequent career see James Morton, *Supergrasses and Informers*.

4. Quoted by E.P. Thompson, *The Making of the English Working Class*, p. 772.

5. Social Policy Director, University of Hull. In this chapter the quotes by Clive Norris, Kathleen Parrott, Ethel Bush, Mel Weinberg and Richard Kelly and Peter O'Sullivan are taken from the BBC's *The Hunt – Surveillance*.

6. Report from Select Committee on Metropolitan Police (675) 1833 Parl Papers (1833) Vol. 13, pp. 409–19.

7. Ibid., pp. 409–10.

8. Bernard Porter, *The Refugee Question in Mid-Victorian Politics*, pp. 114–15. There was quite clearly a great deal more undercover work going on than the police cared to admit. Officers could be put into civvies for particular operations. See also G. Thurston, *The Clerkenwell Riot*, London, George Allen & Unwin, for an account of the demonstration in Coldbath Fields and the death of PC Robert Culley.

9. Bernard Porter, *Plots and Paranoia*, p. 74.

10. Charles Dickens, 'The Detective Police', in *Miscellaneous Papers*,
p. 60 et seq.

11. Joan Lock identifies the clergyman-officer as G.H. Greenham. In his memoirs the Chief Inspector mentions the instance as the only occasion on which he wore a disguise. Joan Lock, *Scotland Yard Casebook*; G.H. Greenham, *Scotland Yard Experiences from the Diary of G H Greenham*.

12. J.E. Archer, *By a Flash and a Scare*, p. 156; *Bury and Norwich Press*, 11 September 1844 and 30 April 1845.

13. *Pall Mall Gazette*, 8 October 1888, p. 3.

14. Bernard Porter, *Origins of the Vigilant State*, p. 84.

15. John Gosling, *The Ghost Squad*, p. 20.

16. John Capstick, *Given in Evidence*, p. 91 and pp. 53–4.

17. Neil Darbyshire and Brian Hilliard, *The Flying Squad*, pp. 83–4.

18. Quoted in James Morton, *Supergrasses and Informers*, p. 212.

19. Mary Allen, *Lady in Blue*, p. 38; Mary Allen, *Pioneer Policewoman*, p. 132.

20. *The Times*, 14 December 1880; 14 March 1881.

21. Anthony Summers, *Official and Confidential*, pp. 25–6 and 108–18.

22. See also 'The FBI stings Congress', *Time* and 'The new FBI is watching', *Newsweek*, February 1980.

23. *Time*, 9 February 1981.

24. For an account of the case see James Morton, *Supergrasses & Informers*.

25. See Laurence Linderman, 'Underground angel', *Playboy*, July 1981, quoted by Gary Marx in 'Who really gets stung? Some issues raised by the new police undercover work', *Crime & Delinquency*, April 1982, pp 165–93; *Chicago Daily News*, 24 September 1975; *Boston Globe*, 26 October 1979.

26. R. Fleming with H. Miller, *Scotland Yard*, pp. 112–13; 115.

27. A pseudonym. See James Morton (1995) *Supergrasses & Informers*

28. Philip Etienne and Martin Maynard with Tony Thompson, *The Infiltrators*, pp. 130–1.

29. *Sun*, 11 August 1994.

30. *The Pink Paper*, 23 May 1997.

31. A pseudonym.

32. See Dani Garavelli, 'The Undercover Sting that wrecked my life', *Scotland on Sunday*, 3 January 1999.

33. For their stories see Joe Pistone with Richard Woodley, *Donnie Brasco*; James Dubro and Robin Rowland, *Undercover*; Thomas C. Renner and Cecil Kirby, *Mafia Enforcer*, and Donald Goddard, *The Insider*. Another long-term undercover agent was a policewoman who posed as a biker's girlfriend – see Michael Detroit, *Chain of Evidence*.

34. Jon Ungoed-Thomas and Matthew Mervyn-Jones, 'The sting that cost £2,000,000,000', *Sunday Times*, 10 February 2001.

35. See e.g. *Guardian*, 18 July 1984 and, for an account of one suburban housewife who changed her mind in time, Philip Etienne and Martin Maynard with Tony Thompson, *The Infiltrators*, Chapter 6.

36. For an account of the case see Duncan Campbell, *Underworld* and James Morton, *Gangland*.
37. Interview for *Catching the Killers*.
38. See James Morton, *Supergrasses and Informers*.

5. Interrogation

1. The quotations in this chapter by Jose Sivuca, Maria Olimpia, Henry Hunter, Marak Mallah, Henry Wallace, Wallace Brown, Fred Holroyd, Jerome Skolnick, Barrie Irving and Tony Collins, Michael Goymour and Tim Shallice are taken from *Catching the Killlers*.

2. 'Truth about famous "Third Degree", *Weekly News*, 12 July 1913. The previous year in the notorious Conway case in Chicago a woman had confessed to the murder of her husband after 48 hours' continuous questioning. She had not been struck or beaten by the officers, merely questioned until, after several fainting spells and an attack of hysteria, she had confessed.

3. See for example 'Repudiation of Third Degree', *Empire News*, 28 February 1926; '13 hours of the Third Degree', *Empire News*, 19 April 1931.

4. At the time the case was something of a *cause célèbre*. Ronald True, who had killed a prostitute, was reprieved three days later. It was widely thought that his social connections had saved him from the gallows whereas Jacoby, who had none, had been a scapegoat. Fior never undertook another murder case as counsel, instead becoming a commercial solicitor. For an account of the case see Douglas G. Browne, *Sir Bernard Spilsbury: His Life and Cases*.

5. Report of the Royal Commission on Police Powers and Procedure (1929); C.P. Brutton, *Police Constable's Guide to his Daily Work* (10th edn).

6. See Ralph Underwager and Hollida Wakefield (1993) 'False confessions and police deception',

American Journal of Forensic Psychology 10(3).

7. S. Welsh (1979) 'Police trickery in inducing confessions', *University of Pennsylvania Law Review* 127(3), January, p. 3.

8. (1987) 86 Cr App R 349.

9. See Alan Grant (1987) 'Videotaping police questioning: a Canadian experiment', *Criminal Law Review*, 375.

10. *Christian Science Monitor*, 16 March 2000.

11. *White v State*, 129 Miss. 182; *New York Times*, 23 November 1919.

12. For a very full account of the case see Richard C. Cortner, *A 'Scottsboro' Case in Mississippi*.

13. Meridian *Star*, 31 March 1934.

14. At the time Mississippi led the country in the lynching of blacks. Six cases were reported in 1934. See *Literary Digest*, 119 (12 January 1935) quoting research by the Tuskegee Institute's Department of Records and Research; Meridian *Star*, 6 May 1934. Jerome Skolnick believes that up to the end of the 1930s there were between 4,000 and 5,000 lynchings of blacks largely associated with accusations that they had raped white women.

15. Four of the boys were released and the other five served lengthy sentences until only Haywood Patterson was left in jail. On 17 July 1948 he escaped to Canada where he later died of cancer while in prison there awaiting trial for killing a man in a fight in a bar. See James Goodman, *Stories of Scottsboro*. Things did not change much over the years in judges' attitudes in the deep south. William Hellerstein, Professor of Law at the Brooklyn School of Law, recalls defending in a civil rights case in the 1960s. 'Every morning I and my colleague would be greeted by the judge "Here comes my favourite kike lawyers." I'd just say "Good morning judge".'

16. See Roy Wilkins, *Standing Fast: The Autobiography of Roy Wilkins,*
p. 141.

17. Letter, Mrs John A. Clark to Arthur Garfield Hays, 12 December 1937 in ACLU Archives, Vol. 941.

18. *Brown v Mississippi,* 287 US 56 (1932).

19. Loren Miller, *The Petitioners*, pp. 277–8. In 1923 the National Association for the Advancement of Colored People managed to show that the 1919 convictions of black sharecroppers should be overturned. The men had been convicted of murder and sentenced to death following troubles in Phillips County, Arkansas. The black witnesses who had given evidence against them had been beaten to make them do so. *Moore v Dempsey*, 261 US 309 (1915).

20. *Miranda v Arizona*, 384 US 436 (1966).

21. August Vollmer (1876–1955) is often described as the father of modern policing. A one-time postman in Berkeley he rose rapidly once he joined the police force. He insisted on recruiting the best people for the job and, unlike many police forces of the period, many recruits had some background in the sciences. He established the first formal training school for the police in America in 1908. In the 1940s by the time of his death there were no less than 25 police chiefs who had served under Vollmer.

22. 'The truth about the Third Degree', *Reynolds Illustrated News*, 8 April 1925.

23. W.M. Marston, *The Lie Detector Test*, p. 45.

24. *Frye v United States,* 293 F.1013 (1924). In 1972, however, Judge Allan Miller sitting in the Superior Court in California made the curious ruling that, since scientific tests had demonstrated the accuracy of lie detector techniques, the rules preventing evidence of the results being given should be changed. The case had concerned the search of luggage at an airport for drugs and much depended on whether permission had been given to a police officer to allow the search. No appeal was made by the prosecutor but subsequent decisions in other venues showed this to be an isolated case. In the years when I defended a number of career criminals, one man charged with bank robbery told me confidently, 'I'm going to ask the judge for a lie detector test before the jury and, please God, he won't let me'.

25. David K. Lykken, *A Tremor in the Blood*, p. 3.

26. L. Burkey (1967) 'Privacy, property and the polygraph', *Labor Law Journal*.

27. For one of many accounts of the case see Nick Harris, *Famous Crimes*.

28. Quoted by Carl Sifakis in *The Encyclopedia of American Crime*,
p. 424.

29. Ministry of Defence (1955) *Treatment of British Prisoners of War in Korea*.

30. For a discussion of sensory deprivation and hooding see Peter Suedfeld (ed,), *Psychology and Torture*, Chapter 8.

31. 'I could solve any crime by use of hypnosis', *Empire News*, 19 April 1931.

32. *Garcia v Scimemi*, 712 P. 2d 1094.

33. *Illinois v Kempinski.*

34. *The Times*, 20 December 1992.

35. Eric C. Copperthwaite (1989) 'How hypnosis can help with crime detection', *The Criminologist*, Spring.

36. 453 N.E. 2d 484 (1983). For a review of the decisions see Roderick Munday (1987) 'The admissibility of hypnotically refreshed testimony', *Justice of the Peace*, 27 June, 4 and 18 July.

37. *R v McCarthy* reported in *Daily Telegraph*, 19 May 1987.

38. 'Dangerous Evidence' in *New Law Journal*, 20 May 1994.

39. *Hansard*, 25 May 1994.

40. *Guardian*, 7 January 2001.

41. Jonathan Alter, 'How sure is sure enough', *Newsweek*, 22 March 1999. A case with a rather happier ending was that of biker 'Crazy' Joe Spaziano who was convicted on the evidence of a 16-year-old who held a grudge and remembered key facts under hypnosis, something the jury was never told. He was eventually reprieved after outstanding work by *Miami Herald* senior editor Gene Miller. See Tena Jamison Lee (1996) 'Anatomy of a death penalty case', *Human Rights*, Summer.

42. Christopher Price and Jonathan Caplan, *The Confait Confessions*.

43. Sir Henry Fisher, *Report of an Inquiry by the Hon. Sir Henry Fisher into the circumstances leading to the trial of three persons on charges arising out of the death of Maxwell Confait and the fire at 27 Doggett Road, London SE6.*

44. Sir Norman Skelhorn, *Public Prosecutor*.

45. *s 76(2).* If, in any proceedings where the prosecution proposes to give in evidence a confession made by an accused person, it is represented to the court that the confession was or may have been obtained —

(a) by oppression of the person who made it; or

(b) in consequence of anything said or done which was likely, in the circumstances existing at the time, to render unreliable any confession which might have been made by him in consequence thereof,

the court shall not allow the confession to be given in evidence against him except in so far as the prosecution proves to the court beyond reasonable doubt that the confession (notwithstanding that it may be true) was not obtained as aforesaid.

(8) In this section 'oppression' includes torture, inhuman or degrading treatment and the threat of violence (whether or not amounting to torture).

s.78(1) In any proceedings the court may refuse to allow evidence on which the prosecution proposes to rely to be given if it appears to the court that, having regard to all the circumstances, including the circumstances in which the evidence was obtained, the admission of the evidence would have such an adverse effect on the fairness of the proceedings that the court ought not to admit it.

46. Nothing, however compares with the Japanese system of *Daiyo-Kangoku*. Under the Japanese Code of Criminal Procedure a suspect must be brought before a judge within three days after his arrest. The judge may, if he wishes, decide that the suspect be detained pending judgement. He is then sent to a detention centre for up to ten days. This is a pre-indictment detention and can be, and usually is, extended for a further period of ten days. In special cases another period, this time of five days, may be granted. Unfortunately under the code a detention centre may and routinely does mean a police cell and during the detention he may be continually interrogated by the police. The cells are ten square metres in size and may be inhabited by a number of other detainees. There are separate, but visible, cells for women who are subject to harassment by other prisoners. The police officer in charge observes and records every movement of the suspect such as waking, washing, eating, reading, sleeping and excreting. Standing up, walking and talking to other prisoners are prohibited. Rules about the correct sitting position are strictly enforced. Baths are taken once a week and there may be exercise in the police station but the exercise area is, in reality, a smoking room. Communication with visitors is extremely limited and prisoners may not communicate with lawyers without permission. Interviews are limited to office hours although the police may continue to question suspects until midnight. If a suspect does not confess, he or she is treated even worse. Conversely, if a confession is obtained, the suspect is accorded preferential treatment. (Japan Federation of Bar Associations). The conviction rate in Japanese courts, where there is no jury system, is over 99 per cent.

47. John Capstick, *Given in Evidence*, Chapter 1.

48. For arguments in support of this theory see for example, Welsh S. White (1986) 'Defending Miranda', 39 V and L Reports. Critics say that each year *Miranda* results in 'lost cases' against some 28,000 seriously violent offenders and 79,000 property offenders as well as producing a similar number of plea bargains.

49. For a discussion on the subject see, for example, G.H. Gudjonsson, *The Psychology of Interrogators, Confessions and Testimony*.

50. Richard Whittington-Egan (1995) 'Corpus delictus or no body worries', *New Law Journal*, 2 June.

51. *Dallas Times Herald*, 14 April 1985. See also Brian Lane and Wilfred Gregg, *The New Encyclopaedia of Serial Killers*.

52. G.H. Gudjonsson (1999) 'The making of a serial false confessor: the confessions of Henry Lee Lucas', *The Journal of Forensic Psychiatry* 10(2), September.

6. DNA

1. See Chapter 1.

2. For an account of the investigation see Joseph Wambaugh, *The Blooding*. The process of testing a whole section of the community was repeated in *Operation Eagle* in the West Country in 2001 following a series of up to 14 rapes in Bath and Bristol beginning in 1991. Around 2,000 men previously questioned about the crimes during the past decade were to be invited to co-operate.

3. There is a very full account of the case in Harlan Levy, *And the Blood Cried Out*.

4. The flamboyant and high profile Scheck went on to appear for such diverse clients as OJ Simpson and the English *au pair* Louise Woodward, convicted of murdering her charge. For an account of one of his campaigns see Edward Humes, 'The DNA Wars', *Los Angeles Times*, 29 November 1992. For a profile of him see Paul Schwartzman, 'The Deacon of DNA has become the defender of last resort', *Playboy*, August 1998.

5. See Eric Lander, 'DNA fingerprinting on trial', *Nature 339*, 501; *People v Castro*, 144 Misc 2d 956 (Sup. Ct. Bx. Co. 1989).

6. P.J. Lincoln (1993) 'DNA on trial', *The Criminologist*, Autumn.

7. *New York Times*, 15 April 1992.

8. *Sunday Telegraph*, 9 April 1995.

9. *Case Studies in the Use of DNA Evidence*, US Department of Justice (1996).

10. Quoted in Daniel Jeffreys, 'Genetic fingerprinting in the dock', *Independent*, 27 October 1995.

11. Paul Schwartzman, ibid.; see also *Case Studies in the Use of DNA Evidence*, ibid.

12. See Chapter 1.

13. *Guardian*, 27 October 2000.

14. Zakaria Erinclioglu (1998) 'British forensic science in the dock', *Nature*.

15. Quoted in Vanessa Houlder, 'Fingerprints of the future', *Financial Times*, 14 May 1998. For a critique of the so-called fallacies of statistics see Christian Jowett, 'Sitting in the dock with the Bayes', *New Law Journal*, 16 February 2001.

16. *Guardian*, 13 February 2001.

17. Francis X. Clines, 'Access by inmates to tests for DNA gains ground', *New York Times*, 19 December 2000.

18. For an account of the case see Stuart Mulraney, 'The Mary Gregson case', *Police Review*, 20 October 2000.

19. Criminal Justice and Police Bill 2001.

20. *R v Weir* (2000), *The Times*, 16 June 2000; *Regina v B., Attorney-General's Reference No 3 of 1999*, (2000); *The Times*, 15 December 2000.

21. See Tony Thompson and Tracy McVeigh, 'There are 600 killers in our midst', *Observer*, 25 February 2001.

22. Quoted by Jason Bennetto in 'A stray hair, and the case is almost over', *Independent on Sunday*, 10 May 1988.

Bibliography

Archer, J.E., *By a Flash and a Scare* (1990) Oxford, Clarendon Press.

Allen, M., *Pioneer Policewoman* (1925) London, Chatto & Windus.—*Lady in Blue* (1936) London, Stanley Paul.

Arons, H., *Hypnosis in Criminal Investigation* (1967) So. Orange, N.J., Power Publishers.

Ashton-Wolfe, H., *The Forgotton Clue: Stories of the Paris Surete* (1929) Klondon, Hurst & Blackett.

Belin, J., *My Work at the Surete* (1950) London, George G Harrap & Co.

Berg, K. (translated from the German by Olga Illner and George Godwin), *The Sadist* (1939) London, The Acorn Press.

Bergreen, L., *Capone* (1994) London, Macmillan.

Bertillon, S., *Vie d'Alphonse Bertillon* (1940) Paris, Gallimard.

Britton, P., *The Jigsaw Man* (1997) London, Bantam Press.

Boot, A., *Psychic Murder Hunters* (1994) London, Headline.

Browne, D. G. and Tullett, T., *Sir Bernard Spilsbury: His Life and Cases* (1951) London, George G Harrap & Co.

Brussel, J.A., *Casebook of a Crime Psychiatrist* (1969) London, New English Library.

Brutton, C.P., *Police Constable's Guide to his Daily Work* (10th ed) (1961) London, Pitman Publishing.

Campbell, D., *The Underworld* (1994) BBC Books.

Campbell, P., *A Molly Maguire Story* (1992) Jersey City, N.J., Templecrone Press.

Canter, D., *Criminal Shadows* (1994) London, HarperCollins.

Capstick, J., *Given in Evidence* (1960) London, John Long.

Cassellari, R., *Dramas of French Crime* (nd.) London, Hutchinson & Co.

Cherrill, F. R., *Cherrill of the Yard* (1954) London, Harrap.

Cobb, B., *Murdered on Duty* (1961) London, Brown, Watson.

Cohen, D., *The Encyclopedia of Unsolved Crimes* (1988) New York, Dodd, Mead & Co.

Cortner, R.C., *A "Scottsboro" Case in Mississippi* (1986) Jackson, University Press of Mississippi.

Darbyshire, N. and Hilliard, B., *The Flying Squad* (1993) London, Headline.

Delong, C., *Special Agent* (2001) London, Headline.

De Marigny, A., *A Conspiracy of Crowns* (1990) London, Bantam Books.

Detroit, M., *Chain of Evidence* (1994) London, Headline.

Deutsch, A., *The Trouble with Cops* (1955) London, Arco Publishers.

Douglas, J. and Olshaker, M., *Mindhunter: Inside the FBI Elite Serial Crime Unit* (1996) London, Heinemann.

Dubro, J., and Rowland R., *Undercover* (1992) Toronto, Octopus.

Etienne, P., and ors., *The Infiltrators* (2000) London, Michael Joseph.

Felstead, S.T., *Sir Richard Muir* (1927) London, John Lane.

Firmin, S., *Men in the Shadows* (1953) London, Hutchinson.

Fisher, H., *Report of an Inquiry by the Hon. Sir Henry Fisher into the*

circumstances leading to the trial of three persons on charges arising out of

the death of Maxwell Confait and the fire at 27 Doggett Road, London SE6. (1977) London, HMSO.

Fleming R., and Miller H., *Scotland Yard* (1994) London, Michael Joseph.

Fletcher, T., *Memories of Murder* (1986) London, Weidenfeld & Nicholson.

Franklin, C., *The Third Degree* (1970) London, Robert Hale.

Galton, F., *Fingerprints* (1892) New York.

Gilbert, M., *The Claimant* (1957) London, Constable.

Giradin, G.R. with Helmer W.J., Dillinger, *The Untold Story* (1994)

Bloomingdale, The University of Indiana Press.

Goddard, D., *The Insider* (1992) New York, Arrow Books.

Goodman, J., *Stories of Scottsboro* (1994) New York, Pantheon Books.

Gosling, J., *The Ghost Squad* (1959) London, W.H.Allen.

Greenham, G.H., *Scotland Yard Experiences from the Diary of G H Greenham* (1904) London, George Routledge.

Gross, H. (adapted J.C.Adam), *Criminal Investigation* (1924) London, Sweet & Maxwell.

Gudjonsson, G.H., *The Psychology of Interrogators, Confessions and Testimony* (1992) Chichester, John Wiley & Sons.

Harris, N., *Famous Crimes* (1933) Los Angeles, Arthur Vernon Agency.

Heppenstall, R., *A Little Pattern of French Crime* (1969) London, Hamish Hamilton.

Herschel, W.J., *The Origin of Fingerprinting* (1916) London, Humphrey Milford.

Honeycombe, B., *Murders of the Black Museum* (1870-1970) London, Mysterious Press.

Houts, M., *King's X: Common Law and the Death of Sir Harry Oakes* (1972) New York, William Morrow.

Jones, D. and Bruce M., *A Psychic Eye* (1992) London, Ebury Press.

Keppel R.D., with Birnes W.J., *The Riverman* (1995) New York, Pocket Books.

Lane, B., *The Encyclopaedia of Forensic Science* (1992) London, Headline.

Lane, B., and Gregg, W., *The New Encycopedia of Serial Killers* (1996) London, Headline.

Levy, H., *And The Blood Cried Out* (1996) London, Basic Books.

Leasor, J., *Who Killed Sir Harry Oakes?* (1989) London, Mandarin.

Lewis, A.H., *A Lament for the Molly Maguires* (1964) New York, Harcourt, Brace and World Inc.

Lock, J., *Scotland Yard Casebook* (1993) London, Robert Hale.

Lykken, D.T., *A Tremor in the Blood* (1988) Reading, Mass., Perseus Books.

Mace, G., *My First Crime* (1886) London, Vizetelly.

Macnaghten, M., *Days of My Years* (1914) London, Edward Arnold.

Mannheim, H., *Pioneers in Criminology* (1960) London, Stevens & Sons.

Marston, W.M., *The Lie Detector Test* (1938) New York, Richard R. Smith.

Michaud, S. and Aynesworth, H., *The Only Living Witness* (1983) New York, Signet Books.

Miller, H., *Proclaimed in Blood* (1995) London, Headline.

Miller, L., *The Petitioners* (1966) New York, Pantheon Books.

Morton, J., *Gangland* (1993) London, Warner Books.

— *Bent Coppers* (1995) London, Warner Books.

— *Supergrasses & Informers* (1996) London, Warner Books.

Gangland International (1999) London, Warner Books.

Owen, D., *Hidden Evidence* (2000) Willowdale, Ont., Firefly Books.

Paul, P., *Murder under the Microscope* (1990) London, Macdonald & Co.

Pistone, J.D. with Woodley, R., *Donnie Brasco* (1988) London, Sidgwick & Jackson.

Porter, B., *The Refugee Question in Mid-Victorian Politics* (1979) Cambridge, Cambridge University Press.

— *Origins of the Vigilant State* (1987) London, Weidenfeld & Nicholson.

— *Plots and Paranoia* (1989) London, Unwin Hyman.

Price, C., and Caplan J., *The Confait Confessions* (1977) London, Marion Boyars.

Pye, M., *The King over the Water* (1981) New York, Holt, Rinehart and Winston.

Renner, T.C. and Kirby C., *Mafia Enforcer* (1988) London, Corgi.

Ressler, R.K. and Shachtman, T., *I have lived in the Monster* (1998) London, Pocket Books.

Rhodes H.T.F. (ed), *In the Tracks of Crime* (1952) London, Turnstile Press.

—*Alphonse Bertillon* (1956) London, George G Harrap & Co.

Rowan, R.W., *The Pinkertons* (1931) London, Hurst & Blackett.

Russell, F., *Tragedy in Dedham* (1963) London, Longmans.

Scheck, B., Neufeld, P. and Dwyer, J., *Actual Innocence* (2000) New York, Doubleday.

Scott, H.R. (ed), *The Concise Encyclopaedia of Crime and Criminals* (1961) London, Andre Deutsch.

Sifakis, C., *The Encyclopedia of American Crime* (1982) New York, Facts on File.

Skelhorn, N., *Public Prosecutor* (1981) London, Harrap.

Smith, S., *Mostly Murder* (1984) London, Panther Books.

Stead, P.J., *The Police of Paris* (1951) London, Staples Press.

Suedfeld, P. (ed), *Psychology and Torture* (1990) New York, Hemisphere Publishing Corporation.

Summers, A., *Official and Confidential: The Secret life of J .Edgar Hoover* (1994) London, Corgi Books.

Symons, J., *Crime and Detection* (1968) London, Panther.

Teresa, V., *My Life in the Mafia* (1973) London, HartDavis, MacGibbon.

Thompson, E., *The Making of the English Working Class* (1963) London, Victor Gollancz.

Thorwald, J., *The Marks of Cain* (1965) London, Thames and Hudson.

Thurston, G., *The Clerkenwell Riot* (1967) London, George Allen & Unwin.

Tullett, T., *Clues to Murder* (1986) London, Grafton Books.

Wambaugh, J., *The Blooding* (1989) London, Bantam Books.

Watson, P., *War on the Mind* (1978) London, Hutchinson of London.

Wilkins, R., *Standing fast: The Autobiography of Roy Wilkins* (1982) New York, Viking Press.

Wilson, C., *Written in Blood* (1995) London, HarperCollins.

Wilson C. and Pitman, P., *Encyclopaedia of Murder* (1984) London, Pan Books.

Wilson, K., *Investigating Murder* (1990) London, Robinson.

Articles

R.L.Ault, 'The FBI's team approach' in *FBI Law Enforcement Bulletin*, January 1980.

Tim Bouquet, 'Professor Canter: Policing's Secret Weapon' in Readers Digest, February 1994.

Robert Brittain, 'The Sadistic Murderer' in *Medicine, Science and the Law*, 1970.

L Burkey, 'Privacy, property and the polygraph' in *Labor Law Journal*, 1967.

Brian Clapham, 'Hypnosis – An Aid to Crime Detection?' in *The Criminologist*, Summer 1989.

Eric C. Copperthwaite, 'How hypnosis can help with Crime Detection' in *The Criminologist*, Spring 1989.

David Ekins, 'Fingerprint Forgery' in *Crime and Detection*, November 1966.

Zakaria Erinclioglu 'British Forensic Science in the Dock) in *Nature*, 1998.

Jan W. Evett and others, 'DNA Profiling: A Discussion of issues relating to the reporting of very small match probabilities' in *Criminal Law Review* 2000 at page 341.

H.B.Gibson, *Bulletin of British Psychological Society*, Volume 35.

Calvin Goddard, 'Firearms as Evidence' in *American Journal of Police Science II*, January-February 1931.

G.H. Gudjonsson, 'The making of a serial false confessor: the confessions of Henry Lee Lucas' in *The Journal of Forensic Psychiatry*, Volume 10, No 2, September 1999.

Edward Humes, The DNA Wars' in *Los Angeles Times*, 29 November 1992.

Christian Jowett, 'Sitting in the Dock with the Bayes' in *New Law Journal*, 16 February 2001.

Edwin R. Keedy, 'The Third Degree and Trial by Newspapers' in *3 Journal of Criminal Law and Criminology*, 1912.

— The Third Degree and the Position of the Trial Judge in Illinois' in *7 Illinois Law Review*, 1912.

—'The Third Degree and Legal Interrogation of Suspects' in *University of Pennsylvania Law Review*, June 1937.

Horowitz Kleinhaus and Y. Tobin, 'The Use of Hypnosis in Police Investigation' in *Journal of Forensic Science Society*, Volume 17, 1977.

A. Lacassange, 'La Deformation des Balles de Revolver' in Vol 5, *Archives de L'Antropologie Criminelle et Des Sciences Penales*. (n.d.)

Eric Lander, 'DNA Fingerprinting on Trial' in *Nature*, Vol 339 (1989)

Tena Jamison Lee, 'Anatomy of a Death Penalty Case' in *Human Rights*, Summer 1996.

P.J.Lincoln, 'DNA on Trial' in *The Criminologist*, Autumn 1993.

Brian Masters, 'Mind over Murder' in the *Mail on Sunday*, 25 September 1994.

William E. Miles, 'Historic Fingerprints', in *The New York Times Magazine*, 22 April 1956.

Ministry of Defence, *Treatment of British Prisoners of War in Korea*, H.M.S.O., 1955.

James Morton, 'Fair means or foul' in *Police Review*, 18 March 1994.

Stuart Mulraney, 'The Mary Gregson case' in *Police Review*, 20 October 2000.

Roderick Munday, 'The Admissibility of Hypnotically Refreshed Testmony' in *Justice of the Peace*, 27 June, 4 and 18 July 1987.

'Murder in Paradise' in *Murder Casebook* No 34, Marshall Cavendish.

National Institute of Justice 'Cases Studies in the Use of DNA Evidence' US Department of Justice 1996.

Wesley W. Stout, 'Fingerprinting Bullets' in *The New York Times*, 5 February 1955.

Paul Schwartzman, 'The Deacon of DNA has become the Defender of Last Resort' in *Playboy*, August 1998.

Ralph Underwager and Hollida Wakefield, 'False Confessions and Police Deception' in *American Journal of Forensic Psychology*, Vol 10, Number 3, 1993.

'Juan Vucetich' in *Revista de Criminologia, Psiquiatria y Medicina Legal, XIII*, January 1926.

S. Welsh, 'Police Trickery in Inducing Confessions' in *University of Pennsylvania Law Review*, Vol 127, No. 3, January 1979.

'Written in Blood' in *Murder Casebook* No 55, Marshall Cavendish.